How World Events Are Changing Education

Critical Issues in the Future of Learning and Teaching

The titles published in this series are listed at *brill.com/cifl*

How World Events Are Changing Education

Politics, Education, Social, Technology

Edited by

Rosemary Sage and Riccarda Matteucci

BRILL

LEIDEN | BOSTON

Cover illustration: Riccarda Matteucci teaching on robotics (photograph by Sally Elvin)

All chapters in this book have undergone peer review.

The Library of Congress Cataloging-in-Publication Data is available online at https://catalog.loc.gov

Typeface for the Latin, Greek, and Cyrillic scripts: "Brill". See and download: brill.com/brill-typeface.

ISSN 2542-8721
ISBN 978-90-04-50644-2 (paperback)
ISBN 978-90-04-50645-9 (hardback)
ISBN 978-90-04-50646-6 (e-book)

Printed by Printforce, the Netherlands

Advance Praise of
How World Events Are Changing Education

"This book challenges and poses dilemmas as to the nature and relevance of effective communication, within teaching and learning, in the present global climate. The evidence presented is important and applicable for both policy makers and practitioners. Academics and practitioners, from diverse backgrounds, offer pragmatic approaches towards a holistic education, which questions the development of the whole person in the context of future life-long learning. *Conversational leadership* is explored as an important concept, a process and a way forward, addressing some of the inadequacies or so-called holes of *Swiss Cheese Learning*, witnessed in traditional educational models. The approaches in the text empower & inspire individuals to be more reflective & reflexive in pedagogy and practice. It is only through sharing best practice from interdisciplinary dialogue that a model of genuine inclusivity can be attained, sustained & valued. The text presents a way forward."
– **Stasia Cwenar, Linguist and Expert in Educational Needs, Leicester and Liverpool Hope Universities**

"The book draws attention to a wide range of factors facing education and training today requiring consideration in the context of global mobility. It draws upon the 2020 OECD evaluation of traditional UK education as narrow and exam driven based on memorisation. Schleicher (2020) argues the role of education is to support and integrate students' personal, practical and academic competencies. The book's contents are therefore wide-ranging and challenge UK and Western values, including the curriculum and pedagogy. Readers may reflect upon the idea that teachers and trainers lacking language, cultural knowledge and experience may judge employee or student competence according to individualist Western culture's mixed expectations e.g. silence, debate and eye-contact. This is contrasted with non-Western interactions, such as those valuing informality, collectivism and cooperation and those in which respect is shown by avoiding eye-contact. The discussion extends to education and training content in a global context, embracing technology, robotics and the media. There is much interesting, stimulating content in the book to engage, interest and challenge industrial and political leaders, as well as everyone involved at all levels of education. It is suitable for stakeholders in education wishing to understand background."
– **Jennifer Rogers, Linguist and Psychologist, Open, Northampton, Leicester and Liverpool Hope Universities**

"The editors have recently produced 2 thought-provoking books – *Paradoxes in Education* (Sense) & *The Robots Are Here* (Buckingham University Press) to show-case the developmental work of Practitioner Doctoral participants. This text completes a winning trio, with the legend of *Two Wolves* a timely reminder of our human nature in the final chapter. This story of a grandfather uses a metaphor of 2 wolves fighting within him to explain his inner love-hate conflicts to a grandson. When the boy asks which wolf wins, the grandfather answers: 'whichever he chooses to feed is the one that wins'. The book evidence explains how in unstable communities and uncertain times people's bad side surges forward. A 2020 pandemic has presented the human good side and this force can rid the world of disadvantage and discrimination as the big barriers to progress and productivity. Billy Ocean's new album *One World*, with the triumph of love, reflects the stories told in this inspiring, gripping text to reinforce education's positive role in development."

– Alice Keens-Soper, Head of Specialist Factual at Oxford Scientific Films and Executive Producer at the Natural History Unit

To the memory of His Royal Highness,
the Prince Philip and Duke of Edinburgh

∴

Contents

Foreword

This book is released at an extraordinary moment for the world. The coronavirus pandemic has forced everybody to lockdown and life has been modified and adapted to ensure some continuity. Formal education has suffered a significant impact and all the traditional ways of doing things have changed to meet present needs of staff and students. Schools, colleges and universities are closed and stakeholders are trying to achieve normality with limited success.

The chapters of this book describe the problems that students face in changing times and conditions. The text relates to primary and secondary schools as well as further and higher education, with pre- and post-graduate students. It shows, that at all levels, institutions are suffering similar problems of teaching and examining students appropriately. We regard these situations as serious challenges and are trying to solve them, using methods, platforms and systems that we have never used before, with questionable results.

One matter, developed in the text, refers to the mismatch of education to the needs of the actual world. In my job, as a university professor in a medical faculty, I know that there are fundamental, specific, learning areas that are necessary to attain the professional competencies described in the curriculum. However, present teaching methods must alter, because the profile of today's students does not meet working requirements, with demands for high-level personal as well as academic achievements.

Today we must work 'smarter', with abilities to collaborate across disciplines for better performances. This matter is developed by Professor Rosemary Sage in the first chapter. She signals, with substantial evidence, how those leaving formal education do not have the range of abilities the job market requires. This reality moves us to pose the question: When and how did academic institutions and the labour market follow such divergent pathways?

Other interesting matters analyzed in the text are the arrival of robots and their increasing influence in daily work activities. Displacement of humans is now a reality and robots always win because they do not need holidays and never are sick. If they fail to function, robots can be replaced quickly by another unit that does the same activity without induction time and human effort required.

It is important to consider robot impact in the job market to understand where we go from here in planning and developing educational institutions for the future. The presence of robots everywhere has unsuspected consequences. Recently, on the television news, a story was presented about Japan. This showed a man formally marrying a robot, with a ceremony, guests and a cocktail party to celebrate the event! There are already robot teachers and now there are robot wives! Where will this substitution for humans end?

The text discusses the actual situation of students at all levels and the fact that everybody needs more encouragement and control over learning rather than transmitted information that may be in an unsuitable form for students. A positive discussion, talking about the feelings of each other regarding a situation/s, will be more effective for learning than a wealth of sophisticated educational resources.

This pandemic age has revealed the inequalities of different student social groups. Some will not have continuous access to the internet and the availability of a computer for learning activities, required by an educational institution. This reflects important differences in learner groups across the world. Although most students own smartphones, a significant number of them do not have the physical space for developing learning activities in their home environments. Many people are living in cramped conditions, accelerating violence within families, plus other visible and invisible barriers preventing an effective educative process.

Institutions are redesigning and remaking course content and sending abundant on-line activities to enrolled students. This is a desperate bid to obtain the same academic results as face-to-face exchanges between educators and learners. These moves, however, are not only ineffective but also encourage burnout for those involved.

The contents, methods and focus of the present educational system are not wholly effective and useful for coping with the actual reality of our global world. There are such fast-changing circumstances that education is not able to run at the same speed as technology developments and inevitably lags behind, bogged down by politics, systems and procedures as well as cultural views and attitudes.

This book presents to the reader an expert, informed view of the present world situation and alternatives that educators must consider and apply, before losing completely the global race. Robots and other new technologies are here to stay. We will disappear and vanish for good if we do not move in the same direction and with superior speed.

Juan Eduardo Romero

The World Is Shifting and Education Must Evolve

We live in ambiguous, complex, volatile, uncertain times.

British television told the story of 6 young people (one a medical student) who have recently committed suicide. British National Health Statistics show 1 in 6 take antidepressants, doubling over the decade 2010–20 (71 million annual prescriptions). The Organisation for Economic Cooperation & Development (OECD) (Burns & Gottschalk, 2019) reports that British 15 year-olds are the saddest and least satisfied of the 37-nation group. Why is this so? Reasons given are:

1. British children spend more time online than others (except Chile) so are sucked into a toxic culture of self-comparison and cyberbullying
2. More tests/exams than other nations bring pressure in a one-size-fits-all system targeting *what* to learn rather than how
3. Social relations suffer from limited communication competencies from time spent online rather than in face-to-face interactions.

Although technology brings benefits there are downsides from global connections and intelligent machines (robots) taking over time-consuming jobs. The ongoing COVID-19 pandemic has accelerated technology use for education and employment. Robots now work alongside humans in manufacturing plants (co-bots) and offer home help and companionship to people with infirmities. In hospitals, they act as surgical assistants and play an increasing part, instead of real people, in the training of medical personnel as well as the police and firefighting professions. You will find robots in homes and offices, as they vacuum rooms and mow the grass outside. Nowadays, because of our bee crisis, robots are pollinating crops. They are also used for land surveying, photography and filming for a variety of purposes. In war zones and natural disasters, like forest fires, drones (unpiloted aircraft) are invaluable for search-and-rescue missions – providing immediate information about the state of a situation from their technological systems. Every day, new uses for robots come on stream. They are definitely becoming our constant colleagues!

Technology has highlighted many issues that although may be worse in Britain, according to OECD reports mentioned above, are a universal trend. Against a background of escalating world events education has to function. This handbook presents the experiences of a range of professionals to reflect on how education can change to meet global challenges. It uses a political, educational, social and technological (PEST) analysis to avoid a myopic view of the world. PEST is a suitable acronym. Students were asked what they thought of on-line learning and used the word 'pest' to describe the pain of enduring daily Zoom lessons, without the solidarity of their mates! These are village dwellers, so 'pest' is a common rural word to describe 'nasties' and has a negative connotation for them.

Summary

The present education system was established to create employees for the 19th and 20th century manufacturing models. The 21st century requires a rethink. Change is happening fast, with students entering a workforce where jobs are not guaranteed. Frey and Osborne (2013) suggested that around 60% of future occupations have yet to be developed and that 40% of 5-year-olds will need to be self-employed for income. The *Who is at Risk* report shows how the COVID-19 virus has accelerated the rise of robots/intelligent machines (Wallace-Stephens & Morgante, 2020). Minimising human contact is how the pandemic is managed, creating a technology boom to perform human tasks. Thus, the economy no longer retains a need for some workers, like people who select goods for warehouse orders or stack shelves in large supermarkets.

We must prepare students for an uncertain future – helping them *think* and *communicate* instead of *retain* and *recall facts* for passing exams. Some curricula content is either irrelevant for today or can be gained at the press of a button. Memorising formula for working out box volume has little value for most jobs and can be googled if needed. Listening and literate talk (narrative speaking) for solving real problems should be the focus – not facts forgotten after tests.

Speaking is our primary representational system and required at narrative levels to enable the secondary ones of literacy and numeracy to become established. Reduced human interaction, from continuing coronavirus threats, is affecting communication competence. If you do not use it you lose it! Thinking evolves from talking with others and one-self, but has less learning emphasis because of the assessment focus, which has increased due to national and international comparison league tables. Speech and language studies (Sage, 1996) found that misdiagnosis of human disorders was due to ineffective human communication. Gaining and explaining information requires expert teaching for talking, thinking, problem-solving, effective judgements and decision-making, so needing attention in education.

Gawande (2011), a surgeon, says around 50% of British patients receive inappropriate management because of scientific complexity and a struggle to process, because knowledge is not properly understood or correctly applied. Communication blunders account for £220 million medication claims alone over the last 15 years, estimated to have killed 22,000 UK patients annually. Pay-outs have doubled since 2014, indicating the importance of prioritizing communication in education and training (Statistics – NHS England, 2020). Misunderstandings have been obvious in the pandemic rollout of changing information.

Traditionally, transferable abilities have been marginalised in formal education because they are harder to measure. They include: *listening, understanding, empathy, communicating clearly informally* (chatting) *and formally* (narrative talk), *flexible thinking, metacognition, creativity, persistence, self-management and being open to continual learning.* Now robots are common, we need to explore, widen and deepen our communication and empathetic connection with others.

A Third Age Trust survey (2019) found that over-60s face a constant barrage of name-calling, insults and patronising language, with 63% saying this happens in public to embarrass them. Young people consider such language "banter" but the words are received as "insults". This shows how language and communication can distress and exclude people. Sharing and creating ideas, refining social capacity, respecting different ages, cultures, beliefs and interests, are primary to experiences in plural societies.

Education must change to become more holistic and precise. While still accepting subject pass rates of 50% (or less) there is a demand for higher accuracy today. What accuracy rate do you want from your builder, mechanic, doctor, dentist, bus driver or airline pilot? This era requires more exactness than the system accepts. Fortunately, there is a world trend for personalised learning, ensuring students and professional trainees are prepared using practitioner models following agreed international criteria. We must work towards competencies not test scores and remain on content until achieving mastery, in relevant, real contexts, rather than studying modular, abstract themes in prescriptive ways.

Our current system is commonly called Swiss Cheese Learning (cheese with holes). This phrase was used by Reason and Hobbs (2003) to describe gaps in human defences. If a student passes exams at a 75% level we praise them. Thus, students think they have done well with a quarter of basic information missing. The issue is the 25% they may not know. Each year the curriculum builds on previously transmitted knowledge. Lack of a foundation compounds as learners move through the system, with some experiencing failure and loss of confidence. There are too many 'holes in the cheese' to apply knowledge effectively. A 50% (or less) pass indicates much learning is questionable, but is satisfactory for progression or a qualification.

Current education means completing set assignments and exams with little room for individuality. Passing prescribed tests does not guarantee students can apply learning in real situations. Currently, 150 American schools have negotiated portfolios of evidence to universities and employers rather than Grade Point Averages (GPA). Portfolios demonstrate personal, practical and academic achievements more clearly than arbitrary tests. Thankfully, project-based learning is more common, demonstrating both knowledge and transferable abilities according to individual interests and capabilities. 'Since learning is so nuanced, so should be the means in which we assess it' (Sackstein, 2015, p. 10). Future education must centre around life-competencies and how to be a contributing citizen, based on individual talents and desires. It must focus on thinking, communication and practical application of knowledge and understanding. This requires rethinking everything we know and recognise about formal learning. Recent reports by world authorities confirm the messages in this book.

The World Bank report "The education crisis: Being in school is not the same as learning" (2020) suggests hundreds of millions reach adulthood with no basic competencies, so that 56% are unable to be fully productive in life and work. The report stresses that educators generally are not given the knowledge to cope with a wide range of diversity. The United Nations 75 Digital Report (2020) suggests that 87% of people globally think that for education to improve there must be better communication and cooperation. Endorsing these views, two World Economic Forum 2020 reports state it is lamentable that trans-missive, lecture-based approaches dominate and so teachers must be trained to re-define their role and focus on the development of learners to become contributing members of society, by helping them to become aware of their specific interests and talents. Opportunities to learn how to communicate and cooperate in project-based, relevant learning facilitates personal, practical and academic development. The Global Technology Governance Summit (Di Caro, 2021) shows how diversity, equity and inclusion have failed, so attention should be given to issues of equality. The chapters expand on these ideas with examples of effective practice to test the present situation and promote future change by considering questions:

- Why do classes start at 9 am?
- Why do we split learning into subjects?
- What is the role of a teacher?
- How can informal and formal learning be encouraged?
- How can students learn from others?
- How might a learning journey be personalised and recorded?
- How could evidence of understanding be better demonstrated?
- What ways might show this progress?

– How might we teach and reinforce abilities for the present and future?
– How will the 2020 pandemic impact on teaching methods?
– How can education deal with inequality issues of diverse learners?

Answers to these questions have political, educational, social and technological aspects, used as the analytic framework for the book content. Students deserve an integrated education that positively challenges and inspires lifelong learning.

The OECD Director suggests Britain has made the slowest educational progress of the 37 OECD nations, because memorisation remains the main learning strategy in a narrow, exam driven culture (Schleicher, 2020). He says that education today is not about teaching people something, but helping them develop a compass to integrate personal, practical and academic competencies. Work-readiness requires an understanding of globalisation, coming from mobility and partnerships. Education must rebalance to develop a more holistic, world approach for coping with life, by fixing on real not abstract issues.

An OECD educational working paper (Bertling et al., 2020) reports schools and colleges will never return to former teaching ways following the 2020 pandemic, with 50% preparing for a future of blended learning. This requires ongoing professional development to monitor new teaching modes, using practitioner recording models to review evidence with colleagues. Since 60% or more students worldwide do not reach required educational standards, it is time to review policies and practices (Luckin, 2020).We are not there yet, but if brave enough to do things differently it is possible. This book explores options from medical, engineering, commercial, linguistic and educational professionals – representing Arts and Science perspectives to present a broad range of possible approaches.

References

Bertling, J., Rojas, N., Alegre, J., & Faherty, K. (2020, October 14). *A tool to capture learning experiences during COVID-19: The PISA global crises questionnaire module.* OECD Education Working Paper 232. https://dx.doi.org/10.1787/9988df4e-en

Burns, T., & Gottschalk, F. (Eds.). (2019). *Educating 21st century children: Emotional wellbeing in the digital age.* OECD Publishing. https://doi.org/10.1787/b7f33425-en

Di Caro, B. (2021). *Global technology governance summit.* GYGS21 WEF.

Frey, C. B., & Osborne, M. A. (2013, September 17). *The future of employment: How susceptible are jobs to computerisation?* [Paper]. Oxford Martin School, University of Oxford. https://www.oxfordmartin.ox.ac.uk/downloads/academic/The_Future_of_Employment.pdf

Gawande, A. (2011). *The checklist: How to get things right*. Profile Books.

Luckin, R. (2020, February 7). I, teacher: AI and school transformation. *New States-man*. https://www.newstatesman.com/spotlight/2020/02/i-teacher-ai-and-school-transformation

Luthra, P., & Mackenzie, S. (2020, March 30). *4 ways COVID-19 could change how we educate future generations*. World Economic Forum. https://www.weforum.org/agenda/2020/03/4-ways-covid-19-education-future-generations/

Reason, J., & Hobbs, A. (2003). *Managing maintenance error*. CRC Press.

Sackstein, S. (2015). *Hacking assessment: 10 ways to go gradeless in a traditional grades school*. Times 10 Publications.

Sage, R. (1996). *An investigation of misdiagnosis of human problems*. RCSSD.

Schleicher, A. (2020, February 4). Preparing the next generation for their future, not our past. *New Statesman*. https://www.newstatesman.com/politics/2020/02/preparing-the-next-generation-for-their-future-not-our-past

Statistics – NHS England. (2020). https://www.england.nhs.uk/

Tam, G., & El-Azar, D. (2020, March 13). *3 ways the coronavirus pandemic could reshape education*. World Economic Forum. https://www.weforum.org/agenda/2020/03/3-ways-coronavirus-is-reshaping-education-and-what-changes-might-be-here-to-stay/

Third Age Trust. (2019). *Survey of views regarding language use*. https://www.u3a.org.uk/

United Nations. (2020, September). *The future we want, the United Nations we need: Update on the work of the Office on the Commemoration of the UN's 75th anniversary*. https://report.un75.online/files/report/un75-report-september-en.pdf

Wallace-Stephens, F., & Morgante, E. (2020). *Who is at risk? Work and automation, in the time of Covid-19*. RSA. https://www.thersa.org/globalassets/_foundation/new-site-blocks-and-images/reports/2020/10/work_and_automation_in_time_of_covid_report.pdf

World Bank. (2019, January 22). *The education crisis: Being in school is not the same as learning*. https://www.worldbank.org/en/news/immersive-story/2019/01/22/pass-or-fail-how-can-the-world-do-its-homework

Figures and Tables

Figures

Tables

Notes on Contributors

Daryle Abrahams

has degrees and post-graduate qualifications in Education and Business Administration. His work experience has been as an equities trader, real estate broker, secondary teacher (Drama & English), Senior Human Resources Development Officer, Corporate Education Consultant, Chief Learning Officer and Information Technology Manager of Managers. He presently is based in New York and travels the world in a training capacity for business corporations, with a role of teaching adults how to learn for both their personal and professional lives. His particular interest is in developing a *Model of Learning Experiences* at work, as situations have shown that present employees struggle with this, as well as often lacking the personal abilities now needed for higher-level job roles.

Nigel Adams

is a Professor of Professional Practice and was first Director of the Buckingham Enterprise & Innovation Unit (http://www.beiu.co.uk) at the University of Buckingham, England. He teaches, advises & mentors undergraduates taking an innovative two-year (8 term) BSc in Business Enterprise (http://bit.ly/bbe_home1) Venture Creation Programme. He was previously the BBE Programme Director, developing it from 2008–2019. This is one of only a few world honours degree programmes that offers undergraduates the opportunity to study whilst also starting & developing a business. Within 4 months of starting the programme, students must pitch for seed-corn capital from *Buckingham Angels* and then run the business/es as an integral part of their degree. He was also Programme Director of a new, different, one-year MSc in Applied Enterprise & Innovation that started at the University of Buckingham in January 2021 & aimed at bright graduates, who have studied subjects not helping them get jobs because they lack experience to be immediately productive for an employer. Nigel also teaches Entrepreneurship & Innovation, advising and mentoring university students, staff and local people who want to develop their "can-do" mind set to start or grow businesses. A *Medical Entrepreneurship* Student Selected Component (SSC) is offered to medical students in the University of Buckingham's Independent Medical School. From 2002–2011, Nigel was Managing Director of Nigel Adams & Company Ltd, providing business, management, international marketing, recruitment and other support and advice to the management of Western companies to establish business operations in Central & Eastern Europe & improve sales. He is an international business adviser, with more than 50 years' experience in business, enterprise, entrepreneurship, marketing & counter-trade. He lived in Poland from 1993-l 2002, working on state company restructuring projects as a British Government *Know How Fund Management* Adviser. He is a Chartered Marketer & Fellow of the Chartered Institute of Marketing (CIM).

Peter Chatterton

is a Chartered Physicist and digital innovator whose work in digital learning started when the first IBM PC emerged, developing interactive multimedia education programmes for companies such as Shell. In the late 1990s, he moved into the higher education sector and was a key innovator in the UK Government's digital modernisation programmes for universities, working "at the coalface" with key Government educational agencies and over 50 universities. He acted in the role of critical friend, evaluator, change management consultant and mentor as universities implemented digital innovation projects to enhance teaching, learning and assessment. He has been a prime mover in setting up industry/education partnerships including the (virtual) Automotive College and was a Visiting Professor at the University of Hertfordshire's Blended Learning Unit (a HEFCE-funded CETL – Centre of Excellence for Teaching and Learning). He was a founder of the Jisc Student Change Agents' network, designed to engage students in supporting academics to digitally enhance teaching. He has authored many books on the innovative use of technology, published by the Financial Times, Pitman Publishing, Routledge and Kogan Page and has produced a range of HE sector resources e.g. the QAA Flexible Curriculum toolkit, the Jisc Technology for employability toolkit and a range of effective practice guides for higher education, including a good practice guide for Critical Friends.

Stefano Cobello

is the coordinator of Polo Europeo della Conoscenza (European Pole of Knowledge – www.europole.org) a permanent network of educational institutions. He has a BA in Philology (Russian and English) and PhD on Models of Educational Inclusion at the Institute of Philosophy and Sociology of the Bulgarian Academy of Sciences. He has been a lecturer of Italian language and History of Art in the East Oriental Siberian Russian Academy – Ulan-Ude (Buriatia). Stefano has long experience of coordinating networks of schools in European projects, webmaster and expert in intercultural education. He has been a trainer of trainers, nominee by the regional administration of Veneto as trainer for teachers. He has been responsible for the Youth for Europe programme in Veneto Region (1992–1996). The network Stefano coordinates is made of about 4000 educational Institutions and includes schools of every type, Universities, adult education organizations, Regional Administrations, VET schools, NGOs, cooperatives working for European social and educational inclusion. It has protocols for collaboration with various institutions in the world from Russia to India. The Europole network works in every field of education, from ITC to in-service training courses for teachers, from Kindergarten sectors to adult education in prison and in rural areas. It works also against social exclusion, xenophobia and racism, helping to break any kind of gender stereotypes among different cultures and religions. It is involved in intercultural learning and the vocational training field. One of the main fields of activity of the network has been in *educational robotics,* focused on prosocial values and human rights. This led to the development of a creative team of teachers and a policy reform Erasmus+ project promoting Robotics against Bullying (612872-EPP-1-2019-1-IT-EPPKA3-PI-FORWARD, www.roboticsvsbullying.net/) with hundreds of teachers involved for the prevention of this increasingly common phenomenon in schools.

Joanna Ebner

is Headmistress of Thomas's Kensington. She was educated at North London Collegiate School, Cambridge University and the Institute of Education, London. An experienced head teacher for the past 15 years, Jo first led the Royal School, Hampstead, an all through girls' day and boarding school, where she turned it around, earning praise from ISI and Ofsted. Jo was appointed to her second headship at Thomas's Kensington in September 2012. Whilst continually driving excellence, the school has been awarded a number of accolades, including the Platinum Award for innovative CPD, the International School Award and the Values Based Education Award. Jo established a bespoke MA for staff across all the Thomas's Schools and Ofsted (Feb 2020) once again deemed Thomas's Kensington as "outstanding in all areas", praising the culture of high aspirations. She is a trained School Counsellor and co-author of *Counselling in Schools* and regularly contributes to educational debate. An associate member of the Girls' Schools Association, Jo was on the panel of expert advisers on mydaughter.co.uk and contributor to the GSA's publication *Your Daughter*. Jo was awarded a Winston Churchill Memorial Travelling Fellowship in 2018, undertaking research into university-school partnerships, with travels abroad to study educational policy and practice to enable an international view of practice. She is nearing completion of a Doctorate in Education. Jo is a visiting lecturer at Roehampton University, a member of the University of Roehampton's Primary Strategic Management Board for Partnerships and was a member of the government led Independent State School Partnership Forum. In summer

2020, Jo set up *School Unlocked* (www.schoolunlocked.org), COVID Response Catch Up Summer Schools for Pupil Premium children.

Pierre Frath

has been Professor at the University of Reims (France). After teaching French and English in secondary schools for twenty years, he completed a PhD in computational linguistics and became a Senior Lecturer at the English Department of Université Marc Bloch, Strasbourg, in 1998. In 2005, he became a Professor at Reims University and taught linguistics, didactics, natural language processing and the philosophy of language until 2013. He created and headed a Language Centre at Reims University in 2008. He is a member of three research laboratories, CIRLEP (Centre Interdisciplinaire de Recherches sur les Langues et la Pensée – Reims), of which he was the Director for many years, CELISO (Centre de Linguistique en Sorbonne – Paris) and GEPE (Groupe d'Étude sur le Plurilinguisme Européen – Strasbourg). He has created a seminar in Reims, *Res-per-nomen,* dedicated to language, which holds an international conference every other year. He has published about a hundred and fifty research articles in the fields of linguistics, philosophy of language, multilingualism and didactics (http://www.res-per-nomen.org). He has recently published an essay on individualism, *Cogito versus Ubuntu,* with the philosopher René Daval (Sapientia Hominis, 2019), an *Anthropologie de l'Anglicisation* (Sapientia Hominis, 2019) and an essay in linguistics, *Linguistique anthropologique et référentielle* (Sapientia Hominis, 2020). He is now working on a book on prehistoric linguistics. He has been involved in the teaching of African languages in French-speaking Africa for the past three years. He was made *Chevalier des Arts et Lettres* in 2014.

Irene Glendinning

began her professional life as a computer programmer and systems analyst, working in UK and Australia, with short spells teaching maths at a secondary school and further education. During a career break caring for her two children she again turned to education, teaching on-glaze china painting to adult learners in a community college and delivering IT in further education. She then taught mathematics, computer studies and IT at secondary level before moving to higher education as a computer science lecturer at Coventry University in 1990. In addition to lecturing, a succession of leadership roles took her on a journey through higher education. First, she managed a range of joint and interdisciplinary undergraduate programmes. In 1999 she was appointed International Programme Manager, with responsibility for establishing and managing collaborative partnerships in Malaysia, Singapore, Hong

Kong, China and Cyprus. Her next role was to manage a portfolio of up to 17 taught master's programmes, before becoming Academic Manager for Student Experience for the faculty of Engineering and Computing. In this role she employed students as peer-mentors, had oversight for organising learning support for students with special educational needs and, as part of the European partnership team, was responsible for recruiting European students to the postgraduate programmes. Only at this late point in her career did she have capacity to undertake research. Her former roles had kindled strong interests in a range of topics, such as preparing secondary students for university, quality assurance, equality and diversity, pedagogical practices and assessment, design of learning spaces, students supporting students. Starting in 2007 she led a series of funded research projects around topics concerning plagiarism, academic integrity, corruption and quality assurance and contributed to several other research projects on similar topics. This research led to the completion of her own PhD and successful supervision of several PhD students. She is now based in Coventry University's Office of Teaching and Learning and is institutional lead for academic integrity. She has had strong links to BCS, The Chartered Institute for IT, throughout her career, being awarded Chartered Fellowship in 2016, taking local, regional and national volunteer roles in BCS at different times. She has also served as external examiner and advisor to many universities and HE providers. She is a member of the UK's Quality Assurance Agency advisory group on academic integrity. Her academic publications, mainly focusing on academic integrity, have led to many invitations as a speaker at events, conferences and webinars.

Susan James
is a teacher of English Language and Literature, as well as a Pastoral Deputy Head at Cheadle Hume School. She has been a Head of Lower School at The Manchester Grammar School; a Drama and PSHE teacher; a Form Tutor and an Academic Mentor for English PGCE Students and NQTs. She achieved a Distinction for her MEd in Educational Leadership, at the University of Buckingham, UK. Following her work on developing resilience in school pupils, Susan has worked to create a new curriculum for Lower School boys at Manchester Grammar School, from 2018. She is a School Governor, with many community interests and is focused on the holistic development of children for their futures in the new Industrial Revolution (4).

Riccarda Matteucci
is an experienced teacher at senior school and university levels, having taught in Italy, Africa, the United States of America and the United Kingdom. She has

held a Research Fellowship at the University of Cambridge, into Italian grammar use in England and led the CamBrit/Rome Scheme, enabling students to study and teach across countries. Riccarda is an expert linguist in European languages, with a specialty in across-language teaching, verbal and non-verbal communication, as well as the language-learning problems of those with special educational needs. In Italy, she has been involved in teacher training and served on the National Qualifications Panel. She has particular interest and experience in the multi-cultural aspects of students in teaching and learning along with the issues that underpin this factor. She was the lead DFCOT doctoral examiner, in the area of *Communication,* at the College of Teachers, then based at the Institute of Education, University College, London. She is presently devising a teacher training programme for African nations. Riccarda is an experienced researcher and author. She is presently working as a collaborator within the Research and Innovation Group on the Polo Europeo della Conoscenza (European Pole of Knowledge) project looking at bullying issues in Education as one of the major problems across the world. Riccarda was in New York, before the COVID-19 outbreak, researching their use of protocols in learning and has kept in touch with progress through media sources.

Gloria McGregor

is a retired Primary Head Teacher, who also by invitation, fulfilled a one-year role as advisory head teacher with responsibility for the support, monitoring and assessment of newly qualified teachers. Gloria took early retirement in 1995 due to a profound hearing loss. Following working with children having specific learning needs support, McGregor taught lip-reading to adults in Essex and Suffolk. She also did some work with the army, including teaching English Language to the wives of Ghurkhas. She has been a Trustee of The British Tinnitus Association. Since 2009, Gloria has run voluntary lip-reading supports groups in her local area and has written contributions to National and Local Hearing Loss Charities. In 2013, she launched her website, as a free resource to anyone wishing to practise lip-reading. She is a visiting professor of Hé University, Shenyang, China. Gloria is a Liveryman of both the Worshipful Company of Educators and of the Worshipful Company of Spectacle Makers. Passionate about raising deaf awareness, in her role as Mistress of the Worshipful Company of Spectacle Makers, McGregor gave a presentation to the City Livery Companies and Civic Representatives to raise deaf awareness in the City. She was joined by two professional musicians who happen to be deaf! Together they sent a powerful message to the group. Gloria continues to work to raise deaf awareness and help overcome the impact of hearing loss.

Elena Milli

is a family and relational psychotherapist experienced in working with children and teenagers with special educational needs or social and behavioural issues. These include those that are abused or with disadvantaged contexts as well as immigrants. She is an expert in educational and prosocial robotics. Elena is a collaborator in the Polo Europeo della Conoscenza (European Pole of Knowledge, www.europole.org) a permanent network of educational institutions, as projects officer. This network of about 4000 institutions (schools, Universities, Regional Administrations, NGOS, cooperatives) is committed to promoting European social and educational inclusion through umbrella activities, European projects, training courses and conferences. Europole network works in every field of education against social exclusion, xenophobia and racism, helping to break any kind of gender stereotypes among different cultures and religions. It is involved in intercultural learning and the vocational training field. Elena has experience in Horizon 2020 research projects and in other Erasmus+ projects about robotics and special needs education, early childhood, giftedness, immigrants and refugee students, bullying and STEM education. She is one of the promoters of the activities of the network in *educational robotics* focused on prosocial values and human rights, especially as project manager of the policy reform Erasmus+ project Robotics against Bullying (612872-EPP-1-2019-1-IT-EPPKA3-PI-FORWARD, www.roboticsvsbullying.net/). She is a teachers' trainer at the national and European levels on different topics connected with psychology and innovative teaching.

She coordinated an educational assistance service for teenagers at risk attending secondary school, structuring psychological, educational and social interventions, working with teachers and parents, in cooperation with the social assistance service.

Elizabeth Negus

is a chartered teacher and for the past twenty years and has been teaching, lecturing, mentoring and offering private tuition to GCSE – College students, undergraduate and-postgraduate students. She has held the posts of Head of English, and Head of English Departments at various colleges and has been a tutor at the University of Dundee. Elizabeth is a Founding Fellow of the Chartered College of Teachers. She is an International Speaker on Education and to a lesser degree politics. In 2017, Elizabeth was a speaker in the House of Lords. The motion was, "What are the challenges for international relations in the 21st century?" Elizabeth also works with secondary schools, mentoring students in oral presentations for that intergenerational debate. She is a researcher, proof reader and book editor. She is Vice Chair of School Governors at Clementswood and was Chair of Curriculum at Gordon Primary School, Ilford. Elizabeth sits as school governor on the Board of the Federated Schools, Gordon Primary and Cleveland Primary. She is a Fellow of the Royal Society of Arts and Member of the English Speaking Union. In 2018, she was honoured with a certificate for her educational role in the Queen's Commonwealth Essay Writing Competition. Elizabeth is on the DSFR LLC Advisory Board, Switzerland. She also sits on the General Committee and Commonwealth and European Diversity and Membership Forum and is Chair of the Diversity Committee at the National Liberal Club, London. She is an Educator and sits on the Membership Committee of the Worshipful Company of Educators. She is author of several books, notably KS 2 English, contributor to *Paradoxes in Education: Learning in a Plural Society* and numerous literary 19th century academic papers. She has reviewed academic books and journal papers. She is a Fellow of the Chartered College of Teachers and the Royal Society of Arts.

Juan Eduardo Romero

is a Kinesiologist at the Universidad de Chile. He is Assistant Professor, in the Department of Kinesiology, Faculty of Medicine. A Master of Education in Health Sciences, Juan is Vice-Director of Continuing Education in the Postgraduate School. He is also Director of the Committee of Programmes for Continuing Education. Memberships include the Co-ordination Committee of Programmes, the Currículum Commission of the Department of Kinesiology and the Central Commission for Development of Continuing Education at the Universidad de Chile. Juan is a past President of the Chilean Association for Respiratory Kinesiology and present President of the Commission for the Development of Competencies in Respiratory Kinesiology, Department for Specialist Accreditation (DENAKE). He is also a member of the American Association for Respiratory Care, the Chilean Society for Respiratory Kinesiology, the Chilean Society for Pediatric Neumology and the Chilean Society for Intensive Medicine. Juan is a participant on the Professional Doctorate at the University of Buckingham.

Rosemary Sage

is a qualified speech pathologist, psychologist and teacher; former Dean at the College of Teachers where she led the first Practitioner Doctorate, sponsored by the European Commission. She was Director of Speech and Language Services in Leicester/Leicestershire; a Teacher in Primary and Secondary schools; Senior Language Advisor to an LEA; an Academic in 4 universities: Head of Department and Professor of Communication at Liverpool and a visiting Professor in Cuba and Japan. Rosemary is on the Queen's Panel for

Education and Industry Awards. She sat on the Lord Chancellor's Advisory Committee as a senior magistrate (Chairperson & Judicial Mentor) and is presently on the judicial executive and a member of the Magistrates in the Community (MIC) project. She was a founder member of the Children's Legal Panel and expert witness for Educational appeals; on Parliamentary Committees for Medicine and Education, the Teaching of Science, Inclusion of Students with Special Needs & Education Advisor to the RCSLT. Rosemary has been a trustee of several charities, a school governor and member (president) of many research boards. She has led international research projects on language, education and employment and published many books and over 150 refereed papers in journals, gaining national/international awards for her work on the Communication Opportunity Group Strategy (COGS). She is a winner of the Kenneth Allsop Memorial Prize, The Bullard Prize, The Gimson Award, The International Human Communication Network Medal and The College of Teacher's Research Award – the Leverhulme Fellowship – amongst others. She is a Millennium and TCOT Fellow. Presently, Rosemary is the SEND Director for the Learning for Life Educational Trust and Scientific Advisor at Abai University, Kazakhstan.

Emma Webster
is Curriculum Leader at a primary school in South East London, building the curriculum since the school's opening in 2014. Her passion for creative learning stems from her previous career as a contemporary dancer, working with internationally renowned choreographers and touring across Europe. Emma has a BA in Dance Theatre and an MA in Dance Performance from Laban, which fostered an interest in the nurturing of creativity within but also beyond the Arts, for success in the 21st century. Emma is a board member of Lewisham Educational Arts Network (LEAN), an organisation committed to building networks between Arts organisations/artists and educators in the London borough of Lewisham. She also works internationally with educational partners in Nepal promoting creative approaches to global learning and collaborates with outdoor learning specialists to improve children's wider experiences of education.

How the World Is Changing Education

Rosemary Sage and Riccarda Matteucci

Never waste a good crisis – reinvented, reinvigorated teaching for today.

∴

Walking past school on the day it was closing, because the coronavirus was sweeping the nation, the children rushed to the fence to view the Jack Russell dog, *Rocket Ronnie*! It was playtime, so we chatted about stopping lessons and working from home. A staff member rushed up to tell the *children* off for talking to strangers and *us* for attempting to engage them in conversation. With a sharp remark, the necessary balance between hope and fear was upset – seen in the expressions of those involved. How you tell things is crucial and understanding the delicacy helps restrain ourselves to avoid *mis-speak*. We went away sad about the enormous terror the world emotes regarding people and events – the present one being the fragility and uncertainty of life. At the start of shutdown, a chap bought all the toilet rolls in a local shop and on exiting someone stabbed him in the stomach for his action. Panic set in with a police presence along the street for hours.

The world is changing and we urgently need to encourage people to be calm, resilient and able to think about the results of actions. The politics and economics of individualism have not forged common identities and built trust. Solidarity is what enables us to survive challenging circumstances. We must examine the general world situation and how education is having to rapidly find more effective, flexible ways to communicate, relate, teach and support people. In the age of Zoom, Microsoft Teams, Skype, etc. it is possible to engage in more personalised learning to address a mismatch between formal instruction and workplace goals.

Whereas education focuses on exam successes, job employers want people with personal and practical competencies to apply knowledge with initiative, independence and effective communication, cooperation and collaboration. We must avoid the equivalent of panic-buying – rushing for dramatic

© KONINKLIJKE BRILL NV, LEIDEN, 2022 | DOI:10.1163/9789004506466_001

solutions, grabbing what suits us and elbowing others out of the way. If wrong decisions are made, we are responsible for consequences. Otto von Bismarck (prime minister of Prussia, 1862–90) once said that the only thing we learn from history is that nobody learns from history.

However, there is an important lesson we *can* learn from life-changing events. The greatest danger faced is social fragmentation from existing threats. The right approach can turn widespread fear into mass courage. We rapidly need to regain a sense of purpose to shape the world according to intended trajectories. Education is not just about helping us *live* our lives but how to *love* and *lead* them. Reflection is followed by review and refinement of educational policies that address proper preparation for jobs and survival. Book contributors are forward-thinking professionals with international research and practical experience, involving a variety of work and cultural backgrounds.

Part 1 Politics of Education will appeal to policy-makers and leaders with background material that presents world trends and changes.

Part 2 Education Policies and Practice is important for classroom teachers to reflect on how to implement a curriculum that develops personal and practical as well as academic abilities to produce student resilience and flexibility.

Part 3 Social Justice centres on values to promote in education for developing the good side of human nature and produce community-minded citizens. This section applies to staff in pastoral roles.

Part 4 Technology in Education is a must for everyone as it considers *positive* and *negative* issues of technology use and reinforces the need for staff to be trained to implement blended learning, with particular attention to those who find this model challenging.

Dr Elizabeth Negus, a Practitioner Doctor, who met Prince Philip at her Award Ceremony, has the final say in this introduction.

Dedication

This book is dedicated to the memory of His Royal Highness, the Prince Philip and Duke of Edinburgh, who was Patron of the UK College of Teachers until 2016. He was passionate about improving education for everyone. His last College role was to ratify Privy Council approval of a Practitioner Doctorate, sponsored by the European Commission to increase impact on policy and practice. The Prince met the pilot 8 Practitioner Doctorates at a 2016 Award Ceremony and the books they produced, *Paradoxes in Education* (Sense) and *The Robots Are Here* (Buckingham University Press) have pride of place in the Palace Library. This book is the third in a series of five texts detailing practitioner concerns. Prince Philip was proud of these achievements. His legacy lives on in all those he has inspired.

He was particularly concerned about students deprived of the means to learn (such as home computers), thereby curtailing their ability to develop. We can find solace or answer in Eliot's (1888–1965) *Four Quartets* (1941). His commitment to *time* draws us into a utopian world if we slow down:

> *Time present and time past*
> *Are both perhaps present in time future?*
> *And time future contained in time past*
> *All time is eternally present*

While we have present time, we must use it for the benefit of the next generation. Teachers are caught within a conflict: the aspiration to improve spoken and literate communication and the increasing emphasis on virtual learning. Countries like Cuba, Finland, Italy and Japan put more emphasis on speaking rather than writing and so are ahead in education and performance. Public speaking is a well proven way of motivating young people to learn and develop confidence to operate in a competitive world. Time is not on our side. The metaphysical poet Andrew Marvell, concerns himself with time and space. In Stanza 2 of *To My Coy Mistress* (1681), he writes: "but at my back I always hear; time's winged chariot hurrying near deserts of vast eternity". We could, however, reverse Marvell's dictum, slow down time and invest energy in promoting a generation that values conversational intelligence".

The Prince would also approve of dedicating this text to our future citizens. One is Riccarda Matteucci's latest grandchild, Luca, born in January 2021. Let us hope the contents make us all reflect more deeply about our present world, with a strong determination to do all we can to improve it!

PART 1

The Politics of Education

∴

Introduction to Part 1

Rosemary Sage and Riccarda Matteucci

We start with politics, the ruling principles of governments deciding education policy and its operating system. Researchers draw distinction between 2 types of educational politics (Scribner et al., 2003). *Macro-politics* define how power is used and decision-making conducted at state and local levels, depending on world events. It is generally considered to exist outside educational institutions. *Micro-politics* is use of formal and informal power by groups and individuals to achieve organisational goals and prepare learners for life. Cooperative and conflictive processes are integral components of *micro-politics*, but researchers note that both types may exist at any level of these systems. There is significant difference between *Politics of Education* and *Politics in Education* – seen in world trends and future predictions which are the content of the opening chapters.

Chapter 1: Global Trends outlines the main developments influencing education. Although how learning is systemised and implemented evolves from government macro-politics, world trends, like people movements, have a big influence over the micro-politics of how individual institutions respond to specific circumstances.

Chapter 2: The Present and Future World begins with micro-political issues, like the 2020 pandemic, and how it has focused on the need for student and staff well-being. This chapter ends with where the future of education might be heading, based on the range of present issues.

Chapter 3: Is School an Outdated System? considers how only 15% of learning takes place formally and examines *micro-political* models giving students more control to develop personal, practical competencies and strengthen individual independence and initiative.

Chapter 4: Preparing for Work describes a unique higher education programme which is practice focused with students having their entrepreneurial enterprises assessed for their qualifications.

Chapter 5: A New Model for Workplace Learning outlines how training can change to meet the education employment mismatch.

1 Reflections

Trends are seen in new technology, economic shifts, education-work mismatches, urban growth, people mobility, education demand, life-long learning

© KONINKLIJKE BRILL NV, LEIDEN, 2022 | DOI:10.1163/9789004506466_002

needs and cultural mixing. These focus on an educational need to cultivate greater resilience, flexibility and the communication competencies underpinning all personal development. In a competitive world, where tests and exams rule, as a result of *macro-political* decisions, it is easy to give personal, practical development a back seat. Teachers must work to government standards, so *micro-political* influences come into play as they need to cooperate and collaborate to meet goals.

Work place surveys suggest that communicative competence is the weakest ability, declining since technology has taken precedence over talk in human exchanges. This is particularly noted in science and engineering professions, where there is much interdisciplinary engagement (Khoo et al., 2020). Therefore, communication issues emerge as a primary area for development in a world where jobs need smarter personnel as robots carry out the routine work. Team-work abilities are required to solve world-challenges. These include a growing, aging population, diminishing natural resources and climate change as well as people movements, to name only a few that need urgent solutions.

References

Khoo, E., Zegwaard, K., & Adam, A. (2020). Employer and academic staff perceptions of science and engineering graduate competencies. *Australasian Journal of Engineering Education, 25*(1), 103–118. https://doi.org/10.1080/22054952.2020.1801238

Scribner, J. D., Aleman, E., & Maxcy, B. (2003). Emergence of the politics of education field: Making sense of the messy center. *Educational Administration Quarterly, 39*(1), 10–40. doi:10.1177/0013161X02239759

CHAPTER 1

Global Trends

Rosemary Sage

Abstract

Education leaders are aware that it is global and not just domestic trends that impact on the way they determine policy and practice, as well as short and long-term operations. World factors change the trajectory and involve consideration of many things that influence the direction of learning and teaching. These encompass political, economic, social and natural issues, so making successful outcomes a complex business. Studyportals,[1] a research organization with about 3,000 education partnerships worldwide, used linear projection modelling of 15 high-income countries to outline trends impacting on the future of education worldwide, with many of these presented in this chapter. Trends are changing learning methods, as well as aspects leaders must consider when planning the future. Nine common ones, are outlined below, with how they can be applied for effective learning.

∴

> Not by speeches are the great questions of the time decided but by iron and blood.
>
> OTTO VON BISMARCK, *Prime Minister of Prussia (1862–90) and First Chancellor of the German Empire*

⁚

1 Rise of Technology and Intelligent Machines (Robots)

Sage (2019) discussed whether robotics, artificial intelligence and machine learning would put people out of work or into competition for existing jobs. Will newly-created job-roles absorb workers displaced by automation? This issue has implications for employment relations and work preparation. Professor Estlund (2018) provides a blue print for reforming *employment law* to cope with insecurity about job automation. This is vital to stem increasing mental health problems because of uncertainty about life and economic futures.

Automation is driven by similar forces to that of *fissuring* (*replacing employees with outside ones*), which transform workplaces to bring lower standards and increasing inequality. Managers are paid large salaries and everyone else a decreasing percentage of earnings (Sage, 2020). Reactions to automation consider the *fissuring* problem and aim to extend legal responsibility for core workers, but fail to meet the mechanisation challenge of reduced costs and human employment risks. As technology becomes a cost-effective, reliable substitute for people, it enables employers to evade laws for protecting staff, so creating insecurity and anxiety. Lack of workplace trust is now common, impacting on effective outcomes. Britain has lower workplace performances than comparable countries and puts less emphasis on people management and training than similar nations (OECD, 2015).

How can staff rights and entitlements be protected, while reducing incentive to replace employees with contractors and technology? Recently, 235,000 university students complained about less face-to-face experiences and more online teaching (Daily Telegraph, 26/03/20: University pupils demand refunds for online lessons). Students feel support and expertise is missing and experienced academics are not being engaged.

Estlund says worker entitlements must be separated from their economic costs. Some personnel rights and privileges entail employer duties and burdens, but for others ways to shift costs or extend these past appointment should be found. Employment rights and benefits are threatened from fissuring, automation and a management elite. They fail to protect all staff and erect barriers for new employees.

A broader foundation of economic security for all is necessary, including those not making a living through regular employment. The coronavirus situation of complete lockdown throws up these issues for review. Work situations are now a major cause of shredded public trust and resulting mental health problems – especially for those exiting formal education to put their feet on the work ladder.

Thus, communication, cooperation and collaboration ate vital abilities, which many employers say are lacking in the present workforce. Education has focused on learning facts to pass standard tests rather than personal and practical ability de elopement. This lack of balance must be corrected, so that students are taught to work independently as well as cooperatively and able to use initiative to solve problems. A survey of 1,012 graduates and 531 senior HR professionals was carried out by Survation in November 2019 confirming employer reports. Since the 1980s, the Confederation of British Industry (CBI) has seen a decline in student formal communication now that technology takes precedence over talk.

A McKinsey Global Institute study (2016) says that 20–30% of the working-age in America and Europe are engaged in 'independent work'. Of those, most said that they did so by choice, either for their primary income (30%) or to supplement it (40%). The remainder said they did for necessity, but would prefer a traditional job (14%), or need extra income (16%). Personal and practical competencies in planning, implementation and marketing are vital for survival – requiring nurturing in education contexts.

Growth of degrees at the expense of personal, practical intelligences and skills, may witness reversal, as technical and skilled manual work (builders, electricians, plumbers, carpenters, cooks etc.) will be hard to automate, whilst many degree occupations (accountancy, banking, computer programming, data processing, education, journalism, law and medicine) show intelligent machines taking over routine tasks. Institutions must prepare students to be entrepreneurial and resilient, to enable reinventing themselves and their careers throughout life.

An undergraduate course, at the University of Buckingham, BSc Business Enterprise (BBE), enables students to apply for funding to start a commercial operation, which forms practical degree involvement. The programme is under the expert guidance of Professor Nigel Adams, who has the experience of commercial life to support students through studies. This is an excellent initiative in tune with workplace needs.

2   Financial Changes

While Higher Education (HE) has shown huge growth, with 50% of British school-leavers studying at this level, most expansion is in middle-income nations, with high-income ones showing inertia. This is partly due to more English-language programmes now available in Europe, with developing countries improving educational resources. Students benefit greatly from learning in another culture in our global world.

UNESCO Institute of Statistics shows lower-middle-income nations beating high-income ones in tertiary enrolling from 2012. Upper-middle-income countries are still top, but with more HE worldwide. Figures suggest that 75% of global STEM (science, technology, engineering and mathematics) graduates will concentrate in Brazil, Russia, India, China and South Africa by 2030, compared with 8% in the United States of America (USA) and 4% in Europe. Britain must attract students by emphasising their special knowledge and how it can be applied, with the English language as an important marketing point.

A third of students are in STEM subjects, accounting for 5.6% of tertiary enrolments, while another third are in business, administration and law. The USA enrolls more international students at undergraduate level than Chile, Poland, Spain and Japan, but lags behind the United Kingdom (UK), Australia and Denmark. The UK marketing edge is English expertise, which is a requisite for global leaders as the language for international business. A rise in anti-immigration policies, along with the need for increased enrolment, means institutions must find new ways to attract international students. How can they globally engage, when policies are against them, especially when needing STEM programme students for the functioning of local economies?

3   Mismatch of Employer Requirements & Education Experience

Payscale (2016), a company researching salaries, benefits and compensation, found that only half of British employers thought recent school leavers and graduates were prepared properly for the workforce. Institutions must understand this disconnect, as they are continually criticised in reports. Creative approaches give students lifelong learning abilities. A start is to increase global collaboration for developing new ideas from mobility and partnership projects in practitioner focused studies at all levels.

Increased automation drives this mismatch, as rapid work changes are not at the rate at which Higher Education can easily adapt. Emerging world-class Asian universities will compete with the West, with more students moving to them. Capacity imbalance increases technology use and blended learning, creating joint ventures within and across organisations. Many UK institutions have links with similar ones abroad, to benefit everyone with a broader view of life and deeper knowledge. Bringing together people with varying perspectives is the way forward if serious about dealing with world problems, such as developing education that meets local, national and international requirements.

4   City Growth

World demographic trends find more people moving to cities, so creating a greater need for local education and job alignment. Cities are growing as job and career centres, so the role of education in regional development is critical, along with industry-institutional partnerships. HE must adapt to needs as urban living demands different teaching, for many personal, national and international reasons.

Daventry International Rail Freight Terminal from Europe, houses some of the largest warehouses in Britain. Houlton new-town has been built to accommodate workers, many of whom are Robotic experts from Europe. Catching a local bus to the warehouses, you will not find many persons speaking English! These people are highly educated in machine technology, as a result of Europole world initiatives, which do not operate in the UK to the same extent as some other nations. Intelligent machine systems for stacking and distributing goods are being developed. European Engineers are designing software for machine operations, building and installing instruments for use. Procedures include picking goods from shelves for delivery, which was done by local residents or students. Now, Robots march the aisles, which take 45 minutes for a human to walk, so machines save human time and energy!

Universities in the area (Coventry, Warwick, Leicester, Northampton) must establish pre/post-graduate engineering courses in *Robotics,* so that intelligent machines can be developed and maintained. Teachers need to be instructed in robotic use, as in the programmes provided by Europole, which I participated in during 2019.

5 Student Mobility

Studyportals (2020) projection model indicates a growth of 412,000 international students from 2015–30 across 15 high-income nations. Nearly 3/4s of the world's mobile students study in developed countries (Millennium Development Indicators). In 2000, 189 national leaders agreed a future partnership vision: with less world poverty, hunger and disease, improved survival prospects for mothers and infants, better educated children, equal opportunities for women and a healthier environment. Eight Millennium Development Goals (MDG), are targets to measure progress.

United Nations (UN) Millennium Declaration statisticians selected indicators to assess progress from 1990–2015, when targets were to be met. Annually, the Secretary-General reported to the UN General Assembly aggregated data at global and regional levels. The 2002 goals, targets and indicators were used until 2007 and then revised to include 4 new targets agreed at the 2005 World Summit (Resolution adopted by the General Assembly – A/RES/60/1 and the Secretary-General's 2006 report).

Agencies and organizations in and outside the UN, with the Statistics Division, coordinate data to assess progress towards the MDG. It maintains the selected indicators database, plus other background supplementing series.

Figures from specialized agencies for the *International Statistical System* (ISS), UN Statistics Division and Agency Statistical Offices, are adjusted for comparability. Data, to calculate national indicators, depend on statistical services to produce it and/or report to the relevant international agencies. Some governments may have more recent statistics not released to the ISS. Others do not produce data required for indicators, so agencies estimate from available related variables, or other methods in the metadata section.

The international statistical community has been concerned about a lack of data to compile required indicators in parts of the developing world. Monitoring has focused on this shortcoming, raising awareness to plan initiatives for statistical capacity building. Progress has been made, but much remains to be done until all nations can produce a common, continuous flow of social and economic data to inform and track progress. Highly educated people are needed for these roles, as much information nowadays is wrongly interpreted, with dangerous consequences for society.

The 2020 agenda for sustainable development, adopted by UN Member States in 2015, provides a blueprint for peace and prosperity, in the present and future, for people and planet. The core mission is the 17 *Sustainable Development Goals* (SDGs (2), which involve all countries (developed or developing) in a global, mutual partnership. Ending poverty and other deprivations must go with strategies to improve health and education, reduce inequality and enable economic growth – while tackling climate change and preserving oceans and forests. The Europole Group – three of whom are book contributors – have initiatives to support this mission.

The right to development must be a reality for all, along with freeing everyone from want. This depends on sustainable economic growth, focusing on the poor, with human rights central to progress. The aim is to promote a comprehensive, coordinated strategy, tackling problems simultaneously. Education is vital to achieve aims, giving knowledge, analytic abilities, judgement and determination, to improve society and build competencies. The Declaration called for halving people living on less than 1 dollar a day by 2015, by finding solutions to hunger, malnutrition and disease, promoting gender equality and female empowerment. A basic education is guaranteed for everyone, supporting the Agenda 21 principles of sustainable development. Support from wealthier nations, with aid, trade, debt-relief and investment provides help to developing countries.

Thus, education is crucial in helping people move out of poverty and achieve a reasonable lifestyle. Professor Riccarda Matteucci is evolving teacher training in Africa and advising on preparing students for the new industrial age, to enable this great continent to compete educationally and economically with the world.

6 Demand for Education

The UNESCO Institute of Statistics (2020) estimates that by 2030 there will be 120 million HE students with 2.3 million internationally mobile. This is a possible 51% increase in international student enrolment. The report said that from 2000–14, there was growth in global Higher Education enrolments from 100–207 million, with 30% at private institutions. However, it is lower and middle-income nations where demand is increasing, with higher-income ones stagnating. As institutions in higher-income nations become more dependent on enrolment, it is vital they access developing areas. Rising incomes and demands for education in these nations mean institutions have opportunities for innovative models.

New delivery modes and institution types are envisaged. Different disciplines must collaborate to provide knowledge and competencies for the future. This cooperation is more common in Europe and Italy leads the way with multi-discipline teams working at all levels in education, to prepare students for future inter-disciplinary work roles through the Education Robotics programme. When lecturing in Child Development, in Japanese universities, there were doctors, nurses, therapists, teachers, architects, fashion designers, nursery staff etc. on the same courses. Disciplines educating and working together are less common in Britain.

7 Need for Continual Professional Development

Estimates suggest that there will be 4.3 million more students over the age of 24 in high-income nations from 2015–30. In 2030, 25–34 year-olds with a tertiary degree across OECD and G20 nations will double as tabulated below, from the OECD (2015) *How is the Global Talent Pool Changing?*
- 2013-137m 25–34 year olds in Tertiary Education – OECD + G20 nations
- 2030-300m 25–34 year-olds in Tertiary Education – OECD + G20 nations

8 Higher Education Budget Cuts

2017 data from 33 American states had revenue below projections to produce budget cuts. *Budget Policy Priorities* (Mitchell et al., 2017; Parrott et al., 2020) show they spent $9 billion less on HE in 2020 than in 2008. The 2020 pandemic accentuated economic problems with diminishing resources affecting progress. Stephen Jordan, Emeritus Professor of the Metropolitan State University in

Denver, in his 2017 retirement speeches, predicts no HE funding in 2025. To demonstrate HE value and evidence of student return on investment, leaders must clarify qualification offers. They need to improve academic standards, as those working in the sector have seen a decline, as student numbers soar and costs are cut. Lifetime education is key to rebalancing the global economy (Sage, 2020).

HE promotes thinking and creativity, with yearn to learn shifting content into experience. The Practitioner Doctorate programmes, researching *within* a participant's own practice, are a move towards this and are sponsored by the American Carnegie Educational Foundation in universities. These degrees need teaching by experienced academics and practitioners, with national and international research outputs. UK universities now functioning as businesses, so there has been a tendency, even within the Russell group, to employ staff without high-level academic qualifications or practical experience to offer students. The dumbing down of UK degrees has been the subject of reports (Kuczera et al., 2016). These suggest that low standards, at the end of initial education, mean that 1/3 of UK students are unprepared for degrees, which lowers academic standards. The OECD latest 2019/2020 report repeats this message. The Italian system takes an interdisciplinary approach to learning, which values spoken, narrative language for assisting critical and creative thinking and improving standards and so is a model of good practice.

9   Cultural Mixing

An influx of immigrants to the West has brought different cultures (backgrounds & lifestyles) to their new countries of residence. Culture includes what people believe and do, influencing how they view the world, understand it and communicate with others. This determines learning and teaching styles. Development depends on being raised by articulate parents, within a stimulating context, which respects the historical values. Upbringing and culture have profound effects on how we perceive and process information. For example, the Asian holistic view differs from the Western idea of object parts or classes defined by rules. Thus, Asians see the world in terms of relationships between things, whereas Westerners view these as distinct entities (Sage, 2020). Such information helps when considering how cultural background might influence learning approaches, as well as the gaps between students and teachers.

A definition of normal student behaviour can be based upon *individualist* Western and *collectivist* Eastern cultures. Teachers lacking cultural knowledge might misinterpret student conduct and judge it as poorly behaved or disrespectful. Asian students tend to be quiet in class and making eye contact with teachers is considered inappropriate. In contrast, Europeans and Americans expect to eye-ball, engage and participate to be considered competent. Educators tend to treat all learners alike despite cultural diversity.

Addressing cultural difference is key but controversial. It is key because we have an increasingly diverse student population with wide achievement gaps. It is controversial because we may culturally stereotype to explain student differences, many of whom do not speak the language of instruction as their mother tongue. Educators aim to teach without discrimination, but this does not always address cultural diversity. They cannot escape the fact that their communication styles reflect cultural background. What they say and how they articulate, along with student, parent and colleague relationships, are influenced by how they have been socialised.

Race and ethnicity play a role in identity, contributing to behaviour and beliefs. Recognizing this helps students succeed when communications and expectations are unfamiliar. Despite learner differences, uniformity dominates practice. Students use the same textbooks and materials. They may work at a different pace, but have the same content, curriculum and tests measuring success. The curriculum should include different voices and ways of thinking, experiencing and understanding life. It is important for students to discover and value their own voices, histories and cultures for their confidence and self-respect.

Institutions are biased toward uniformity over diversity, because sameness is easier to manage than difference, with practices promoting student equity. Few teaching models integrate both educational values and human diversity. The issue is to identify what should be the same and different as people existing together must have core values and goals to minimise tensions. Uniformity brings disadvantages for students, whose culture has taught them different beliefs and behaviours from majority norms emphasized in education. Students, whose culture values collaboration (like the Japanese) are told to be independent. Those valuing spontaneity are asked to exercise self-control. Others rewarded in families for being social are told to work quietly alone. Students embrace the one where they live, but must take on behaviours to become upwardly mobile and have to cope with this duality. Thus, clashes cause struggles when individual strengths are not respected. Without understanding individual unique histories and meanings, helping students effectively is impossible. Courses in intercultural communication and understanding are important and some nations require these for immigrants. One which I led on the INTERMAR (Sage, 2011) European Commission project was seen essential by students and employees in order to study and work well together. This was called: *Getting to Grips with Intercultural Communication* and became a popular on-line course when the College of Teachers functioned as a training institution.

10   Review

Education is driven by political, economic, social and cultural considerations. Population world movements create plural societies with complex learning needs. Italy is an example of a cultural regard for spoken communication in education practice. This is seen in their focus on oral examinations at all levels. It means students acquire effective ability to communicate, cooperate and collaborate. These attributes are viewed by engineering professions as mandatory, as they work in international consortiums. Sage (2020) shows in the book *Speechless* that people have different learning attitudes affecting *what* and *how* they communicate, due to cultural, ethnic and religious backgrounds. *Received Pronunciation* has been debunked in a London Royal Academy of Dramatic Art (RADA) *Anti-Racism Action Plan,* showing disregard for Standard English, which employers deem vital for easy understanding.

Thus, all teachers must be mindful of the many influences on policy and practice, as well as knowledgeable about global requirements and social impact. This chapter summarises trends as a background for looking at new educational developments in later sections. Educators need creativity to promote learning that takes account of holistic human development and values academic, personal and practical intelligences equally. A lack of attention to the full range of human competencies means that people are more prone to mental health problems, with inability to cope with life uncertainties and a need to be constantly adaptable. With 50% of students admitting to being sad and afraid for the future, according to an OECD education and skills working paper (Bertling et al., 2020), we must take social and emotional development seriously.

Note

1   Studyportals.com is the international study choice platform to find & compare study options across borders.

References

A/RES/60/1 World Summit Outcome. (2006). *The secretary-general of the United Nations report.* http://www.un.org>desa>docs>globalcompactPDF

Bertling, J., Rojas, N., Alegre, J., & Faherty, K. (2020, October 14). *A tool to capture learning experiences during COVID-19: The PISA global crises questionnaire module.* OECD Education Working Paper 232. https://dx.doi.org/10.1787/9988df4e-en

CBI (Confederation of British Industry). (2019, November 29). 45% of employers value academic and technical qualifications equally. *FE News*. https://www.fenews.co.uk/fevoices/39023-45-of-employers-value-academic-and-technical-qualifications-equally

Estlund, C. (2018). What should we do after work? Automation and employment law. *Yale Law Journal, 128*(2), 254–326. https://www.yalelawjournal.org/pdf/Estlund_40pp7v2g.pdf

Kuczera, M., Field, S., & Windisch, H. C. (2016). *Building skills for all: A review of England*. OECD. https://www.oecd.org/unitedkingdom/building-skills-for-all-review-of-england.pdf

McKinsey Global Institute. (2016, October). *Independent work: Choice, necessity, and the gig economy*. https://perma.cc/RE86-CFZ6

Mitchell, M., Leachman, M., & Masterson, K. (2017, August 23). *A lost decade in higher education funding*. Center on Budget and Policy Priorities. https://www.cbpp.org/sites/default/files/atoms/files/2017_higher_ed_8-22-17_final.pdf

OECD. (2015, April). How is the global talent pool changing (2013, 2030)? *Education Indicators in Focus, 31*. https://doi.org/10.1787/5js33lf9jk41-en

Parrott, S., Aron-Dine, A., Leachman, M., Stone, C., Rosenbaum, D., Pavetti, L., Bailey, P., Marr, C., & Romig, K. (2020, March 19). *Immediate and robust policy response needed in face of grave risks to the economy*. Center on Budget and Policy Priorities. https://www.cbpp.org/research/economy/immediate-and-robust-policy-response-needed-in-face-of-grave-risks-to-the-economy

Payscale. (2016). *Salary, benefits and compensation*. http://www.payscale.com/data-packages/jobskills

Sage, R. (2011). *Getting to grips with intercultural communication*. INTERMAR: Project no. 519001 – LLP – 2011 – PT – KA2 – KA2MP.

Sage R. (2019). *The Robots are here: Learning to live with them*. Buckingham University Press.

Sage, R. (2020). *Speechless: Understanding education*. University of Buckingham Press.

Studyportals. (2020). *Mega-trends on world education*. Studyportals.com

UNESCO Institute of Statistics. (2020). *Education growth of demand*. http://uis.unesco.org

Webber, A. (2019, December 18). Graduates "lacking key skills", HR managers say. *Personnel Today*. https://www.personneltoday.com/hr/graduates-lacking-key-skills-hr-managers-say/#X4c sOcQBCo.whatsapp

CHAPTER 2

The Present and Future World

What Education Needs to Consider

Rosemary Sage

Abstract

It is fascinating to learn that since the lockdown for the COVID-19 pandemic in March 2020, the sale of Seneca's letters from a Stoic have increased by 747% and the Meditations of Aurelius by 356% (Daily Telegraph, 5 May 2020). We might wonder what a Hellenistic School of Thinking, founded by Zeno of Athens in the 3rd century BC, could teach us today. In an uncertain world, there is much to examine in these ancient writings as preparation for the future. Stoic philosophers believed that the key to a reasonable life is learning to live in the moment and not regretting the past or worrying about the future. Therefore, to focus on the present is the cure for anxieties hovering around and ready to hit at any moment. If a situation displeases and distresses, the Stoics advise leaving or changing and stop complaining about it. I remember my mother advising: "like it, lump it or leave it", as the recipe for dealing with difficult situations. The pressure of constant testing makes education tough for many students. The recent pandemic revealed anecdotal evidence that some students with additional needs coped better away from school or college pressure. This chapter considers learning strategies for political review and ends with reflecting on the big changes afoot in our rapidly expanding age of technology.

1   Learn to Accept

Acceptance of grim circumstances is often the only course of action – as to leave or change these is impossible for most of us in societies dominated by politics. Choices are limited by many context factors. Recently, we have witnessed the opposite of Stoicism in the pandemic, with people hoarding goods (like toilet rolls) and breaking social distancing rules. This can be contrasted with the selfless acts of people at the front line who have put their lives at risk for others. We were all blown away by Captain (made Colonel and Knight of the Realm) Sir Tom Moore, with his gold Blue Peter badge, who as a centenarian showed himself a real trooper. He trudged daily to raise around £33 million to assist the National Health Service and his sad death from COVID-19 was ironic (February 2021).

Modern opinion encourages us to express our feelings and emotions but has this gone too far? As a volunteer, I go into many schools and colleges on the *Magistrates in the Community* (MIC) project, aiming to help students become aware of the consequences of their actions, now that serious crime in the youth population is escalating. It is staggering to witness how some youngsters treat their teachers and the way they speak to them. No restraint or respect is shown. We are told not to bottle things up, but there is an appropriate time and place for this. It is important for educators to assist students to examine their reactions and consider how best to respond to situations and relationships. This is basic to a teaching approach where effective personal development is considered as important as academic success.

To find a calm approach is to acknowledge that bad things happen continually, like fires, famines, plagues, wars, failing exams, falling out with friends, or finding oneself without employment and the means to live. These are all part of experience. Bad events can be endured, reviewed and mastered. They should not be unexplored worries and shoved away to fester, or they will always unsettle us.

Story books give mostly happy endings but this often does not mirror reality. Students need to grasp this from informal and formal educational experiences. Stoics advised running through the worst scenarios – public disgrace, loss of possessions, death of loved ones, betrayal, poverty, failure, ill health etc. – to examine such terrors head on. I ran sessions called, *Coping with Problems/Disasters* (see Sage, 2017, p. 186), which gave opportunity to look at things that students would face in life. The British Ofsted school inspectors always regarded this input favourably. Not only was the content important, but students had choice of joining groups to explore the topic,with tasks at different cognitive-linguistic narrative levels to assist processing and production. They were able to engage in activities at their developmental stage and learn from others operating at higher levels. Experience shows that students choose things they can cope with comfortably.

The way to achieve inner strength and thinking strategies to solve problems is not to run away from anxiety but focus on the fear. If you fail exams   how would you cope? If someone stole your precious things – what would you do? If left without relatives – how would you manage? If people plot behind your back – how would you respond? Working through fears shows resilient thinking. It is not accepting that fears will disappear and everything will be alright. Treating fears as trifling and attempting to dismiss them is not the way to cope. Doubts will still be there and develop rather than diminish. In an age when mental health is a significant student issue, facing fears positively is priority within the curriculum.

2   Fight Fear with the 4 Ds

- *Dreaming* – reflection and choice.
- *Drafting* – plan to bring fulfillment and contentment
- *Discovering* – sense of life to elevate energy, commitment & passions
- *Deciding* – how to deal with present fears and anxieties

This is a continual process. We must be constantly engaged to stay alive in the present and be hopeful for the future. Dreaming or imagining is proactive and vital to continually assess our position and ask if choices are sustaining or becoming intolerable. The steps in this process should be in an age/stage appropriate way. The following suggestions were devised by English Baccalaureate students and known as *Rosie's Remedies!*

2.1   *Reflect*
Are we going nowhere? Are we in a dash to act in a flash? Is life crushing us? If so, we must review. Time-out is needed if feeling on edge. Plan for daily personal space and take 6 deep breaths through the nose, exhale slowly, asking: "Am I doing what I want?" When a teacher, I started lessons with a *Pace Learning Technique* (PLT) (Sage, 2000, p. 98) and a brief reflection on how everyone wanted the day to be like. This brings mental focus and action.

2.2   *Relate*
Successes result from support. If people praise rather than pillory us – we develop a positive self-image and confidence. What are our helpful relationships? Recall these people. What questions would you ask them? How would you like them to respond? What help is needed? To imagine and reimagine, one must deal with a natural inclination to delay. Take action not analysis to avoid apathy. Sound out a friend to support your action.

2.3   *Remake*
Talents are our creative force. What are our abilities? Do we use them fully? If not, how can this be done? The peak of vitality *flow* (see Appendix) is when talents, interests and passions meet, engaging us mentally and physically. Choose something in which you have felt *flow* – complete absorption in something. Describe it in words to remake experiences.

2.4 *Revise*

Are you living another vision of life? Create your own ideas. Dream and achieve them. What is success and fulfillment for you? We add things to life to make it intolerable. What is the answer? First, decide what you want to cope with – what goes and stays. Sort things to unpack and repack.

2.5 *Respond*

Fulfilling not filling time brings satisfaction. Revise schedules and redesign life. Without time control, autopilot occurs. When we own time, excuses of too much work do not govern us. We must not become captive to email, phone checking and the internet. National Health Service data shows that children are more likely to need treatment for complaints linked to screens, like repetitive strain injuries, than anything else, increasing by 65% in 2019. There is a 432% increase of youngsters self-harming with sharp objects, from viewing internet content (National Health Statistics, 2021). Repossess time by reducing social media mindless connections. This pattern is learnt early and must be confronted in education, as it encourages us to delay things, like course assignments! Are you happy with how you organise tasks? When did you say: "This was a well-spent day?" Are you saying *no* to less important things and *yes* to priorities? Choose one priority and act on it today. Do something daily that gives pleasure. Hang out with people supporting your goals and bringing out the best in you.

3 Review Life Experience

Monitoring progress brings awareness. This quiz, devised by psychology students at the University of Leicester, is in 3 sections that define: what you *own, act* and *recognise* – your OAR to row you out of trouble!

Mark statements with a *number* (1–4) to define appropriate response.

1. *Disagree* (over 75% of the time) 2. *Partly disagree* (under 75% of the time) 3. *Partly agree* (under 75% of the time) 4. *Agree* (over 75% of the time)

Own
I like my life _____
I keep fit through exercise _____
I like where I live ____
I am happy with my relationships ____

I have a clear idea about my future ____
I am creative and pursue this ____

Act
I make decisions in line with life goals ____
I continually learn and develop ____
I focus and think through things clearly ____
I am resilient when difficulties arise ____
I am kind, understanding and forgive others ____
I am content to be alone sometimes ____

Recognise
I make time to help others ____
I feel peaceful and relaxed in natural places ____
I am grateful for the good things in life ____
I maintain a regular spiritual practice ____
I believe in human power ____
I know what I want to be remembered for in life ____

A possible total is 72 (Grade 4–75% of the time). Score often & check progress.
  Students enjoy this type of quiz and like to devise their own for various purposes. In an English lesson we considered things we were good at and this is what 16-year–olds decided in a group task.

> Creating and making things, developing trust, moving physically, exploring new things, growing plants, fixing possessions, constructing things, solving problems, analyzing information, remembering things, composing music/poetry/stories/art, assembling resources, helping people, caring for others, making relationships, organizing events, attending to details, seeing the whole picture, coping with change, grouping things, making others happy, communicating well, managing activities, organising people/events, leading teams, writing for work/pleasure, gaining information, achieving something special.

Following this task, students listed possible jobs and matched abilities for these. Personal, practical and academic competencies develop from a clear purpose and passion which brings energy, enthusiasm and commitment. Build ideas and responses needed and consider use in the future. Look at life in response to circumstances and pose answers to present problems, even if not perfect. Small daily moments bring learning and living purpose. Count blessings regularly!

4   Future Education

Personal, practical and academic abilities develop from a clear resolve. When using talents for something passionate, we have energy and drive. Build ideas and responses needed, thinking how to transform them for the future. Reimagine life and learning in response to world situations. Provide answers to present issues. Have you identified your goal? If not, what can you do to gain it? A challenge for 21st century Education is the growing divide between a demand for learning and the supply of teaching. There is a global shortage of appropriately trained educators, a scarcity of highly-qualified leaders and a lack of schools. According to UNESCO's Institute of Statistics (2013) the world will need 3.3 million more primary teachers and 5.1 million more secondary ones by 2030. There is no easy solution to this issue, but how the Middle East is addressing this provides one answer.

Why would this not come from Europe or North America? The reason is in what the Harvard Business School calls 'disruptive innovations'. These are improvements transforming the organisational and management structure of established institutions. Disruptive innovations originate in low-end and new-market footholds. Thus, it is more likely that a learning-teaching solution is found in Dubai than in traditional Britain, America or independent sectors. What can we learn from Dubai? How might this be implemented world-wide? Are there other alternatives?

5   The For-Profit Sector

Dubai is driven by return-on-investment, economies of scale, scalability, differentiated markets and limiting costs, like staffing. There are 3 characteristics that shape future for-profit global education.

5.1   *Different Priced Education*
The for-profit groups offer premium, mid-range and budget schemes, like Airline first class, business and economy seats. Price differences are between type of institution, class size, range of facilities offered, educator qualifications and the amount of teacher-student weekly contact time.

5.2   *Central IT Systems*
Nord Anglia developed the Nord Anglia University, as a global continual professional development portal for teachers. The Global Education Model (GEMS) has a shared Virtual Learning Education (VLE) for schools with blended

learning programmes. This has moved away from the traditional model of a teacher standing in front of a class transmitting information for students to memorise for passing national tests.

6   Investment in Top Talent for Key Leadership Roles

People with a high-level personal, practical and academic education and train-ing (like the Practitioner Doctorate Model) are wanted for present complex educational needs to meet demands of the new industrial world. Emphasis is on research *within* practice, producing evidence of acquisition and application of knowledge, continual professional development, mobility and partnerships. The aim is to gain a global perspective and achieve a wide knowledge and per-sonal competencies to drive policy and practice. GEMS attracts top education-alists worldwide, to progress educational and IT learning strategies. However, many are cautious of the business model as the route to opportunity for all. We have seen the downside in our university system, with a decline in standards overall and employer disillusion.

Many prefer a free school system, where everyone learns the same things under the same conditions, as necessary for a more equal society. However, it does require well-educated teachers, to the level of other professions and changes to bureaucracy to enable more flexibility. The *one-size-fits-all* philoso-phy for learning, that is academically focussed, results in many students failing to make the grade and leaving education with limited achievements. We are all different and plural societies exacerbate this, as curricular issues, like early sex education, have shown in certain ethnic cultures. The recent pandemic empha-sised this, as the world reacted to events differently. When the crisis began, American people started to buy up guns furiously, the French red wine and the British toilet rolls and hand sanitiser! Professor Pierre Frath, from France, says:

> I do not much like the British system with its many public (private) schools, where the well-off population provide separate tuition for chil-dren. This is a recipe for a class-ridden society. Our rightists want this too because they hope they can pay less taxes and they do not want their chil-dren contacting the riff-raff. What the governments since Sarkozy have been doing, both socialist and conservative, is ruin the state system and in 10 years' time they will claim that it is unable to provide a good education & then clamour for subsidised private schools like in Sweden (the Swedes are thinking again). If there are problems with state schools, and there are, let us solve them. They have provided top-level education up to now. If they had not, our country would not be the 5th/6th world economy. If

parents pay for their children's tuition, they expect them to be delivered a diploma. They are customers then. This is already plaguing British universities and sooner or later is bound to become an obvious problem. It would just take the collapse of a building or a bridge built somewhere by an incompetent architect or civil engineer who 'bought' his degree in the UK. Universities put much pressure on academics. When they fail a student, it is hassle and they get the message – just let them pass. I have many examples. I don't believe the market has any wisdom at all and I am sure it is a rather sinister place, full of greed and perfidy. I also think it is much less cost efficient than public organisations. Look at health care in the US: hugely expensive and unable to cope with a pandemic like COVID-19. Millions of people are unable to pay for their expenses, basically because the system is geared towards profit, not solidarity.

Here are quotations, taken from a *Diary of a Bad Year*, by Coatzee (2007):

Conservatives believe that the role of government should be self-limited: to create conditions in which individuals can bring their aspirations, their drive, their training, and whatever other forms of intangible capital they have, to the market, which will then (the moment when economic philosophy turns into religious faith) reward them more or less in proportion to their contribution (input).

Surely God did not make the market – God or the Spirit of History. If we human beings made it, can we not unmake it and remake it in a kindlier form? Why does the world have to be a kill-or-be-killed gladiatorial amphitheatre rather than, say, a busily collaborative beehive or anthill?

For-profit schools will develop a reckless society geared towards individual wealth and this means poverty for those who do not adapt, i.e. for the original members of society, not common good.

Pierre Frath's philosophy is right for providing a more equal society. He points out that the state system needs to change. This has been taken up by Matthew Lynn in an article, *Where is the public sector's can-do-spirit* (Daily Telegraph, 14 May 2020, p. 16). He suggests that although the private sector has adapted well to the new world of the pandemic, 'the public sector is fighting change tooth and nail and, even where it is willing to adapt, it is holding the Government and public to ransom by its demands'. An example is a public sector worker asking for help in delivering official notices through letter boxes in residential areas and told it was not possible as no risk assessment had been done. There is an obstinate refusal to consider even a phased return to normality. Matthew Lynn is pessimistic about national unity. However, let us be positive and give it a try. As Professor Frath suggests, wisdom is needed for this and it comes from experience. The OECD has continually pointed out the failings in the UK system which has produced the slowest educational progress of all nations. It is urgent that we act with wisdom to produce the unity that progress requires.

7   Future Forecasts

If we apply principles of Dubai's for-profit sector to the global learning problem, what will the future hold for education? Five forecasts were discussed at the Rome Education for Robotics programme (2019).

7.1   *Education for-Profit*
This will become common worldwide. Not-for-profit education is unequipped or unable to meet global demands, so the result is that the for-profit sector will fill the void. In Chapter 1, a decline in Higher Education funding was examined. Many state school, college and university classes are taught by educational assistants with minimal training in subject areas and pedagogy. However, this could change if state systems invested more wisely in provision that acknowledges differences and society needs for personal, practical and academic talents. The pandemic has highlighted the importance of all roles for producing effective outcomes.

7.2   *Teaching by a Specialist at Secondary Level*
This will be less common. Technology may not replace teachers everywhere – but will in many places. In future, it will only be premium secondary education that delivers teaching by experts in classrooms. A range of real and virtual resources is increasingly available to supplement face-to-face teaching. Budget secondary education will not have subject teachers, but be delivered through online courses on learning platforms. However, for many youngsters worldwide this will be better than the present situation of receiving no education at all. Mid-range secondary education will be delivered by *super-teachers* via virtual-reality conferencing. The for-profit sector will invest in new technologies to maximise teacher impact. Universities, like Leicester, have used this model. For example, when Warwick developed their Medical School, under the auspices of Leicester, lectures were viewed by medical students in both places using technology. Similarly, my key lectures on *Communication in Education* went to Leicester Centres worldwide.

7.3   *Virtual Reality Teaching*

This will disrupt secondary education. We already have video conferencing, which enables pupils to be taught live by a remote teacher. It enables students to travel through time and space and experience Rome's ancient relics, wartime life in the trenches and examine world wonders, like the Egyptian pyramids. Once these technologies are combined, so that we have virtual reality teaching, it will be possible for a student to put on a headset and *feel* as if they are in a real classroom with a world-class teacher, or be taken on a school visit to any place in time and space.

7.4   *Super Teachers*

These are commanding high salaries with high levels of education. A result of virtual reality teaching is that super teachers will increase. The for-profit sector has a proven record of investing in talent to provide the best quality education. It will pay to attract top talent, particularly in shortage subjects and their global networks will deliver a platform enabling outstanding virtual reality teachers to reach millions of students. These teachers will be famous celebrities with social media *likes* and fan clubs!

7.5   *Primary Teachers*

They will be assisted by robots. Children, at a foundation stage, need human contact and face-to-face interaction to shape learning and provide real support. Therefore, it is unlikely that teachers at this level will be replaced with technological solutions. Secondary education predictions suggest that primary schools must teach competencies to enable youngsters to access non-classroom based forms of education. Robots will possibly replace some teaching assistants, performing basic instruction, like teaching English and Mathematics or listening to children read. Robots can be programmed by experts (therapists/psychologists) to manage learning problems.

Nevertheless, the pandemic proves that artificial intelligence (AI) is not always smartest. Many AI systems, which control inventory, marketing, retail and even fraud, have needed tweaking because they could not compute why the lives on which they made predictions had changed so much. As people habits have rapidly altered, the AI systems had to be transformed. Algorithms need to be robust and able to change quickly. The modelling behind lockdown has been an unreliable mess. Experts say that results vary from different machines and in some cases using the same ones. There appears to be a bug in either the creation or re-use of the network file, according to people writing on the Github online forum. This prompts questions that models must be capable of passing the basic scientific test of producing the same results given the initial set of parameters, otherwise there is no way of knowing they will be reliable. Global predictions are made using deterministic models that factor in randomness. We must understand the limitations of mechanisms we use to make judgements and decisions.

8   Implications for Education

The COVID-19 pandemic has changed the way we view things and how we might work in the future. It is possible that it will alter how we live permanently, although it is a transition to a different state, which we were moving to more slowly. Regarding education, video conferencing has become common during lockdown, with Zoom meetings prevalent. Statistics compiled by secure-connection provider Okta, in April 2020, showed a 200%+ increase in daily users. Freemium terms are popular, like ability to have group calls with 100 people free for 40 minutes. *Teams* is a common system in universities.

Technology has long been involved in the complexity of human systems and importance of multi-discipline approaches. When at the University of Leicester, in 2000, we had joint courses integrating science and humanities. A human cannot just be conceived in medicine's conventional biological and developmental terms, but also in philosophical, psychological, sociological, cultural and educational perspectives. Students had all these inputs in integrated course modules. It was Einstein who said, in an hour you spend 55 minutes thinking about the problem and the last 5 on the solution. The more perspectives bearing on the issue the better the final result.

University business models have largely dispensed with inter-discipline approaches, particularly in Schools of Education. Some have no psychologists or speech pathologists on teaching teams. This contrasts with cultures like Cuba, where Heads of Educational faculties have backgrounds in these areas, on the basis that learning is a communicative experience and unless you understand this development and how it breaks down or fails to occur, you cannot teach effectively. Bringing together the humanities and sciences is vital, as Elizabeth Negus argues in Chapter 7. Education in the liberal arts emphasises dialogue, empathy and ethics, alongside understanding of human behaviour, culture, values and attitudes. It prioritises reflection as much as rote learning, which is valued in the Japanese Hansai tradition, bringing greater personal awareness, judgement and more effective learning.

However, the pandemic lockdown meant collaborative, hands-on, face-to-face teaching and learning has been impossible, so virtual reality (VR) augmented (AR) and mixed reality has come to the fore. What has been the best way to deliver learning when everything has shut down? It is feasible to deliver practical training via mixed realities now there is confluence of technologies. This means that VR may live up to the publicity of recent years – cheaper headsets (£320 each), improved broadband and availability of cloud computing. Recently, medical students have been brushing up or perfecting skills in the virtual world. Using Oculus Rift headsets, they practise treating patients on an immersive ward, using technologies. More widely, there is disconnect between the promise of VR and AR and what is happening in practice. A minute of VR content can cost many thousands of pounds to create, which makes it beyond the possibility of some users. Also, not everyone feels comfortable with headsets.

9   Relevant VR Use

To understand when and where VR might be suitable, we need to understand what must be achieved. People learn best by *doing*, in live situations alongside others, where they can share understandings, guided by experts. When you compare this experience to online learning, used for conveying information, the forgetting curve is cruel, as nobody remembers anything after a few days, say teachers. Where VR might be useful for teaching facts and theories, real learning takes place in social situations, where students support each other and teachers monitor non-verbal language to assess comprehension. Much knowledge is tacit and cannot be communicated through spoken or written words. Learning needs to be hands on in context. VR companies are making progress in developing haptic controls to give an individual physical feedback from the virtual world, but presently progress does not live up to expectations.

Learning does not need VR or AR to be interactive. The Open University has successfully refined online learning for 50 years. E-learning in early days was viewed negatively – you listened to someone muttering a monologue and faced routine multiple choice questions. Now experts understand how to design content, using knowledge of communication information processing and performance, as well as splitting hour-long lessons into bite-sized chunks of 3–5 minutes (Sage, 2020). What works best is live virtual classrooms with small groups of around 8 students, so teachers can 'see' what people understand. Interaction, in a virtual classroom, is really important. Online learning works for delivering factual information but for practical instruction it struggles to deliver.

For VR to fully arrive the business model is yet to develop. VR companies must make integration of content simpler, so that education can incorporate it easily into curricula. Economies of scale are relevant in hard economic times.

Ability to educate and train students in large numbers remotely, to standard requirements, will be important. The use of robots to individualise learning is proving successful, as students with specific needs can have programmes devised by experts, like psychologists and therapists, which removes the need to be taken out of class for specialised help.

10   Review: Final Thoughts ...

Foretelling is more about reading signs of the time and working out a likely future position from events, rather than predicting from revelations on high or intelligent machines. Prophets are rarely popular, because they usually deliver a message that people do not want to hear, which might involve unacceptable changes. The signs for a future of education are for all to review. There are unforeseen events that crop up, like the COVID-19 pandemic, but this was forecast by the late Professor Stephen Hawking and others, as population control over the course of history is by illnesses and wars.

In an ideal world every child would receive the education quality that is available at the British elite Public and Grammar Schools, but this will be unlikely to happen. In reality, there is inequality of educational provision at all levels worldwide, which is difficult to change because of costs and cultural influences. The challenge to every passionate educator is how we can give every student opportunity to have an appropriate education, so technology has an important, increasing role to play in enabling this prospect. However, the most imperative issue is teacher quality, methods of instruction and a system accounting for diverse student talents, interests and needs, using various learning approaches. Dr Peter Chatterton, an expert in education technology and recently Professor at the University of Hertfordshire, says:

> The average number of simultaneous uses of Blackboard (education product like Zoom) in February 2020 was 100 but now is 6000 in a university where I am a consultant. The problem is that now academics are focusing on real-time conferencing as their distance learning model to directly replace a lecture. The goal must be to change mind-sets about on-line delivery. For example, think about synchronous approaches but rethink course design. Trying to replicate existing ways of doing things in the virtual world will not work.

Peter mentions in Chapter 15 that a problem of online learning is the proper monitoring of feedback to students. This is highlighted in a recent National

Union of Students Survey (2020), which showed significant dissatisfaction with the quality of provision both on-line and face-to-face. Students suggest that they are taught by people with no experience and limited knowledge, as the tendency is for universities to buy in cheap labour.

Both Peter Chatterton and Juan Romero (Foreword) pose problems of distance learning for students not having regular access to computers at home. This was an issue in a project for continual professional development of teachers, involving the universities of Cape Town, South Africa and Leicester, England. In the African bush there is no reliable computer network, but teachers have mobile phones that work, so instruction takes place through this medium and is effective. This is cheap, flexible delivery and prevents people having to attend pricey off-site courses. Such learning could become more widespread.

Dr Kim Orton was investigating this method when Academic Development Officer at the College of Teachers. Closure of the institution for teaching meant ideas were not pursued further than talks with IT specialists, who could implement this technology. French et al. (2019) show how 11 million British people do not have reliable internet connections in the Midlands and the North. Now that we are dependent on digital connections for daily life, this issue needs urgent attention if large sections of the population are not to be disadvantaged.

There is obviously much we need to learn and the challenge is to make education better for everyone. To achieve this we need a unified approach from international disciplines and the will to make things work! Political manipulation needs to be abandoned and this is the real test for today's global, competitive world. Are we up to it? Let us hope so for all our futures! There is a famous saying: "Yesterday is history, tomorrow's a mystery, but today is a gift and why it is called present". It is time we gave back to the world the gift of wisdom to understand consequences of actions and make decisions that benefit everyone.

There are signs that the pandemic is alerting everyone to the necessity of change, with greater reflection about education. The European Distance and E-Learning Network (Eden) have run webinars discussing research into project-based learning (Bell, 2010; Musa et al., 2012). Studies have stressed that 21st century employers are looking primarily for transferable abilities – communication and social ability, self-confidence, responsibility, flexibility, team spirit, work attitudes, self-motivation and management. Research shows these are learnt through student groups investigating work-place problems in real settings, with teachers offering merely guidance and support. Open minds to new collaborative approaches augur well for the future. Politicians must listen and learn from the pandemic situation, as this is an opportunity to make radical changes to systems.

References

Bell, S. (2010). Project-based learning for the 21st century: Skills for the future. *The Clearing House: A Journal of Eduational Strategies, Issues and Ideas, 83*(2), 39–43. https://doi.org/10.1080/00098650903505415

Christensen, C., Raynor, M., Dyer, J., & Gregersen, H. (2012). *Disruptive innovation: The Christensen collection*. Harvard Business Review Press.

Coatzee, J. (2007). *Diary of a bad year*. Penguin Books.

Csíkszentmihályi, M., Abuhamdeh, S., & Nakamura, J. (2005). Flow. In A. J. Elliot & C. S. Dweck (Eds.), *A handbook of competence and motivation* (pp. 598–698). The Guilford Press.

French, T., Quinn, L., & Yates, S. (2019). *Digital motivation: Exploring the reasons people are off-line*. University of Liverpool Study. https://www.goodthingsfoundation.org/

Musa, F., Mufti, N., Laftiff, R., & Amin, M. (2012). Project-based learning: Incalculating soft-skills in the 21st century workplace. *Proceedings of the Social & Behavioural Sciences, 59*, 565–573.

NUS Survey. (2020, February). *Consistency, controversy and change*. https://www.officeforstudents.org.uk/publications/the-national-student

Sage, R. (2000). *Class talk: Successful learning through effective communication*. Bloomsbury.

Sage, R. (2017). Rationale for communicative teaching. In R. Sage (Ed.), *Paradoxes in education* (pp. 178–198). Sense.

Sage, R. (2021). *Speechless: Understanding education*. University of Buckingham Press.

UNESCO. (2013). *Statistics: Global education monitoring, 1990–2013*. UNESCO Report.

Appendix

Flow. If feeling completely immersed in an activity, you might have been experiencing a mental state called *flow*. What is flow? Imagine you are running a race. Attention is focused on body movements, muscle power, lung force and road surface feel. You are living in the moment. Time seems to stand still. You are tired but hardly notice. The psychologist, Csíkszentmihályi, says this experience is *flow,* a state of complete immersion in an activity for its own sake. Time flies. Thought, action and movement follow in a smooth sequence to use skills to the best of ability. Flow experiences are different for people. Some might experience flow while engaging in a sport like skiing, soccer, tennis, cricket, dancing, or running. Others might have the experience, while painting, drawing, writing, sewing or constructing something. It occurs when absorbed in an enjoyable, skilled activity.

How Does It Feel to Experience Flow? Csíkszentmihályi suggests 10 factors accompany flow. While many components may be present, it is not necessary to experience *all* of them for flow to occur:

- *Clear*, challenging goals that are attainable
- *Strong* concentration and focused attention
- *Intrinsically* rewarding activity
- *Feelings* of serenity: loss of self-consciousness
- *Timelessness* focused on the present so that time passing is lost
- *Immediate* feedback
- *Knowing* task is doable; a balance between skill level & challenge
- *Feelings* of personal control over the situation and outcome
- *Lack* of awareness of physical needs
- *Complete* focus on the activity itself

How do you Achieve Flow? How can you increase chances of achieving flow? Csíksze-ntmihályi et al. (2005) explains that flow is likely when an individual is faced with a task having clear goals requiring specific responses. A game of chess is an example. For the competition duration, the player has specific goals & responses, allowing attention to focus entirely on the game in play.

If you are trying to achieve a state of flow, it can help if:
- You have a specific goal and plan of action
- It is an activity that you enjoy or are passionate about
- There is an element of challenge
- You are able to stretch your current skill level

Flow in Education. Csíkszentmihályi suggests that overlearning a skill or concept helps people experience flow. Another critical concept is the idea of slightly extending one-self beyond current ability level. This stretching of current skills helps the individual experience flow.

Flow in Sports. Just like in educational settings, engaging in a challenging athletic activity that is doable, but presents stretching of abilities is a way to achieve flow. Described as '*in the zone*', reaching this state of flow allows an athlete to experience loss of self-consciousness and performance mastery.

Flow in the Workplace. Flow occurs when engaged in tasks and focused entirely on a project. A writer might experience this while working on a novel, or graphic designer working on a website illustration.

Benefits of Flow. It makes activities more enjoyable and can lead to improved per-formance. Researchers have found that flow can enhance performance in a variety of areas, including teaching, learning, athletics and artistic creativity.

Further learning and skill development. Achieving flow indicates mastery of a cer-tain skill, so the individual must continually seek new information and challenges to maintain this state.

CHAPTER 3

Is School an Outdated System?

Alternatives to Traditional Classrooms

Rosemary Sage

Abstract

School is not the only way to gain an education. Chicago University academics at a Manchester University 2004 conference: *It is Good to Talk,* shared research showing that only 15% of what we learn is in a formal context like school, college or university. Historically, formal education is a recent invention in the United Kingdom (UK) since 1893. Mass schooling established because of the rise of industrialisation in 19th century Europe. This required employees with more knowledge and skills to comply with directions and implement machine routines and their support systems. An experienced teacher instructed student groups in the information and competencies needed for future work. Teachers were the most active in the class – transmitting information, instructions and demands. Today, there is more knowledge about interactions between learners and their teachers in the context of the local culture. However, most teaching today follows a traditional model, because of government standard targets to be met and international league tables that measure institutional differences. Therefore, these requirements encourage a transmissive teaching style. The chapter discusses issues as our diverse society, with new employment possibilities resulting from machines taking over job routines, demands more flexible learning.

1 Introduction: Learning Differences

Research supports that the environmental effect on a child is mediated by their genes. In *The Gardner and the Carpenter* (2016), Professor Alison Gopnik says that children act like scientists, creating hypotheses and testing them out. Studies show that youngsters make predictions about their surrounding world and behave in line with these projections. Children are active and not passive negotiators. Teachers transmit the same lesson to a class, with students interpreting the information differently and only really absorbing and memorising what interests them.

This was seen on a British and Japanese project (2002–10) to prepare the 21st century citizen (Sage et al., 2003, 2006, 2010). Observing teaching in Japan, a third of the lesson is *Hansei* (reflection), when each student reviews the lesson topic, in a 30 second presentation to the whole class. The range of observations is surprising and a great learning experience for everyone. Each participant takes away a range of perspectives on the material presented. Students are encouraged to speak concisely, within their time slot, so it was illuminating to observe how much could be communicated effectively in such a brief period.

Variability is a human strength to be valued and nurtured. However, the UK *one-size-fits-all* education philosophy means people differences are a problem. An example is a child starting school not knowing her letters. The teacher summoned mum, after the first week, saying these must be drilled at home. She is not yet connecting her left and right brain well, which is a common experience. The right develops first (4–7 years) with the left coming later (7+ years). Children vary enormously in the time it takes to thicken the myelin sheaths surrounding brain neurons and until this happens connections between hemispheric areas are erratic. Typically, these children are labelled "slow learners", but should not be regarded as lacking in intelligence or potential. There are many people who did badly at school but have developed successful lives and careers, once out of a prescribed, controlled education system that failed to meet their particular requirements. Abilities should be managed according to individual, developmental needs. We must value personal and practical gifts as much as academic ones and not expect similar performances from students.

School is necessary in our present economy, with both parents working to pay for high living standards. However, formal learning contexts are not as important as we think. Other learning types are effective. In 1921, Alexander Sutherland Neil started *Summerhill*, a school where lessons are optional. Many experts have argued that children should not be forced to learn. Maria Montessori, an Italian medical doctor, designed an education system, over 100 years ago, to enable pupils to reach potential through small-step activities, so they could control all operations and work independently. This depends on inner language development. She wanted focus on *autonomous learning* rather than passing tests. I studied London Montessori schools on a post-graduate Neurology course, finding they produced self-determining learners who demonstrated confident actions. Emphasis on effective communication with self and others, in the Montessori approach, ensures that children have the narrative language structures and inner thinking for self-governing learning. In Montessori schools, children are active, using self-directed activities and play, supported by teachers taking a hands-off approach. The Lillard (2018) studies confirm the method's success.

In spite of evidence that child-centred alternatives work and demonstrate more independent learners, UK education is becoming more formal, narrow and rigid, with the introduction of further national testing in the primary sector. Children can view themselves as failures very early on in their formal learning experiences. Many drop out or are excluded for bad behaviour, which research found was often due to high level language difficulties (HLLD) making understanding and responding to teacher instructions a problem (Sage, 2000). They would rather present themselves as bad than dull! Schoeneberger's 2012 report suggests that dropping out of school is linked with incarceration, unemployment, lower life-time earnings and premature death.

In reviewing this issue, as a member of a National Health Service (NHS) Child Development Team, assessing children with learning difficulties, I found *choice* and *control* were important about what was experienced and learnt. Self-directed education does not exclude any specific approach, but proves pressure has negative impact. If a child wants to stop what they are doing, they can when in control of their actions. Ability to regulate events builds self-awareness and confidence. This is achieved in student project work, with choice over what to investigate and later communicate in class presentations.

2   Informal Learning

As a speech therapist (my first profession) one looks carefully at interactions between child and parent, teacher and peers. This is hard for teachers to do and uncommon in large group contexts. Children with communication problems need adult intervention, with many parents/carers basing this on their own school experiences. However, 3 factors suggest more informal methods. Firstly, informal learning is needs-related to help motivation. Secondly, formal one-to-one learning is intensive and only tolerated in short spurts. Thirdly, many children with problems resist direct teaching and fail to listen, with glazed eyes suggesting it is useless to continue tasks. Parents then encourage informal learning through play or home tasks. For example, if a child is not understanding and using reference words (I, you, me, they etc.) this can be facilitated and reinforced in talk during activities, like dressing, eating or shopping. *The Raven*, by Edgar Allan Poe, has a 5 Lesson Mini-Scheme useful for an older child working on *narrative inferences*. These are situations when information has to be deduced as in *Rosie and Helen were alarmed*. Other facts in the narrative might help one to *infer* their relationship and reason for alarm. The Raven package focuses on clear understanding of a sophisticated, difficult poem, which targets symbolism, tension and inference abilities. A time-line provides activities with many attractive pictures. After studying the poem, a student joined a school *Communication Opportunity Group* (COGS) to enhance abilities and performed *The Raven* in a concert to audience acclaim (Sage, 2017).

Harriet Pattison (2017), a home-educating parent and childhood studies lecturer at Liverpool Hope University, researched how children learnt to read at home, involving 400 subjects. Outside school it did not matter if a child could not read later than 7 years. Learning, in this informal context, was mainly accessed through *spoken* not *written* words. The survey showed children learnt to read between 2–16 years, with ages varying in the same family. Whether parents used reading schemes or provided high-literacy environments was not a significant factor. When children understood and produced spoken narratives they naturally began reading.

Japan follows this principle. I have never seen educators teaching reading in the formal British way. The Japanese believe that if children have acquired spoken narrative language and thinking they will shift into reading effortlessly. With almost 100% of the population being literate one must take this view seriously. In Britain, children are pushed into reading, who do have the spoken language and brain thinking structures to support this secondary, linguistic activity. Their left brain, which copes with parts, develops from 7+ years and their right one, dealing with the meaning of whole events, does not get the right attention at the growing phase between ages 4–7. Therefore, analytic phonics, a popular reading approach, may be beyond students. Speech and language therapy clinics are full of such cases. It is no wonder that we have many students with learning difficulties. Such experiences throw up questions. What if many education theories are only true about *formal* school learning? Certainly, schools are only *one* way of becoming educated and gaining knowledge and abilities. One reason I went into teaching was because I could get children communicating well in a more informal clinic atmosphere, but they lost these abilities when going back into formal classrooms.

3 Alternative Schools

In *Free to Learn* (2015), Peter Gray talks about his *Damascus* – seeing the light. As a Psychology Professor at Boston College, he was a successful outcome of traditional education. However, his son, Scott (9 years), was not cooperating with school demands, so an alternative was sought. Peter Gray founded *Sudbury Valley School* (SVS), Massachusetts, which is not what one imagines about formal education. Children choose what they want to do and run the school, making decisions with teachers. They play outside, construct things, draw and paint, make music, write notes/letters, watch television and even read! How are they learning? It appears they are messing about and only doing what they fancy. It is certainly not our notion of schooling!

These ideas were replicated with young adults. Gray and Riley (Psychologist & Clinical Professor of Adolescent Special Education at Hunter College) surveyed 75 informally educated young adults (2013). They went on to Higher Education and were happy about their early learning experiences. Most were financially independent, with only a few feeling they had missed out on traditional education. The cohort could be called *drop outs*, as they attended formal school at some stage. However, they were not disengaged and viewed themselves as *dropping in* to alternative provision rather than *dropping out* of school.

This rebuts a view that orthodox schooling, with graded curricula, is vital for life success. If able to educate oneself, according to interests and ability, whilst controlling learning, the results are positive. *Home Education UK* is a website with resources and support for home learners. An online facility, *Inter-High*, provides tutors, with live or pre-recorded lessons on subjects, to assist those learning out of school. The pandemic has meant all children experiencing home-schooling during lockdowns, with some preferring this approach, offering greater freedom and more personal control. The media reported in July 2021, that there had been a 75% increase in UK home-schooling as a result of the pandemic. More than 40,000 pupils were formally taken out of school between September 2020 and April 2021 and in north-west England numbers were 92% up on the previous 2 years (Daily Telegraph, 20 July 2021, p. 7).

Not all children educated outside school will have guaranteed life success, but conventional education is not vital for achievement. Academic careers are possible from informal learning contexts and some children succeed in this way who otherwise would fail. We all know people fitting this description. Education must be flexible and allow more student control over content and learning style, so that they can succeed in their preferred way.

When teaching a BSc. Medical and Communication Sciences degree, I briefly introduced the day's topic and allowed students to investigate this as they wished. Some chose to do this in groups and others wanted to go it alone. They could gain information from the library, internet or other people. The last part of the 3-hour-session was to present findings to the whole group. This enabled students to learn in the way they wished and from each other – either in small or large gatherings. It gave a chance to communicate, both in speaking and writing, to broaden understanding and aid retention and recall. This model is common in Japan and Cuba, where I have worked.

4   Informal Learning

If acknowledging that informal education is possible, how does this work? Traditional learning goes through regular testing regimes. In Britain, these are called Standard Assessment Tests (SATS) and happen at intervals across all levels. Understanding is secondary to reaching the required norm in this model. The grade is what matters, with learning narrowly directed towards this goal. In the term that SATS occur, students practise them continually to side-line other activities and limit learning. If holistic education is the goal, continual assessment may divert from this intention.

Today, many children have video games at home, which differ from school demands, but are as complex regarding intention, attention and problem solving. Game inventors know how to motivate players, who will endure task failures. Is this because they can choose the activity? When bored they can stop playing. This suggests the importance of autonomy, interest and learning control, offered by video games.

This agenda has been behind the *Practitioner Doctorate Programme,* commissioned by the European Commission from 2011–16 to encourage professional development. Participants *choose* the perspective they wish to research *within* their work roles. Providing they present a range of evidence, that confirms knowledge and personal competencies, that is agreed internationally for leading professional roles, they have freedom to choose learning goals. Ryan and Deci's *Self-Determination Theory* (SDT, 2017) is based on understanding how curiosity, interest and purpose develop over time. External factors can damage intrinsic (inside the person) motivation.

For example, when a student is rewarded for completing a task, they are less likely to continue with it when prizes stop than if never receiving them. Thus, a relative lack of external, extrinsic motivators for the home-educated might preserve *intrinsic* reasons, to learn more flexibly and dynamically than is possible formally. They also learn within real situations to make this meaningful, interesting and relevant for them. When studying academic subjects they then bring this attitude to these activities. Adults, however, are important in giving support, as well as sharing subject expertise and personal experiences.

You cannot force intrinsic motivation but only facilitate it. Cognitive Evaluation Theory (see Appendix) suggests this comes from competence, autonomy and relatedness. Increasing student control over their environment keeps them interested and determined. The issue is knowing what motivates each one. What if a child does not want to read, write or do arithmetic? How do we deal with this issue?

5   Confident Learning

We must trust that children will acquire relevant knowledge and abilities for their survival. Humans are biologically disposed to observe surroundings and learn from what other people do in their culture. Unconsciously, they ask: What is everyone doing? Why are they doing it? What do I need to learn to do the same? How will I do this?

Gray's studies (above) suggest that humans have 3 innate drives, curiosity, play and sociability, which complement each other. Curiosity is how you answer questions about the world and its functions. Play practises skills to become an effective community member. Children appear repetitive at play, as practice makes perfect from observing actions and behaviour of others. Watch them on play equipment. They become more daring as they become competent and challenge themselves to be their best. Sociability aids learning, as children watch, listen and learn from others, particularly peers.

When language is acquired children can question and discuss what prevents progress. Thus, they integrate into their cultural context and accept norms. Each generation depends on previous ones to help them acquire what is needed for survival. Ability to talk with others and share ideas spreads knowledge and discoveries and cannot be taken for granted. Many times I have assessed struggling students, to find that even 15-year-olds cannot ask and answer questions or follow talk easily. Five conversation abilities must be acquired before formal learning is possible (Sage, 2000, see Appendix).

Hide and seek or treasure hunts are ways of helping children to explore, observe and communicate findings with each other. In Britain, Sugata Mitra (2018) uses school Self-Organising Learning Environments (SOLE). Groups of 6 share a computer and teachers give questions to answer by working collaboratively. Children are free to move around, talk, discuss and share views. Sugata finds this enables primary children to answer GCSE questions. They remember facts, because they have shared and combined knowledge. You do not really know and understand something until having to communicate it to others, who then expand ideas. In this way, information is best retained and recalled (Sage, 2020).

Children are active agents but only learn what is accessible to them. It is difficult to study without adult help, but a different educator role is advocated. Instead of transmitting knowledge and abilities and forcing students to learn, the focus must be on creating a stimulating environment to explore what interests them. Teachers must observe student interactions to monitor behaviour and offer support when needed.

Recently, I asked a young friend how he was finding senior school, which he started in September 2019. His reply was: "It's good being with friends but lessons are boring. The teacher talks for 35 minutes, often in ways that we do not understand and just before the bell rushes through the homework. Most lessons are like this". We must consider our approach to students, so that learning is effective. Introducing a lesson topic and devolving tasks to groups, at different narrative levels for them to choose how to complete, involves students actively. Following group interaction, students can present findings to the class, as this is an effective way of giving them opportunity to learn from each other and make choices (Sage, 2017).

6 Review

Education may suit one person but not another. It is not just a question of learning style and whether we absorb best through auditory, visual or haptic (experiential) sensory systems and top down (overview) or bottom up (details) cognitive preferences. These are important and teachers must know how to present information that encompasses all sensory and cognitive thinking modes (Sage, 2004). However, culture, customs, beliefs, attitudes and interests are also important factors influencing learning patterns and how, where and with whom we wish to study. In Britain and elsewhere, different approaches to teaching and learning have multiplied. Those instructing others must be acquainted with what helps or hinders education.

This chapter discusses studies that illuminate formal and informal learning practices. We need both approaches to meet society needs, but must appreciate that in formal systems we should give students more control over learning to encourage communication, confidence and motivation. It is likely that the coronavirus and its lockdown strategy, over a long period, will change behaviour that lasts. Children and adults now rely more on interactive technologies for connecting and informing. It allows more flexible approaches to routines which have been positive. Now that we have mastered systems, like Zoom and webinars, they will probably integrate into learning tasks permanently.

References

Deci, E., & Ryan, R. (1985). *Intrinsic motivation and self-determination in human behavior*. Plenum.

Gopnik, A. (2016). *The gardner and the carpenter*. Vintage.

Gray, P. (2015). *Free to learn: Why unleashing the instinct to play will make our children happier, more reliant and better students for life*. Basic Books.

Gray, P., & Riley, G. (2013). The challenge and benefits of unschooling, according to 232 families who have chosen that route. *Journal of Unschooling and Alternative Learning, 7*(14).

Lillard, A. (2018). Rethinking education: Montessori's approach. *Current Directions in Psychological Science, 27*(6), 395–400.

Mitra, S. (2018). *The Hole in the Wall Project and the power of self-organised learning.* http://www.edutopia.org/blog/self-organised-learning-sugata-mitra

Pattison, H. (2017). *Rethinking learning to read.* Educational Heretics Press.

Ryan, R., & Deci, E. (2017). *Self-determination theory.* Guildford Press.

Sage, R. (2000). *Class talk: Successful learning through effective communication.* Bloomsbury.

Sage, R. (2004). *A world of difference.* Bloomsbury.

Sage, R. (2017). Rationale for communicative teaching. In R. Sage (Ed.), *Paradoxes in education* (pp. 178–198). Sense.

Sage, R. (2020). *Understanding the doctoral system: The practitioner doctorate* [Paper]. Commonwealth Conference.

Sage, R., Rogers, J., & Cwenar, S. (2002–2011). *The DIAL Project: Dialogue, Innovation, Achievement, Learning: Sharing, developing and spreading good practice.* Reports 1, 2, 3: EW Collaboration to Raise Educational Achievement.

Schoeneberger, J. (2012). Longitudinal attendance patterns: Developing high school dropouts. *The Clearing House: A Journal of Eduational Strategies, Issues and Ideas, 85*(1), 7–14.

Appendix

Cognitive Evaluation Theory (CET) is a psychological theory explaining external consequences on internal motivation. It is a sub-theory of the self-determination model, focusing on competence and autonomy, while examining how intrinsic motivation is affected by outside forces, called motivational 'crowding out'. CET has 3 propositions to explain how consequences affect internal motivation (Deci & Ryan, 1985).

External events will impact on intrinsic motivation for challenging activities influencing perceived competence, within self-determination theory. Events promoting greater perceived competence enhance intrinsic motivation, whereas those that diminish this will decrease it. Behaviour initiation and regulation have 3 potential functional aspects.

– The informational aspect facilitates an internal perceived locus of causality and perceived competence to positively influence intrinsic motivation.

- The controlling aspect assists an external perceived locus of causality (person's perception of cause of success/failure), so negatively influencing intrinsic motivation & increasing extrinsic compliance
- The a-motivating aspect facilitates perceived incompetence, undermining intrinsic motivation & promoting disinterest in the task

Personal events vary in qualitative aspects and like external ones have differing functional significances. Events deemed *internally informational* facilitate self-determined functioning and maintain/enhance intrinsic motivation. Those deemed *internally controlling* are experienced as pressure toward specific outcomes and undermine intrinsic motivation. Internally a-motivating events make incompetence salient and also undermine intrinsic motivation (Deci & Ryan, 1985).

Five Conversational Moves (Sage, 2000)

1. Answer closed *what, who, where, when* question needing specific response
2. Contribute idea even if not entirely appropriate showing turn-taking ability
3. Listen & shows maintenance moves-eye-contact/smiling-75% of time
4. Answer an open *how or why* question needing explanation
5. Initiate new ideas that fit with the topic under discussion

CHAPTER 4

Preparing for Work

Nigel Adams

Abstract

This chapter considers the workplace and how students can be prepared for it in this 4th Industrial Revolution. As a business professional, before entering Higher Education, I was very aware of the obvious disconnect between learning policies and working practices. I have developed courses that aimed to tackle this problem, as the economic, emotional and social costs have a significant impact on everyone.

1 The Present Situation

> Just 13% of graduates were seen by HR as ready to hit the ground running when they entered the workplace according to Pearson Business School research, while two-thirds were seen as somewhat ready to work. (Pearson Business School, 2019, p. 12)

You can see from this survey and many similar ones that even before the world was hit by the COVID-19 pandemic, it was clear that in the United Kingdom (UK) something was not right. Universities are not developing graduates who are prepared for employment with personal, practical as well as academic competencies.

Some academics argue that universities should not be preparing their students for work, as their role is to expand minds and develop research and critical thinking abilities. Surely that is also what graduates will need in a world of Artificial Intelligence (AI) and the 4th Industrial Revolution? Even academics who claim not to be preparing students for later employment are doing so for new job roles, but this would improve if there was better insight into workplace needs.

This book adds to the discussion by gathering together a wide range of expert views in how world events are influencing education and training. The editors also have recognized that education is not changing fast enough and it is students and graduates who are losing out, with the workplace also suffering from a lack of graduates with appropriate professional skills.

2   How Can We Prepare Students for Work?

How can we better prepare our students for the world of work? This is an important question to reflect on and produce an effective answer. At the independent University of Buckingham in England, we have been aiming to do this for the last fifteen years, by creating and running our BSc. Business Enterprise (BBE) programme.

We believe that in 2006, BBE was the world's first undergraduate *Venture Creation Programme* at a university. What is a Venture Creature Programme? According to Dr Martin Lackeus of Chalmers University in Sweden:

> In a Venture Creation Programme, students are expected to start real-life business ventures as a formal part of their studies. Common characteristics of these programmes are that the students are expected to interact with real-life potential customers and partners, that they are expected to manage real-life resources, such as money, products, sales materials and sometimes even staff. (Lackeus, 2012)

How does our innovative BBE programme prepare students for work? Well, it provides them with the opportunity to combine learning academic theories and models with real-life work experiences – creating, launching and developing a business as in integral part of their honours degree. In addition, at Buckingham our students must achieve their honours degree in just two years, as we work four terms each year. This starts to prepare participants for the working environment, where they are likely to get only one month's annual holiday.

3   Venture Creation Programmes

The main objectives of the BBE programme are to enable undergraduate students to start to achieve their own goals in life and careers by:
– *Achieving* a good honours degree
– *Developing* entrepreneurial self-efficacy and a 'can-do' mind-set
– *Cultivating* an ability to 'think on their feet'
– *Being flexible* and able to adapt in a fast-changing world environment

We are not just enabling students to start a business, as the aim is to develop their enterprising or 'can-do' mind-set, so that they can be successful in whatever they choose to do in life. As well as providing academic business theories and models, we aim to develop emotional intelligence, communication and presentation competencies and the ability to work in teams, along with curiosity and creativity. Participants must be able to deal with the unexpected and have the ability to hit the ground running in any situation they meet in life and work.

Have we been successful? Even from an academic and quantitative research viewpoint, I can claim partial success, having started to survey our students and graduates and shown that:

> The experiental nature of the VCP develops the students' entrepreneurial self-efficacy (ESE) and flexibility, which should enable them to develop successful careers.

4   Review

This chapter discusses a degree programme that is designed to breach the reported disconnect between university and workplace needs. The author's paper also presents anecdotally the way in which VCP students mature very quickly, by learning about themselves, confronting risk and working together in teams to develop their ideas in a real business start-up and learning environment (Adams, 2006).[1]

Note

1   You can hear for yourself the types of successful graduates we have helped to develop, by listening to the Buckingham Enterprise and Innovation Unit Entrepreneurs' Podcasts, available on http://www.beiu.co.uk/podcast

References

Adams, N. (2016, September). *Does an undergraduate VCP in a university achieve its objectives?* [Paper presentation]. The European Conference on Innovation and Entrepreneurship ECIE 2016.

Lackeus, M. (2012). *This is a venture creation program.* Pearson Business. https://vcplist.com/2018/10/23/this-is-venture-creation-programs-vcp1/

Pearson Business School. (2019, December 18). Surveys: Conference on business: The CBI education and skills survey, 2018. *Personnel Today.* pearsoncollegelondon.ac.uk

CHAPTER 5

A New Model of Workplace Learning

Daryle Abrahams

Abstract

The trend towards replacing classroom-based learning events with e-learning ones continues, driven for the most part by the persistent move for cost reduction. Unless you happen to have a Chief Executive Officer, who is fully experienced in the value of classroom-based learning, education and training is the first thing to suffer when businesses face a downturn. Clearly classroom-based learning is not the be all and end all for acquiring the knowledge and competencies needed for work roles. When professionals are given the authority to teach and learn alongside their daily requirement to produce, individuals come up with many interesting, creative approaches to learning – very few of which involve a classroom. However, despite an initial flood of creativity in e-learning design in the late 1990's, at the prospect of someone learning effectively while sitting in front of a computer, the majority of online education has sadly boiled down to a *tick-box* activity, which for legal purposes, covers the organizations' obligation to ensure people have read a compliance document or some other required piece of material. Thus, the problem remains; how do we really educate people remotely?

1 Teaching Models for the Future

The second quarter of 2020, with the COVID-19 pandemic rampant globally, forced the issue. The first aid dressing was ripped off, as students of all ages around the world were sent home and required to attend online learning events. Professionals, in white-collar jobs, were also sent home. There, they were forced to not only work from home but *learn* from home, if they could. As many have found, during the COVID-19 pandemic of 2020, a significant portion of education still requires a social element. The learning input is not the problem and neither is the learning output.

– For *input* – computers allow us to use digital imagery, listen to audiobooks, play learning games and even indulge in virtual reality to explore concepts.
– For *output* (assessment) purposes, computers allow us to take tests to be marked immediately, write and submit digital documentation instantly and even test our understanding by solving puzzles.

The missing piece is the bit in the middle, the learning; the integration of the input into our understanding so that we can actually say we have retained and can recall information, rather than just witnessed, read or heard the new material. The proof of the pudding still remains in the eating; no recipe book or food critic's evaluation will suffice if you cannot *taste* the cake. From this practitioner's point of view, the *eating* (synthesis of new information into new behaviour, aka learning) is still best done in a group setting for adult learners, by sharing views and knowledge to review and refine information and consider how to apply it to individual situations.

2   Group Learning in a Remote World

The topic is building trusted advisor relationships. The students are geographically dispersed: Fabio is in Milan, Bruno is in Germany, Pierre is in France, Cem is in Turkey and their six remaining colleagues are split between the UK, US and Canada – two in each country. Of the 10 students involved in this English-speaking education event, six of them are learning in their second or third language. The class is scheduled for 11 am Eastern Standard Time (EST). Toby, in California, joins at 8 am. Cem in Turkey makes the link at 6 pm. This fictional class is not as unlikely as it may seem. Quite often in the business world teams are spread globally by discipline. Using this example, which model of adult teaching is going to help us?

We cannot fly them all into the same place as it costs too much. Sending them a book to read will not suffice in teaching them an abstract, or so-called soft skill. Having them complete an e-learning activity, where they pick multiple-choice answers, tick a check-box to say that they have read a policy document, or answer questions from a video interaction, will only cater to their *knowledge* of a topic. It will not necessarily enable them to *understand* the topic for implementing lessons learned in real life and behave in a different way. Thus, if we cannot use traditional e-learning modes – what can we do?

3   Classroom Experiences

Classroom-based learning or teaching, in this example, can actually be a very useful model. If we think of the classroom as being the format that we are trying to replicate – experience rather than merely a geographic location – the first thing we need is to be able to see and hear our fellow students as well as the teacher. Technology can help with that requirement. Assuming the teacher knows how to use a graphics tablet, the whiteboard or chalkboard can be replicated too. In fact, many modern video conferencing solutions provide the functionality of raising one's hand or sending questions to the teacher privately or to the entire group, while the class is in progress.

While tools, such as the Cisco WebEx conferencing platform, attempt to mirror the classroom, there are still two, critical, missing ingredients – it cannot replicate group work and chitchat. Each of these enables students to understand what is going on when the teacher moves ahead too quickly and check with others the technical jargon if this confounds them, or they get distracted and need to be put in the picture. Experienced and informed teachers understand how critical small-group work is in a classroom. They also realise that just because they have said something, does not mean that everybody heard and understood it. Importantly, technology can help with this. It just takes some preparation.

4 Communication Channels

To effectively enable learning to take place across time zones, geographies and a range of remote learning environments, there needs to be at least two separate communication channels: one for the whole group discussion and one for the side conversation. As first demonstrated in ancient Greek theatre, you need the chorus and the players. The players represent what the audience are seeing and hearing in real time – the content of the classroom. The chorus represents what the audience potentially thinks about what they are seeing, hearing and experiencing.

The second communication channel allows for reflection on the content between learners in tandem to enable understanding and therefore integration into future practice. Clearly the teacher needs to set up the learning event with all of this in mind, which is where best practice in adult education comes into play. By best practice I mean that the students should be given an opportunity to understand the learning objectives for the event before it takes place. Additionally, the students should be given some form of preparation task before the planned session, which warms them to the topic by orientating them to the subject matter.

In addition to a second communication channel to allow small group conversations, activities, and synthesis of the information being presented to the whole group, there should also be an emphasis placed in the adult classroom on the student being the teacher. Whether or not this is new, or in any way related to today's changing world, is questionable.

Great teachers have been asking their students to take the role of the teacher in order to cement a narrative structure of the content in their mind for decades; they know that the act of teaching aids understanding and learning. If anything having so many people sitting in front of a computer, while also being in a virtual classroom, presents an opportunity. Students can now be searching the Internet for content, while sitting in class observing the teacher; speaking with their colleagues on a second channel and preparing to teach on that topic at the same time. Previously, one could ask students to bring laptops to class, but this means every desk needs a power supply, which is not always possible.

5   Review

World events are changing education, forcing people to work from home. As long as they have access to a computer, a mobile phone and a decent Internet connection, this represents an opportunity. A well-prepared teacher should do the following. Ensure students are given access to materials ahead of the class, which will enable them to prepare to engage. Set students a task of answering a question using those materials so that when they appear in the virtual learning event they are warmed up and have some grasp of the topic.

Instruct students to have their mobile phone available, in addition to the computer, as they will be using it as a second channel of communication. During the class task students will be searching the Internet for potential answers to questions. Set students some tasks, requiring them to break away from the whole group into smaller ones, in a second channel. Have the smaller groups no larger than four people so that everyone has a chance for good discussion. Finally, task students with teaching the whole group what they have learned on a given topic in their small group activities. This shares knowledge and widens thinking from the varied interpretations made from the information presented.

PART 2

Education Policies & Practices

∵

Introduction to Part 2

Rosemary Sage and Riccarda Matteucci

On any working day, over 1 billion students worldwide head to class, according to UNESCO (United Nations Education, Scientific & Cultural Agency). More young people today are enrolled in education than ever before. Yet, for many, education does not lead to learning. A lack of appropriately trained teachers, a diverse population, inadequate learning methods and materials, makeshift classes and limited facilities make education difficult for students. Others come to formal learning too stressed, hungry, sick, exhausted from work or home tasks to benefit from lessons. The consequences are grave. UNESCO estimates 617 million young people worldwide are unable to reach minimum proficiency levels in oracy, literacy and numeracy – even though two thirds are in education. This learning crisis is the greatest global challenge for preparing students for life, work and active citizenship, with understanding of their additional learning needs.

Chapter 6: Creativity for Creativity builds on previous ideas to show how developing an innovative learner environment is vital for becoming open-minded and imaginative in approaching everyday problems. How this ethos can be built into all learning is discussed.

Chapter 7: Conversational Intelligence outlines what the 2020–2021 pandemic and other influences mean for actual classroom practice. It focuses on the importance of integrating both Arts and Sciences for helping students understand global issues more effectively and communicate this learning efficiently.

Chapter 8: University-School Partnerships present world research to demonstrate the impact of *scholars in residence* to facilitate continual professional staff development. The quality of teaching is key to improving education standards and this initiative shows how to achieve this aim.

Chapter 9: Imaginative Alternatives to the 'Macabre Constant' introduces the crucial concern of how present regimes result in exclusion of students who do not respond well to traditional tests and examinations. A portfolio of actual work accomplished produces a clearer, more holistic record of student achievement.

Chapter 10: Third Generation Doctorates describe a personal record centering on workplace research *within* practice to gain a *Practitioner* doctoral qualification. This has greater impact on educational progress than PhD and Professional models, showing limited impact from research *on* practice. Harvard University now concentrates on PhDs, using a greater range of investigative

© KONINKLIJKE BRILL NV, LEIDEN, 2022 | DOI:10.1163/9789004506466_008

methods, along with Practitioner models, focusing on participant work problems and solutions.

1   Reflections from Part 2

The chapters indicate that education is changing positively in response to recent trends and world events. The need to be open-minded and creative in thinking and action is paramount. The importance of integrating Arts and Science knowledge into all learning is stressed, in order to better comprehend the world and articulate ideas to others for sharing and developing thinking and problem solving. It is notable that world geniuses always have a strong Arts and Science background, which is fundamental for citizenship and future earning potential. The final chapters introduce problems of tests and examinations as narrow evaluations of learner attainments. These traditional assessments exclude those who cannot readily respond to this approach. The portfolio personal record of actual achievements provides a more accurate picture of an individual. This mode is becoming more common in countries, like the United States America, for entrance to colleges, universities and professional occupations. It enables logging of personal and practical feats alongside academic ones, to provide a complete picture of someone that jobs require. Many large corporations are opening up employment to non-graduates as they experience people with degrees often lack the range of competencies demanded in work roles. Communication always is a top attribute mentioned, necessary for engaging with colleagues across cultures, but viewed as a declining competence in a world where technology supplants talk. The chapters suggests ways to improve this aspect of learning and teaching.

CHAPTER 6

Creativity for Creativity

Emma Webster

Abstract

In order to improve our education systems, Rogers (2020) highlights a need for educators to be open-minded and prepared to reflect, utilising their own creativity abilities to foster those of students. This chapter will explore how creative change for creativity's sake starts with an approach to leadership that guides teachers to celebrate creativity processes for nurturing student abilities.

1 Introduction: Why Creativity?

During the challenging times faced currently, as global citizens, we are forced to evaluate the important things in life, with Education one of them. A new appreciation of teachers is emerging and the wider positives of education, including personal development, socialisation and creativity are being celebrated, but how can we ensure that education and curriculum experiences are truly fit for purpose in an unpredictable, challenging 21st century?

In 1976, James Callaghan, British Prime Minister, in the Ruskin College Speech, defined the aims of Education were to ensure students are equipped to make constructive contributions to society and be ready for work. Also, he recognised a need for a child's whole personality to be catered for, allowing it to 'flower in its fullest possible way'. Fast forward to the 21st century and the need to prepare children effectively for their future is still a fundamental aim, but under a very different guise.

Creativity has been identified as one of the most important, desirable abilities of the 21st century, highlighting that the workplace and the world looks very different to when the National Curriculum was first introduced in 1988 (Florida, 2002). Although the curriculum has changed since its first implementation, Richardson and Mishra (2018) question whether current education systems are fit for purpose, as the thinking required is not promoted in the current curriculum. The National Curriculum document (Department for Education, 2014) refers to engendering 'an appreciation of human creativity' (p. 6), supportive of Smith and Smith's (2012) view that creativity and education are '*natural allies*'. Fostering creativity in education has many benefits, including improving motivation, confidence, openness and resilience (Bereczki & Kárpáti, 2008; Davies et al., 2013; Ryan & Deci, 2000).

Creativity has power to move Education beyond the traditional classroom and perceived limits. Creativity can unify knowledge, utilise ability, enrich experience and promote innovation.

2   Creativity at a Glance

Creativity has been defined by many and, reflective of its richness, it has been tricky to pin down. Runco and Jaeger (2012) discuss a standard definition, identifying a need for both originality and effectiveness, as well as useful novelty. These attributes are also acknowledged by Robinson (2007), asserting creativity as original ideas that have value. Products of creativity are referenced in MacKinnon's (1962) definition that suggests an initial idea will lead to a tangible product. The process is identified as a key aspect of creativity by Csikszentmihalyi (1996); "a process by which a symbolic domain in the culture is changed" (p. 8). Likewise, The Durham Commission (Newton, 2019) states that creativity is "the capacity to imagine, conceive, express, or make something that was not there before" (p. 2). The definition provided by the Arts Council England (2020) describes detail of the creative process, as the application of "knowledge, skill and intuition to imagine, conceive, express or make something that was not there before" (p. 12).

These definitions are relevant to the implementation of creativity in Education. They can further be explored within Rhodes' (1961) 4 'Ps' of creativity – person, process, press and product. Understanding the importance of these elements to the creative process is particularly important. This chapter highlights the process of creative leadership in addition to teaching practice and student learning experiences. Guilford (1950) connects the definition of creativity to education, making a case for a holistic view, inclusive of personality, environment and motivation, concluding that the act of creativity is "an instance of learning" (1950, p. 446). This also draws upon the work of Kaufman and Beghetto (2009) on the 4-C model of creativity, which indicates 'mini-c' creativity as the most appropriate to the learning process.

The development of definitions has emerged from the evolution of research into creativity since the 1950s. Glǎveanu (2010) explores the tetradic framework of creativity research that sees a move from positivism to interpretivism through the He-I-We paradigms. The shift from focusing on the Big-C products of eminent artists, to understanding the person, process and context involved in creativity, helps us articulate the place it has in education. By focusing on the wider context for fostering creative abilities, we are better equipped to emphasise them in our curricula. Our understanding of creativity has become more relevant to the needs of it within our society and culture.

3   Creativity in Education

As a leader, passionate about the fostering of creative abilities from a background as a professional dancer, I am constantly faced with the misconceptions that these are exclusive to the arts. My work, initiatives, actions and research challenge this, aiming to prove that creativity is an integral part of the whole learning process, as well as each individual subject. Experience in the arts has influenced my role as a curriculum leader, enabling effective utilisation of transferable skills. Eisner (2002), in his address to the Dewey Society, highlighted lessons learned from the arts for education practice. These are qualitative relationships, making judgements without rules, formulation of aims, form and content as inextricable (in most cases), knowledge articulated in non-linguistic ways, relationships between thinking and motives for engagement.

In primary schools, with few specialists, a general approach is adopted. The journey, with staff over the past 3 years, demonstrates how the creative process can support effective change leadership, as well as improve teaching practice and the education experience for students. My move from a domain-specific to a domain-general context of creativity highlights the importance of the dichotomy for both students and teachers. As a leader, the knowledge of a specific application of creativity lends itself well to fostering domain-general creative abilities in teachers, supporting increased autonomy of them in this area (Worth & Van Den Brande, 2020; Department for Education, 2016).

A positive view of creativity can act as an enabler in the classroom (Bereczki & Kárpáti, 2018) and creative actions, as a leader, ensure that these positive views are disseminated. Nurturing creativity begins with creative leadership. This means having a good understanding of the creative process and supporting teachers through it, so that students thrive as a result. This can be done through the curriculum, pedagogical approaches, environments and attitudes. Creativity must be considered generally, to pave the way for creative specialisms in the arts, sciences and technology. As Kampylis and Berki (2014) suggest, the promotion of creative thinking can happen in all subjects and important for educators to consider it as a pedagogy itself.

4   Designing and Leading Creativity

Understanding the reality of a school curriculum is the first step towards implementing change. This takes time (Stefanini & Griffiths, 2020) and buy-in (Sharples et al., 2018). The journey towards developing and implementing a creativity-centred curriculum starts with identifying the problems as well as successes, noticing gaps and establishing aims. Experience of leading change for creativity, I identified two gaps in the knowledge of teachers that are not exclusive to my individual setting. Firstly, a lack of awareness of the creative process and secondly a limited teacher subject knowledge. How can we promote creative abilities in children without a sound knowledge ourselves? Teachers are a vital component in the education jigsaw, so a curriculum design that also supports professional development is essential (Ramakrishnan, 2019).

Planning to address the problem of lesser creative abilities in teachers must be done carefully and in accordance with the process itself. Taking inspiration from Craft's (1999) *possibility* thinking can help design a curriculum that focuses on open-ended questions. This provides teachers with the autonomy to guide the creative process to suit learners; identifying a problem, producing ideas to solve it, selecting, implementing then evaluating ideas. However, this design, alongside naïve optimism towards solving the problem quickly, must be avoided. Knowledge is key to launching creativity, but other approaches to curriculum design and resulting pedagogies must be considered, to provide a balance of originality and appropriateness, as well as knowledge and skill that leads to experience, innovation and success.

Willingham (2009) considers the importance of a strong knowledge foundation, as a means to develop critical thinking, applicable to both teachers and students. Knowledge is essential not only as a springboard for innovation, but for determining the level of innovation, with a better awareness of what already exists (Sternberg & Lubart, 1991). Therefore, we must acknowledge that students must be provided with opportunities to listen to teachers imparting knowledge that can be creativity-inspiring (Jeffrey & Craft, 2004, p. 83).

To afford this opportunity to students and address this information gap in teachers, a knowledge-rich approach to curriculum design that intertwines with skills should be adopted. Young (2014) defines *powerful knowledge* as key to avoiding disadvantage in later life. Roberts and Kidd (2018) emphasise a need to understand the purpose of knowledge and how it can be used, making skills an important factor when designing a curriculum for creativity. A further emphasis on use of knowledge is highlighted by Ramakrishnan (2019), who suggests that skills, like problem-solving, experimentation, communication and teamwork should also be developed within a curriculum design.

Assessment is an important part of our education system, but assessing creativity must be considered carefully. The product of a creative process should be open to evaluation and scrutiny, but a formal assessment of a child's achievement can have detrimental effects. Hennessey and Amabile (1987) suggest that extrinsic goals and rewards, like formal assessment, hinder the ability for students to intrinsically motivate themselves, so hindering their creative abilities. However, Pederson (2007, in Sternberg, 2015) suggests "what is measured is treasured" indicating the status placed on subjects formally assessed. If we want to raise the profile and value of creativity, do we have to assess it? In addition to final products, or assessments, the way in which students communicate, collaborate, formulate ideas, ask and answer questions, address social situations and value themselves and each other are all indicators of creative abilities that can be measured by creatively-aware teachers.

5   Review

This chapter has explored the benefits of nurturing creativity. Encouraging teachers to understand creative process steps and how this influences practice can lead to effective fostering of student imaginative abilities. Effective leadership is essential for nurturing student creativity and by promoting understanding of the process. Leadership can effectively support the shifts in teaching, learning practices and approaches.

Although creativity is arguably one of the most valuable traits for the 21st century workplace, the present, challenging situation must be raised. This sees people, in many industries, out of work due to the COVID-19 pandemic. What does creativity mean in this case? If we enrich education and life, with creativity, we equip people with abilities to enhance their existence. It then becomes straight forward and intuitive to respond creatively to challenging problems, whatever the context. Csikszentmihalyi (1996) refers to our language, values, artistic expression, scientific understanding and technology as the creative elements that make up the most interesting parts of human life that distinguish us from animals and deepen our existence (pp. 2–3).

As well as enhancing workplace abilities, creativity has the potential to have a positive effect on our mental wellbeing, offering relief and support in overcoming challenging times. This will only happen if we have nurtured creativity effectively in early education stages and continue it as we grow.

> The flexibility of creative persons is what gives them the capacity to cope with the advances, opportunities, technologies, and changes that are a part of our current day-to-day lives. (Runco, 2004, p. 658)

- *Narrative talk* in the classroom should be encouraged and extended
- *Contexts* must provide safe spaces to build resourcefulness
- *Take risks* and value creative inputs and innovation
- *Student ideas* should inform planning and be incorporated into activities
- *Encourage autonomy*, initiative & group work to extend thinking
- *Word assignments* to promote creative thinking, problem finding &solving
- *Give students direct feedback* on creativity asking the class to contribute
- *Help students and teachers* to know why it is important to be creative
- *Leaders must be consistent* with messages, flexible, adaptive & reactive
- *Model* how to connect across learning, 2030utilising all knowledge & skill

References

Arts Council England. (2020). *Let's create: Strategy 2020–2030.*
https://www.artscouncil.org.uk/sites/default/files/download-file/Strategy%
202020_2030%20Arts%20Council%20England.pdf

Bereczki, E. O., & Kárpáti, A. (2018). Teachers' beliefs about creativity and its nurture: A systematic review of the recent research literature. *Educational Research Review, 23,* 25–56. https://doi.org/10.1016/j.edurev.2017.10.003

Callaghan, J. (1976, October 18). A rational debate based on the facts. In *Education in England: The history of our schools.* http://www.educationengland.org.uk/ documents/speeches/1976ruskin.html

Craft, A. (1999). Creative development in the early years: Some implications of policy for practice. *The Curriculum Journal, 10*(1), 135–150.

Csikszentmihalyi, M. (1996). *Creativity: Flow and the psychology of discovery and invention.* Harper Collins.

Davies, D., et al. (2013). Creative learning environments in education – A systematic literature review. *Thinking Skills and Creativity, 8,* 80–91. https://doi.org/10.1016/ j.tsc.2012.07.004

Department for Education. (2014). *National curriculum: Framework document.*
https://assets.publishing.service.gov.uk/government/uploads/system/ uploadsattachment_data/file/425601/PRIMARY_national_curriculum.pdf

Department for Education. (2016). *Educational excellence everywhere* [Policy paper].
https://assets.publishing.service.gov.uk/government/uploads/system/uploads/ attach ment_data/file/508447/Educational_Excellence_Everywhere.pdf

Eisner, E. (2002). What can education learn from the arts about the practice of education? *Journal of Curriculum and Supervision, 18*(Part 1), 4–16.

Florida, R. (2002). The rise of the creative class. *Washington Monthly, 34*(Part 5), 15–26.

Glăveanu, V. P. (2010). Paradigms in the study of creativity: Introducing the perspective of cultural psychology. *New Ideas in Psychology, 28*(1), 79–93. doi:10.1016/j.newideapsych.2009.07.007

Guilford, J. P. (1950). Creativity. *American Psychologist, 5*(9), 444–454. https://doi.org/10.1037/h0063487

Hennessey, B. A., & Amabile, T. M. (1987). *Creativity and learning: What research says to the teacher.* National Education Association. https://files.eric.ed.gov/fulltext/ED312835.pdf

Jeffrey, B., & Craft, A. (2004). Teaching creatively and teaching for creativity: Distinctions and relationships. *Educational Studies, 30*(1), 77–87. https://doi.org/10.1080/0305569032000159750

Kampylis, P., & Berki, E. (2014). *Nurturing creative thinking* (Educational Practices Series, Vol. 25). International Academy of Education.

Kaufman, J. C., & Beghetto, R. A. (2009). Beyond big and little: The four C model of creativity. *Review of General Psychology, 13*(1), 1–12. https://doi.org/10.1037/a0013688

MacKinnon, D. W. (1962). The nature and nurture of creative talent. *American Psychologist, 17*(7), 484–495. https://doi.org/10.1037/h0046541

Newton, L. (2019). *Creativity in education.* Durham Commission.

Ramakrishnan, V. (2019). Creating a broad and balanced curriculum. *Impact, 6.* https://impact.chartered.college/article/creating-a-broad-balanced-curriculum/

Rhodes, M. (1961). An analysis of creativity. *The Phi Delta Kappan, 42*(7), 305–310.

Richardson, C., & Mishra, P. (2018). Learning environments that support student creativity: Developing the SCALE. *Thinking Skills and Creativity, 27*, 45–54. https://doi.org/10.1016/j.tsc.2017.11.004

Roberts, H., & Kidd, D. (2018). *Unchartered territories: Adventures in learning.* Independent Thinking Press.

Robinson, K. (2007). *Do schools kill creativity?* [Video]. YouTube. https://www.youtube.com/watch?v=iG9CE55wbtY

Rogers, J. (2020). The need for critical engagement when using academic research and evidence. *Impact, 10.* https://impact.chartered.college/article/the-need-for-critical-engagement-academic-research-evidence/

Runco, M. A. (1988). Creativity research: Originality, utility, and integration *Creativity Research Journal, 1*(1), 1–7. https://doi.org/10.1080/10400418809534283

Runco, M. A. (2004). Creativity. *Annual Review of Psychology, 55*(1), 657 687.

Runco, M. A., & Jaeger, G. J. (2012). The standard definition of creativity. *Creativity Research Journal, 24*(1), 92–96. https://doi.org/10.1080/10400419.2012.650092

Ryan, R. M., & Deci, E. L. (2000). Self-determination theory and the facilitation of intrinsic motivation, social development and well-being. *American Psychologist, 55*(1), 68–78. https://doi.org/10.1037/0003-066X.55.1.68

Sharples, J., Albers, B., & Fraser, S. (2018). *Putting evidence to work: A school's guide to implementation* [Guidance reports]. Educational Endowment Foundation. https://discovery.ucl.ac.uk/id/eprint/10068468/1/EEF-ImplementationGuidance Report.pdf

Smith, J., & Smith, L. (2012). Educational creativity. In J. Kaufman & R. Sternberg (Eds.), *The Cambridge handbook of creativity* (pp. 250–264). Cambridge University Press.

Stefanini, L., & Griffiths, J. (2020). Addressing the challenges of using evidence in education. *Impact, 10.* https://impact.chartered.college/article/addressing-the-challenges-using-evidence-education

Sternberg, R. (2015). Teaching for creativity: The sounds of silence, psychology of aesthetics. *Creativity & the Arts, 9*(2), 115–117. https://doi.org/10.1037/aca0000007

Sternberg, R., & Lubart, T. (1991). Creating creative minds. *The Phi Delta Kappan, 72*(8), 608–614.

Willingham, D. (2009). *Why don't students like school?* Jossey-Bass.

Worth, J., & Van Den Brande, J. (2020). *Teacher autonomy: How does it relate to job satisfaction and retention?* National Foundation for Educational Research. https://www.nfer.ac.uk/media/3874/teacher_autonomy_how_does_it_relate_to_ job_satisfaction_and_retention.pdf

Young, M. (2014, March 25). *The curriculum and the entitlement to knowledge* [Presentation]. Cambridge Assessment Network. https://www.cambridgeassessment.org.uk/ Images/166279-the-curriculum-and-the-entitlement-to-knowledge-prof-michael-young.pdf

CHAPTER 7

Conversational Intelligence: The Basis of Creativity

Learning from Others

Elizabeth Negus

Abstract

The world is changing at a phenomenal rate. The old world order is past and the new one so different that it is almost unrecognisable. This is evident in education, where new methods are challenging thinking. Education has entered a new stage, where personal as well as academic abilities are the currency, with teaching often within the confines of homes rather than in traditional classrooms. Traditional teaching, in face-to-face class meetings, has shifted to a new norm of teaching and learning digitally as well as face-to-face, as a result of the worldwide pandemic, COVID-19. In light of this, the chapter addresses *conversational intelligence* – the basis of creativity. It will discuss how this vital ability has been eroded/interrupted and attempt to seek new ways of restoring it for a healthy, productive world. It is both exciting and timely. My views are grounded from experience as a teacher and lecturer in English language and literature. Educators must embrace new disciplines and new capabilities to be more effective. Education is affected by self-isolation of students and staff because of contact with COVID-19. What was once the capitalist's mainstays: financial resources, corporate buildings, human resources and financial assets are becoming history. In order for conversational intelligence to cope with world changes it must:

– Be diverse, remote or virtual
  Offer different approaches across generations
– Adapt to rapid change in the nature of work
– Meet the rising demand for communication competencies

• • •

> Imagination is more important than knowledge. Knowledge is limited. Imagination encircles the world.
>
> EINSTEIN (1879–1955)

• •
•

1   **Introduction: Creativity: Imperatives for the New Educational World**

Prior to the 2020 pandemic, conversational intelligence was an important force that created strategic value for education. In my primary, secondary and university education life, investments focused on physical buildings like the British library, stacked sky-high with books, reading rooms with nicely polished desks and chairs, canteens and rest-rooms. Today, sophisticated technology has eclipsed the use of libraries. There is a growing sense that they are no longer needed, with *intellectual capital* the only meaningful form, which we must continue to strive for despite the changing ways of how we teach and learn. The evolution of communication technologies is at the heart of these changes. The internet and other technology forms have to an extent lessened critical and creative thinking. Consequently, communication, oracy competencies, management and knowledge-sharing have been weakened, but are highlighted as never before. Educators derive self-worth from the work they do and feel a huge sense of achievement from the intellectual contributions made. Some world artists and thinkers are revered today because they were compelling communicators. Whilst there have been many great orators throughout history, only a few transcend time. Examples are: Martin Luther King (1929–1968) Winston Churchill (1874–1965) and Charles de Gaulle (1890–1970).

2   **Printing Press Communication Impact**

The invention of the printing press by Johannes Gutenberg (1400–68) changed how we communicated. This allowed for books and pamphlets to be mass produced and read aloud in public. It enabled wider distribution of information around the world. People could go out in the public squares to protest, preach and chat while handing out leaflets. Consequently, in 1501, Pope Alexander VI (1431–1503) passed a decree to excommunicate anyone, who printed manuscripts without church permission. Twenty years later, during the Reformation, books spread the word about Martin Luther (1483–1546) and Protestantism.

In Europe, there was religious, political, intellectual and cultural upheaval, which deepened a desire for people to argue, discuss and present ideas in a more coherent, vehement way. From such wide spread speeches, history tells us that the Protestants claimed that the Catholic Church was rich and corrupt. They rejected the pope's authority and believed that the Bible should not be read in Latin but in the common language. Trouble was brewing in every sphere in society. Throughout Europe, Christians argued fiercely over religion and this splintered the Catholic community. The Protestant Reformation ultimately triggered wars, persecutions and the so-called Counter-Reformation. This part of history is important, because not only does it show how speaking can affect positive change, but it instils in learners the idea of the importance of oral competencies in taking a message to the world.

Alongside these religious debates, Nicolaus Copernicus (1473–1543) published *On the Revolutions of Heavenly Spheres*, which the church vigorously rejected. His thesis proposed that the earth revolved around the sun on its axis. The effect of this profound hypothesis on the intellectual community resulted in scientists and philosophers coining the phrase the *Copernican Revolution* to describe world changing ideas. This development of Western thought gave birth to the scientific age and helped remove the many superstitious and ignorant beliefs of the time. It led to the positive or negative decline of the church and gave rise to a new age of scientific inquiry and intervention. The point here is that there is power in conversational intelligence to revolutionise society.

3   Threat of Technology

Technology has paved the way for greater sophisticated interaction, as in telephone conversations with friends, families and businesses. Now, computers and social media applications support teachers and students to handle assignments within time frames. Thus, better communication between stakeholders, through webinars on topics, tutorials and online socialising, enable quick connectivity to many people at once, wherever they are, to enhance a broad range of abilities. However, educational institutions are mindful that with more students learning from home (with those at university level more likely to maintain this model particularly for post-graduate students) there is now a greater emphasis on protecting students from identity theft, cyberbullying and social isolation. A report from the City and Guilds Institute (2021) claims: "A quarter of children (27%) say that online bullying has increased during periods of lockdown, with two million experiencing the problem over the last year". This research was carried out by Uswitch.com, the comparison and switching service.

Over half of the children (56%) bullied online say they have suffered name-calling, while two fifths (39%) have seen lies published about them on social media sites and messaging apps. A quarter (28%) have had pictures or videos of them shared without their permission. Parents say their children spend more than half (17 hours) of their 30 hours a week online for learning purposes, unsupervised. While three fifths of parents (60%) worry about what their child might be looking at and two fifths (38%) say they are too busy working to keep a regular eye on them.

We have already seen how the invention of the printing press made communication easier and impacted on human lives. Teaching communication competencies should be given priority in education despite the pandemic. The benefits of oracy go far beyond academic achievement and employability. Children who engage in the Winston Churchill (1874–1966) school debate events, display a dynamic range of social, interpersonal and emotional abilities, together with self-confidence, self-awareness, resilience and empathy. Children need to develop a voice to prepare them for life negotiations.

According to John Maxwell (1947–), in his book, *Good Leaders Ask Great Questions* (2014, p. 27), he discusses how engaging with profound enquiries can be life changing. He references the speaker, Anthony Robbins, who observed, 'Quality questions create a quality life. Successful people ask better questions, and as a result, they get better answers'.

Having spent over 23 years in education leadership positions, I found this to be true. Teaching, lecturing and speaking at international conferences are valuable opportunities, as audiences desire to learn and grow knowledge in whatever field they are following. The confidence and ability to ask profound, probing questions provokes us to think and respond with life-changing answers and comments. As the world continues to morph, deeper, meaningful conversations become imperative, to enable individuals to express their innermost thoughts, ideas and feelings. This is an opportune time to change practice and make a difference. Exploring our creativity adds value to what we do in education and influences future generations. From a personal perspective, my contribution to this book aims to show the impact that intelligent conversations make to life and learning. Hopefully, everyone reading it will have a greater desire to become a great communicator in this increasingly mechanical, remote world.

4   Views of Great Writers

The famous novelist, Charles Dickens (1812–70), did not favour technology. In fact, many of the 19th century Romantic writers argued that machinery puts people out of work. Dickens saw it as a real threat, perhaps like the 21st century society sees Artificial Intelligence (AI) as a danger and voices concerns that robots may take over our jobs. In the novel, *The Signalman* (1866), he presents two critical ideas: how human beings are fragile and how technology makes us think deeply about their well-being. Dickens draws attention to the unforgiving brutality of industrial machinery. It is the story of a solitary rail worker, plagued by a ghostly apparition's continuous warnings, which result in his death. Therefore, the novel's message is one of cultivating well-being.

Five years after the Clayton Tunnel completion and one year after the Staplehurst rail accident (1865), *Mugby Junction* (1866) was published. Dickens was a passenger on the accident train and his urgency for humanity to be wary about machines is understandable. He asserts that people have ditched religion for the worship of technology. This idea is further justified in *Dombey and Son* (1848). Dickens highlights the fears generated by the new steam engines and railways. After this publication, Dickens experienced the tragic rail derailment, which left many passengers dead or severely injured. He was left traumatised by the pain, suffering and deaths that he witnessed. Victorians had a genuine fear of trains.

5   Present Fears

Is this fear akin to that we have of AI? Whether or not we favour technology to communicate, people still need a creative voice. The mysterious workings of robots, computers and vehicles implanted with AI (deep learning) have proved robust at solving problems, like face and voice recognition or language translation. Deep learning can be deployed in implementing new oral techniques, enabling input to suit the individual needs of each student, as in learning a new language and achieving practice in accurate pronunciation. Therefore, teachers must help students understand the value of communication, both with fellow humans and robot assistants. As technology advances, so should student communication and creativity to perform in smarter ways. I have observed many teachers conducting *speaking and listening* tests in their classes and found that they concentrate on student ability to use correct vocabulary and grammar rather than how to develop well-organised, appropriate narratives for audiences. This is how I was taught. The danger is that we focus on just part of the whole process of communication to limit the awareness and possibilities of students. Our learners desperately need more holistic approaches, because they are now operating in a virtual world. Effective communication is vital for academic and professional success, whether it is face-to-face, group, organisational or international. Today's educational institutions need to be able to learn and teach in a broader way to be competitive.

As world events change lifestyle, we must focus on human oral talents to discover who we are, develop our abilities, motivate each other and energise our mind, body and soul. Stimulating communication has profound effects for us all. In Great Britain, we are privileged to be surrounded with many theatres, art galleries, museums, cinemas, opera houses etc. that provide the inspiration for talk and thinking to expand our minds and bring us wider understanding.

6   COVID-19 Losses

To meet demands for more conversational learning, responsibility, ownership, instant feedback, greater work/life balance and stronger relationships, education must alter culture and management approaches and adapt to learning changes. My favourite Shakespeare (1564–1616) plays are *Measure for Measure* (1623) *Julius Caesar* (1623) and *Hamlet* (1623). These plays are timeless, because they have enabled students to understand the world in which they live, simply because they address themes relevant for today. For example, *Measure for Measure* (1623) addresses virtue, liberty, justice and the role of women. Hamlet (1623) deals with themes such as: the nation as a diseased body, the complexity of action, the impossibility of certainty. Julius Caesar (1623) focuses on the power of speech, ambition, conflict, identities as well as public and private issues. Such themes resonate with us as classrooms cope with lockdowns. What makes them great plays is the combination of *intelligent speech* and *dynamic creativity* in the ideas expressed in beautiful language. Just think of the *St. Crispin's Day* speech from Shakespeare's (1564–1616) Henry V (2000). Speaking is a connective force in every culture and society. It transcends race, ethnicity and gender. Shakespeare's speeches have influenced us, and students who study these say they underpin and stimulate their oratory ability. This is important as the longer students remain in lockdown situations, the more their speaking is likely to weaken.

Over the years, popular and high culture texts have drawn from Shakespeare. Nick Lowe's (1949–) *Cruel to be Kind*, took its title from the play, *Hamlet* (1609) addressing his mother: 'I must be cruel only to be kind', said the Prince of Denmark in a wriggling apology for killing a courtier and meddling in a new relationship. *Hamlet* also influenced the title of Agatha Christie's (1890–1976) theatrical smash, *The Mousetrap* (1952) and Alfred Hitchcock's (1899–1980) evocative spy thriller, *North by Northwest* (1959). Hamlet has inspired countless writers in various genres and become famous for many eloquent speeches. Whilst Shakespeare is still 'alive' in 2021, it is not much discussed in mainstream UK education. We spend most of our time in a virtual world, so real acting and conversing are difficult. In virtual reality meanings are often lost, interpretations are confused and enjoyment may be minimal. In fact, there is a sense that even with the most sophisticated technology like Zoom and Teams, the emotions, senses and ambiance of face-to-face contact are lost. Students who find it challenging to speak may distance themselves further as opportunities diminish and visits to theatres decrease. Thus, minds are less stimulated with the growing threat of boredom.

Educators have an uphill task unlocking student capacity for communication and creativity. In accordance with Maslow's (1908–70) *Hierarchy of Needs*, teachers should suggest alternatives to help students reach "self-actualisation" (full potential). They could practice speaking in front of a mirror, dress up, speak, sing and dance to music on You Tube. Aretha Franklin (1942–2018) referred to as the Queen of Soul, Whitney Houston (1963–2012) Otis Redding (1941–67) and Marvin Gaye (1939–84) Ed Sheeran (1991–) and Mariah Carey (1970–) are examples of singers who used their voices to communicate in a powerful way. Educators must take drastic measures to resurrect a motivation that provides learners with a sense of anticipation, hope and interest in using their voices intelligently.

7   The Importance of Arts

Psychologists argue that arts are essential because they tell a story:

> In Russia, realists such as Repin (1844–1930) had popularised art in a very rare but interesting way. Folkloric art was a vibrant source of inspiration, while organised groups of schools remained important. Pop art emerged in 1955 in America and England concurrently .... The idea was simply to bridge the gap between mundane contemporary life and art .... Ironically cheerful and airy, it reflected the way of life that had emerged from a postwar economy of abundance with cheap and ubiquitous consumer goods, comic books, movie and television entertainment, and advertising. From 1960 onwards society engaged in video art ... by way of television or computer screen. Video artists showed a concern with everything typical of the contemporary age ..., they initially employed TV monitors, and later turned to computer imagery. Video cameras also played a role when it came to recording transitory performances and other events for posterity. Video art indicates the extent to which contemporary approaches to art can diverge from traditional definitions. In fact at one point, it seemed on the verge of supplanting traditional art entirely. (ART from Impressionism to the Internet, pp. 50, 114)

Conversation forms part of the arts and prepares children for academic and personal success. Thus, by looking at art, in terms of sculptures, books, plays, poems, speeches, films, theatres etc. we can learn much about the attitudes of the time they were produced, as well as the technological developments which are reflected in the styles and forms of artwork.

COVID-19 has curbed how much learners and teachers can participate together face-to-face. On-line conversations have limited eye contact, distorted body language and a sense of alienation. The structure of classrooms has altered, the wearing of masks and gloves disturb natural human interaction.

8   Creativity: Shaping the Future

Accelerating demands for new capabilities, combined with worldwide skill shortages have made learning a strategic necessity for all organisations. In a global economy, educators need to create adaptable workforces. The arts provide creative languages for shaping and expressing our understandings. London is a multicultural city where a wide range of languages are spoken. These include mainstream ones, like English, French, German and Spanish. Below is an example of sub-languages, you might hear, like Creole and Caribbean Pigeon English:[1]

The opening words of the Apostle's Creed:

I believe in God the Father almighty, creator of heaven and earth and in Jesus Christ, his only son, Our Lord, who was conceived by the Holy Ghost ....

A belif fo wan God, di Fada wei I get ol trong, wei I mek heven an grong. An a belif fo Jisas Kraist wi masa, di wan piken fo God, wei I bon fo di Holi Gost ....
[Literal translation: I believe for one God the Father who he get all strong, who he been made heaven and ground. And I believe for Jesus Christ we Master, the one child for God, who he born for the Holy Ghost ....]

In pidgin grammar, this is the personal pronoun system of Tok Pisin – more complex than English:

me I, me
yu you
em he, she, it, him, her
yumi we, us (exclusive, ie you + me)

    mipela we, us (exclusive, ie not including you)
    ol they, them

We learn languages best when living in the country where it is spoken and a teacher's job is to make sure the national language is given priority in learning as necessary for developing their talents in their resident communities. In 2001, some schools handed out certificates to the *Best Talented* child – such as my son, Michael Negus. Now a young adult, he engages with the piano and plays like a professional to gain satisfaction and joy from developing something he is good at doing. This brings self-esteem and confidence to learn.

    According to Wilkinson and Pickett in *The Spirit Level* (2009, p. 36)

> ... in the 1950s only 12 percent of teenagers agreed with the statement 'I am an important person', but by the late 1980s this proportion had risen to 80 percent. So what could have been going on? People becoming much more self-confident doesn't seem to fit with them also becoming much more anxious and depressed. The answer turns out to be a picture of increasing anxieties about how we are seen and what others think of us which has, in turn, produced a kind of defensive attempt to shore up our confidence in the face of those insecurities.

9   The Collapse of Social Structure from COVID-19

Classrooms, lecture halls, canteens and restrooms are places where learners congregate, form friendships and interact. These meeting environments survive because of norms in our society. The alarming rate at which world events are changing normal behaviour means that these very structures are collapsing. How do we monitor good behaviour in children? How do we grade a child fairly after participating in a group discussion, in line with the changes due to the pandemic? With this in mind, it is important for us all to have a stake in shaping the future. As humans we work best when we collaborate and the arts catapult us into greatness. We break boundaries by moving from the pedagogical model of teacher-as-boss to that of making the classroom feel like a West End studio. The pupils at Gordon Primary School, where I am a Governor, delighted the audience with their Christmas play. They were engaged in a collective process that forced them to take responsibility for each other. Pre COVID-19, classrooms connected art with the heart and soul of learners, even when art based curricula were overshadowed by science based subjects. This balance of arts and science is vital for the proper development of the human mind.

10   The Human Mind

Robert Winston's (2003) in *The Human Mind*, discusses measures of intelligence. In January 2003:

> A 12 year-old boy, from the Midlands, won finals of a television show
> called Britain's Brainiest Kid, selected by taking a test on the Mensa web-
> site. Mensa is a global organisation for people whose IQ scores place them
> in the top two percent of the population. The boy's interest was sparked
> from watching the US cartoon show, The Simpsons, in which a child
> prodigy, Lisa Simpson, joins a high-IQ society not dissimilar to Mensa.
> Lisa Simpson provides a journey down the memory lanes of human intel-
> ligence as a child genius. She follows in the tradition of Mozart, who mas-
> tered the harpsichord at age 3 and was composing symphonies by 6 years,
> spending his adolescence as the musical darling of the European aristoc-
> racy. Lisa Simpson does not enjoy the same benefits. Ignored by her beer-
> guzzling father (Homer) and teased mercilessly by her demonic brother
> (Bart) she was patronised and belittled by teachers at school. Lisa's life is
> closer to many gifted youngsters' real experience – a hard time. It is not
> surprising that parents of many child geniuses decide to educate them at
> home, for better or worse. (p. 419)

Winston points out that Lisa's background is middle-class American. Her surroundings are comfortable but not affluent. She attends a state school. Her parents are mostly loving and kind but not intellectual. Lisa's ability came from
her innate brain. As an educator – 11+ to GCSE A Level to university – I have
witnessed the brain's adaptive, plastic ability to rewire itself continually (within
limits) according to the specifics of the environment – home and classroom.
The Scottish government announced in the media that 9 in 10 children were
seriously worried about the coronavirus pandemic, needing encouragement
to help their conversational intelligence cope. How do educationalists explain
intelligence? Are child geniuses the product of pressurised parenting or do
they possess an innate quality waiting to be released? Do we all have capacity
to free the genius inside ourselves, becoming efficient at problem solving, swift
to remember and creative? Winston says 'yes'. Whilst the potential of becoming
Pulitzer-winning novelists or Nobel-winning scientists might be slim, we can all
boost our intelligence (Winston, 2003, p. 430). In light of this, it would appear
that literature can help us to be moral, intelligent experts. Moral thinking is
probably not a single domain but functions variously in different circumstances.

Perhaps we can find kinds of moral reasoning, where experts trained partly by exposure to the fictional literature of complex moral choice do better than those who do not? Novels written by Lamb, Macaulay and Mill are deemed literature, whereas Bentham, Marx and Darwin are not. Why is this? The first three are considered fine writing (belles lettres), with much learnt from their study. Karl Marx (1818–1883) was troubled by why ancient Greek Art retained *eternal charm*. It is enjoyed because ancient tragedy is discovered. Such concerns are different for a 21st century audience, but give insight into our own issues to retain value across the centuries. They have ability to stimulate and educate. Homer, in cartoon stories, is not identical to the Greek one. Different historical periods construct a different Homer and Shakespeare for their own purposes with elements to value. All literature is re-worked, if only unconsciously, by those that read them. I have students with a view that literature is for an elite and so do not appreciate the aesthetic merit. There are long-lasting pleasures, rewards, inspirations and understandings to be gained from reading. The effort makes us enlightened.

11   Can Art Revive Conversational Intelligence in the New World Order?

The world is changing at a phenomenal rate. The old world order has been totally eclipsed and forgotten only to be replaced by one which is unrecognisable. This is most evident in education, where new ways of working are challenging our thoughts, ideas and actions and how we relate to each other. It is important to note that historically the world was first an oral society before literacy was established when printing became possible. Educators have entered a new stage of globalisation where intercultural communication is key to success. This is ever present, as COVID-19 has forced humanity to work and relax in their homes – now converted to classrooms, gyms, offices and whatever else they need to be, with technology allowing remote connectivity. The key to life success is to become a master of conversational intelligence. Prior to lockdowns, some institutions provided for students to learn effective strategies that prepared the brain for reciprocal exchanges. We converse on a one-to-one basis, in small or large groups and also with our inner selves. The future depends hugely on conversational intelligence, because what we say and how we say it contributes significantly to our success. In Wilkinson and Pickett's book, *The Spirit Level* (2009), they produce a wealth of data, suggesting that good education is the basis for a healthy society whereas the lack of it can result in one that is crime-ridden, violent and in poor health.

12   Impact of COVID-19 on Conversational Intelligence in Education

In a digital world, it is difficult to interact properly with a robot or with students in an effective way. COVID-19 has destroyed the authority of conversation and removed it from the mainstream of life to lose power. Few people are aware of this, because the means of communication are mainly virtual, promoting the illusion that nothing has changed. The result is that people feel disempowered and are less likely to succeed. The pandemic has polarised society, as some elite schools ensured that students received good quality teaching and learning. Unfortunately, the disadvantaged ones have seen their level of performance suffer greatly.

The use of smart boards, interactive whiteboards, online lessons and various types of computer programmes has made education a sophisticated art. The pandemic witnessed many unorthodox ways in which individuals absorb information and attempted to address all learning styles with new technology options. Over the years, knowledge has rapidly grown with virtual technology transforming homes into classrooms. However, it is ironic that as knowledge escalates, so do reports claiming that standards of literacy (speaking & writing) and numeracy are falling. What has gone wrong? The UK is a leader in science, the arts and technology. *The Evening Standard*, Thursday 2 June 2021, had an article: "Illiteracy in London, My Pupils can't read Basic English words" (Davis, 2021). The internet has made conversational intelligence difficult because technical issues like lagging, poor sound quality, electricity failure, lack of full visibility and loss of physical touch means half of the interaction is lost before started. Students lacking adequate computers are disadvantaged thereby curtailing their ability to develop. Perhaps we can find solace or answer in Eliot's (1888–1965) *Four Quartets* (1941). His commitment to *time* draws us into a utopian world if we slow down:

> Time present and time past
> Are both perhaps present in time future?
> And time future contained in time past
> All time is eternally present

While we have present time, we must use it for the benefit of the next generation. Teachers are caught within a conflict: the aspiration to improve spoken and literate communication and the increasing emphasis on virtual learning. Countries like Cuba, Finland, Italy, Japan and Finland out more emphasis on speaking rather than writing and so are ahead in education and performance. Public speaking is a well proven way of motivating young people to learn and develop confidence to operate in a competitive world. Time is not on our side. The metaphysical poet Andrew Marvell, concerns himself with time and space. In Stanza 2 of *To My Coy Mistress* (1681), he writes: "But at my back I always hear; Time's winged chariot hurrying near Deserts of vast eternity". We could however, reverse Marvell's dictum, slow down time and invest energy in promoting a generation that values conversational intelligence.

13   Review

This chapter has sought to identify the importance of conversational intelligence and the effects COVID-19 has had on it; conversely, it has attempted to show the positive implications for global educational institutions if we prioritise oracy. Education has been disrupted by the pandemic, thus limiting the intellectual growth and minds of children. Today's classrooms have children speaking many languages, with English a minority in over 2000 UK state schools, according to Department of Education figures, thus making traditional teaching monologues difficult to follow. Teachers and students need time to reflect and grow, with opportunity to imagine, exchange and share ideas, engage in public speaking and able to express feelings to produce deep learning. Fundamental to this, is competence and confidence in spoken understanding and expression of ideas and emotions, which enable inner thinking and narrative speech to develop. Conversational intelligence, narrative thought and linguistic structures are facilitated to underpin literacy and numeracy (National Association for Language Development in the Curriculum[2]).

Our society is at a critical point and should make more informed judgments about present issues, within the context of our rapidly evolving world. Today, oral activities play a limited role in the educational curriculum, as written exams dominate for league tables and virtual reality cannot compete effectively with actual reality. The works of William Shakespeare, cannot be performed effectively if performers are not able to see, hear, touch, smell and taste to achieve tone, mood and atmosphere. We all need to be cognisant of our surroundings to feel alive.

Therefore, it is imperative for speakers and listeners to be in accord. Shakespeare's performance of *Henry V* required a myriad of different stage settings. A presentation of England and France in 1413–20 had to inspire and attract the audience. The Chorus description of the night before the battle of Agincourt had to excite and intrigue. For an audience to be enraptured by a play and get a holistic flavour, they must be in a physical building, like the Globe theatre, instead of sitting in front of a 2-dimensional screen, with classmates and teacher. The digital world has made it possible to enact plays, discussions, speeches, presentations online. However, we cannot deny that human feeling is lost! Is there anything that can replace the human touch? John Baldoni (1952–) in his book, *Great Communication: Secrets of Great Leaders* (2003), made clear that speaking is not just about standing up to talk, but involves ability to deliver a message verbally, mentally and metaphorically. Moreover, he insists that everything we do demands effective communication. If society is to survive, we must rise up above the daily challenges and put conversational intelligence at the forefront of education to give students a distinct voice, which is the stimulus for both creative and critical thinking.

Notes

1   www.google.com
2   www.naldic.org.uk/research-and-information/eal-statistics/lang

References

Angelou, M. (1984). *I know why the caged bird sings*. Virago.

Baldoni, J. (2003). *Great communication: Secrets of great leaders*. McGraw Hill.

Davis, A. (2021, June 2). Illiteracy in London: My pupils can't read basic English words. *Evening Standard*.

Dickens, C. (1848). *Dombey and son*. Penguin.

Dickens, C. (1854). *Hard times*. Wordsworth.

Dickens, C. (1866). *The signalman*. Profile Books.

Dickens, C. (1868). *Mugby Junction*. Chapman & Hall.

Eliot, T. S. (1971). *Four quartets*. Harcourt Brace Jovanovich.

Marvell, A. (2003). To his coy mistress. In *The poems of Andrew Marvell* (N. Smith, Ed.). Pearson Education.

Maslow, A. (1943). *Hierarchy of needs*. https://www.simplypsychology.org/maslow.html

Maxwell, J. C. (2014). *Good leaders ask great questions: Your foundation for successful leadership*. Center Street.

Orwell, G. (1949). *Nineteen eighty-four*. Secker & Warburg.

Richter, K. (2001). *Art from impressionism to the internet*. Prestel.

Shakespeare, W. (1623). *Hamlet*. Wordsworth.

Shakespeare, W. (1623). *Julius Caesar*. Wordsworth.

Shakespeare, W. (1623). *Measure for measure*. Wordsworth.

Shakespeare, W. (2000). *Henry V*. Wordsworth.

Stokes, P. (2006). David Hume. In *Philosophy: 100 essential thinkers*. Arcturus.

Stokes, P. (2006). Jeremy Bentham. In *Philosophy: 100 essential thinkers*. Arcturus.

Stokes, P. (2006). Nicolaus Copernicus. In *Philosophy: 100 essential thinkers*. Arcturus.

Todd, L. (1984). Cameroon Pidgin English. In *Modern English: Pidgins & creoles*. Blackwell.

Wilkinson, R., & Pickett, K. (2009). *The spirit level*. Allen Lane.

Winston, R. (2003). *The human mind and how to make the most of it*. Bantam.

CHAPTER 8

University-School Partnerships

Scholars in Residence within a School

Joanna Ebner

Abstract

I was awarded a Churchill Fellowship in 2018 to establish the efficacy of a Scholar-in-Residence (affectionately known as SiR) within a school environment. This could be in relation to initial teacher training or continuing professional development (CPD). The terms *Scholar, Academic* and/or *Professor in Residence* are used interchangeably, depending on the setting and country. The academic is seconded from a university whose specific function is to work within a school developing teacher professional learning. I had already piloted this scheme by appointing a Scholar in Residence from Roehampton University at my own school, Thomas's Kensington in London. Initially, I was anticipating that this would be an academic seconded from the education department of a university and that my research would continue to support the presence of a Scholar in Residence in my school.

This chapter considers the impact of a scholar in residence and the benefits within and outside schools.

1 Introduction: Impact and Benefits

This project has gained valuable insights into the potential benefits of the SiR model. Academic research has already resulted in on-going schemes across the US and Australia and raised awareness of the concept of a SiR will hope to extend this active engagement by challenging pre-existing UK assumptions regarding the value of SiR and their potential for raising academic achievement both for staff and students. SiR might, thus, become a regular feature of the English school landscape. One natural extension of this raised awareness might be a broader acceptance of the value of a professional academic, or other external input, as a vital element of everyday classroom practice rather than a distracting intrusion.

The SiR initiative might, more broadly, lead to increasing partnerships and collaborations between schools and (teacher training) universities or community organisations. This might, in turn, directly influence government policy with the aim of implementing this model nationwide and furthering teacher professional development in a focused, structured manner. Questionnaires, semi-structured interviews, field notes and case studies were the methods used to collect evidence.

2   Background

I am the headmistress of Thomas's Kensington – a co-educational, independent school with 400 pupils aged 4–11 years. Established in 1971, the school is proprietary owned, run by the sons of the founders and comprises four schools – Kensington, Battersea, Fulham and Clapham, a kindergarten and one sponsored school – *Thomas's Academy* – in the state sector. All the head teachers work closely together to ensure that the schools maintain the founders' stated aim:

> To offer the highest academic standards, within a broad, rich curriculum, which inspires enjoyment learning and achievement. We expect everyone within school communities to be kind. In a recent report by School Ofsted inspectors (2017), Thomas's Kensington was judged outstanding.
>
> The headteacher and the proprietors have created a caring and aspirational culture to ensure pupils make rapid progress in their learning. Staff morale is high and there is a shared sense of community in this family-orientated and outstanding school.

Also, again in February 2020:

> The proprietors, head teacher and senior leaders are highly ambitious in what they want pupils to learn. Teachers deliver these very high expectations effectively. As a result pupils achieve exceptionally well.

All schools within the group are deemed by Ofsted to be '*outstanding*'.

In order to uphold and maintain these values, I am a strong believer in focused Continuing Professional Development (CPD). As a result, I was responsible for establishing a Masters (MA) degree in Educational Practice across all the Thomas's Schools. After a bidding process, the University of Roehampton was selected as the host institution and Roehampton's first bespoke MA was established with the initial cohort successfully graduating in June 2016.

This process was the beginning of a practical commitment to CPD at Thomas's Kensington with teachers profoundly involved in their own professional development, informing both their teaching and that of the pupils. The MA is now offered to all Thomas's staff, with particular encouragement given to early career teachers and action research projects are undertaken that feedback directly into the school. Projects have included the examination of Carol Dweck's *Growth Mindset*, the development of a creative curriculum and the impact of homework. MA candidates are encouraged to offer feedback in staff meetings and to share their knowledge and expertise with teachers and parents across the Thomas's schools. This work has led to a conference for parents, led by academics, and the publication of a journal containing summaries of the MA projects. Thomas's part funds (60%) the MA programme as part of its on-going commitment to CPD, while the 40% self-funding element ensures that MA candidates remain active stakeholders.

3   Influence of the USA and the Professional Development School Model

The expanded links between Thomas's and the University of Roehampton, led me to begin an exploration of other ways in which the University and the School could collaborate to enhance staff learning and development. It had become apparent as part of the MA research that, for a variety of well-documented reasons (often connected to a lack of resources), a policy shift has taken place across the English teacher-training model. This has evolved away from its traditional base within a university to a more school-based system, taught, led and accredited within the relevant school.

The new model had brought its own challenges, as it appeared that CPD in schools frequently lacks structure and rigour. I had become increasingly engaged in the notion of continuous, in situ teacher training – a model which appeared, on the surface, to be closely related to the Professional Development Schools' framework frequently employed within the US. I was keen to explore this new model both by embedding a scholar or academic-in-residence within my own school and by observing well-established case studies in the US and Australia.

Through the University of Roehampton, I made contact with Professor Ferrara of Manhattanville University, who invited me to observe a PDS model in action at her partner school – Thomas Edison School, New York. This initial visit (September 2014) gave me the impetus to develop a project, based on Ferrara's PDS model, the design of which we worked on together.

4 Scholar in Residence: The Rationale and Pilot Study

Thomas's Kensington's first SiR was appointed from the Roehampton University staff and engaged to work within school once a week for 2 terms (January–July 2015). The stated objective was to instill academic rigour into the school's on-going CPD in order to fill a perceived learning vacuum. The SiR provided relational and informal support to staff, including those who were undertaking their MA degrees and/or the Leading Practitioners in the school. The SiR also developed a whole school staff project on creative teaching and learning in the curriculum. The embedded nature of the SiR was instrumental in the school's ability to offer a model in which teaching theory and practice could be experienced in tandem. This embedded programme led directly to the school's attainment, in September 2015, of the Professional Development Quality Mark Gold Award for Professional Development practice (and subsequently the Platinum Award 'recognising the school as a centre of innovation and excellence in Professional Development' in Feb *2019*). The report stated that Thomas's Kensington has: "a very systematic, planned and organised approach towards PD in the school".

Following this, and through the school's links with Manhattanville College and Thomas Edison Community School, alongside the assistance of Professor Ferrara, Thomas's Kensington was awarded the International Schools' Award (January 2016) and I was invited to write a chapter for Ferrara's most recent book outlining our project and my continued interest in pursuing research into both the theory and practice of CPD via an academic-in-residence model.

5 Winston Churchill Memorial Travelling Fellowship

Further to the pilot *Scholar in Residence* programme, I successfully applied for a Winston Churchill memorial Travelling Fellowship, in order to carry out further research into the parallels between my pedagogic aims and the Professional Development Schools (PDS) in the USA and Australia. Part of my motivation for this research was my increasing awareness of the de-professionalisation of teachers, as well as the flaws that my team had encountered in the English initial teacher training programmes. I felt strongly that university-school relationships and partnerships work (preferably with an embedded academic in-residence) in a model that is replicable across English schools. The development of such a model would be a way to ensure that the very best staff will experience lifelong learning, which will benefit all pupils.

6   The Model in Australia

In *Becoming Critical* (1986) Carr and Kemmis presented a rationale for the *'teacher as researcher'* movement. Claiming that informed understanding about the practice of teaching emerges from reflexivity on the part of practitioners, Carr & Kemmis suggested that research and theorising have been largely ineffectual in improving the quality of teaching because educational research is not the exclusive preserve of experts but also in the domain of practitioners. They argued for a shift away from an empirical-analytic tradition with its traditional expert/novice split to a new paradigm in which knowledge is created by people in situations and is best understood by participants in such situations (Jacknicke & Rowell, 1987).

Stenhouse (1975, p. 159) suggested that the most promising way of overcoming the social and psychological barriers to teacher participation is through mutually supportive cooperative research between teachers and full-time researchers. Carr and Kemmis (1986, p. 161) built on this theoretical foundation to propose that it is the relationship between researcher and teacher that is most important. The researcher should become a *'critical friend'* who helps the insider to make wise judgements in the process of educational transformation. This approach appears highly appropriate for school staff, who often remain sceptical of external interventions.

The theoretical work of Carr and Kemmis has a long history of practical implementation in Australia where programmes of 'scholarly teachers' working as "critical friends" were developed throughout the 1990s, and where such practitioners were introduced into schools to put theory into practice in a mutually beneficial way. The active pursuit of this process led to the University of Melbourne foundation of the country's first *clinical teaching* MA programme led by Professor John Hattie at the Melbourne Graduate School of Education. This innovative centre has made the city a hub for teaching research.

In a separate development, the Australian Office for Learning and Teaching has funded a two-year project to investigate the experiences of the newly appointed *Scholarly Teaching Fellows* (STF) and how their role might be developed across the sector. By the end of 2018, there will be more than 800 STFs across four Australian universities: UTS, UNSW, U Canberra and Griffith. Amongst academics, there has been some resistance to this development, since their creation might be seen as threatening and a means to create more zero-hours contracts for freelancers to serve a student body that has doubled over the last decade. Trade unions, in particular, suggest that the scheme has become a cheap way to deliver teacher training.

An amended STF programme aims to overcome these obstacles by promoting STFs into teaching-research roles and thus bringing scholarship and job security back into academic teaching. The Office for Learning and Teaching has initiated further research to investigate the STF experience and to build a consensus on how to expand the programme.

The Office has, however, recognised that the most effective professional learning occurs on site (Cole, 2012) and in context (Harris, 2014). It has, thus, become Australian school policy to encourage schools to work directly with experts. (Sharon Clarke, Australian Council for Educational Research 2013, Camberwell, Victoria). Teacher-Scholar-Community Partnerships are being formed across Australia with a primary aim of improving student motivation, attendance and behaviour plus enhancing teacher development.

7   Policy in the Unitied States of America (USA)

Dr Sonia Janis is the Clinical Assistant Professor in Social Studies Education at the University of Georgia (UGA). During the academic year 2014/15, she was invited to undertake a year in residence at Cedar Shoals High – a local school, which had been selected to work in partnership with UGA. During that first year, 50% of Janis' workload took place within the Cedar Shoals High premises where she was invited to co-teach one government class (one period) in the Freshman Academy, alongside an in-house 'government studies' teacher. The government class was specifically designed to take place early in the school day so that Sonia was able both to participate in school staff meetings and to return to fulfil her university responsibilities each afternoon. In this way, she fulfilled the requirement to be socially, as well as pedagogically, embedded in both institutions.

Sonia initially served as the *lead teacher* with the co-teacher and students in this government class continuously reporting to the Professional Development (PD) Classroom. She collaborated with the teaching faculty and leadership team at CSHS through the following settings: Government Data Team meetings, Social Studies Department meetings, Freshman Academy meetings, Faculty Meetings and School Improvement (SILT) meetings. The learning concept was to enable an experienced social studies instructor to practise in a horizontal collaborative, not vertical or top-down model. This collaboration could then support the planning of a quality curriculum and learning experience throughout the high school.

After the successful outcome of Sonia's first year at Cedar Shoals High, she was invited back during the school year 2015–16 with her hours at the school now increased to 75% of her timetable. She was again invited to co-teach one period of American Government/Civics in the Freshman Academy as the "lead teacher" in a co-teaching partnership with an in-house teacher who acted as the official instructor-of-record.

The horizontal model had proved so effective during its first year that Sonia was also invited to lead a section of the CSHS Social Studies Department Meeting in November 2015. She used this to share her stance on teaching and to demonstrate how enquiry-based learning could lead to the development of a series of formative assessments, which would access student understandings in innovative ways. She provided the department with six different formative assessment models that included opportunities for students to develop supported conclusions around big idea (Wiggins & McTighe, 2005) questions associated with American Government/Civics (i.e. Is there liberty and justice for all?).

Sonia's innovations and ideas proved so popular that she was invited to extend her outreach beyond CSHS. The leadership team at another local school, Clarke Central High, asked Sonia to mentor three recent graduates who had been hired as American Government/Civics teachers. By the spring of 2016, Sonia had undertaken responsibility for the school-based mentoring of 29 teacher candidates across two sections of their education degrees. She also helped to set up formal and informal lines of communication between the leadership team and teachers at four local secondary schools. Sonia's curriculum suggestions were also incorporated into the district's online curriculum portal for American Government/Civics teachers.

8   Analysis of Questionnaires

An analysis of the responses in the questionnaires that were handed out to teachers reveals universal support for the concept of the Academic-in-Residence. All teachers found it a rewarding experience with teachers making declarations such as: "This relationship is a win-win-win" and "I truly did not realise my growth potential".

Everyone mentioned that it has been genuinely helpful to their professional practice to learn from a more experienced individual with extra insight. The only mild caveats to this almost total approval were suggestions that even more interaction and time would prove beneficial.

Academics' responses to the questions on their questionnaire were equally positive. A few stated that their confidence in the classroom prior to the residency was quite low but that, while the experience had been challenging, it had also been much more rewarding than they had anticipated and it had helped to enhance their professional practice. Others stated that, while their original confidence levels had been high, there were still many aspects of classroom

teaching that had surprised them. They had not expected to encounter resistance from the student teachers (several thought that the academics might be
out of touch with the reality of the classroom). All academics declared that
they are now more aware of the daily stresses and strains of classroom teaching practice and several stated that, as well as broadening classroom learning
more generally and acting as a *critical friend*, they felt that the great advantage
for the student teachers was that:

This "third space" allows freedom for new opportunities to be develop. All
the academics stated that they had genuinely enjoyed the experience and felt
that their own teaching had been enhanced.

9   Review

My research questions and the rationale behind each school and university
visit were framed as follows:

1.   *Is a Scholar-in-Residence a valid and useful concept?*
Further to my own employment of the Scholar-in-Residence model, my collaborative discussions at the Professional Development Schools' Conference
(Jacksonville, Florida, March 2018) and visits to a number of schools across
the US and Australia, it has become abundantly apparent that the Scholar-in-
Residence model can become a powerful tool for improvement and development both for members of teaching staff and for the pupils themselves. An
unexpected finding is that it is also a valuable growth tool for the Academics.

2.   *If it is, what needs to be implemented in a school in order for the Scholar-in-*
       Residence to be most effectively employed?
The schools in which the SiR model was most effectively employed are the ones
where the SiR has been properly, and profoundly, embedded in the school's
daily framework. Relationships need to be built up in order for the Scholar
to feel supported and for the staff to feel engaged and included in the design
and implementation of the programme. Scheduled informal and social interactions appeared to be one key factor in the success of such programmes but
other important factors were constant observation, self-reflection and mutual
support. The academic-in-residence programme needs to be embraced and
actively supported, in order to be successful. Both the partner school and the
university need to commit to the programme over an extended period of time
for it to become truly worthwhile.

10   Recommendations

Following my Fellowship, I have incorporated the positive aspects of my observations into my daily school practice. My recommendation to my own school's proprietors was to appoint a new Scholar-in-Residence, but one with an improved and modified role, fully supported by an engaged academic institution. This is still in the early stages, but staff across the group pf schools are encouraged to collaborate, plan and engage with the resident academic as much as possible and to enjoy the opportunities that this academic relationship enables. I have disseminated my findings to staff and the proprietors so that they can see that the concept of the SiR is useful, interesting and fundamentally positive as I have found it to be following my visits to the US and Australia.

11   Postscript

An Academic in Residence was appointed across Thomas's London Day Schools in the academic year 2019/2020 seconded from the National School of Education and Teaching, University of Coventry. The role is still developing but a university-school(s) partnership has now been established, alongside Thomas's Teacher Training which is based at the Thomas's Academy. A training pathway is being developed for post graduate training and continuing professional development in our schools, which includes an MA programme and opportunities for our own bespoke *Thomas's Leading Teaching Certificate*. Elements of this are provided remotely and online, which has proved useful especially during the recent COVID-19 pandemic. My role has been to play a significant part in leading the CPD offering across the Thomas's group of schools in partnership with a Scholar in Residence.

References

Carr, W., & Kemmis, S. (1986). *Becoming critical: Educating knowledge & action research.* Falmer Press.

Cole, T. (2012). The development of growth references & growth charts. *Annals of Human Biology, 39*(5), 382–394.

Harris, A. (2014). *Distributed leadership: Perspectives, practicalities and potential.* Corwin Press.

Jacknicke, K., & Powell, P. (1987). Alternative orientations for educational research. *The Alberta Journal of Educational Research, 33*(1), 62–72.

Stenhouse, L. (1975). *An introduction to curriculum research and development.* Heinemann Education.

Wiggins, G., & McTighe, J. (2005). *Understanding by design.* The Association for Supervision & Curriculum Development (ASCD).

CHAPTER 9

Imaginative Alternatives to the 'Macabre Constant'

Pierre Frath

Abstract

It is generally acknowledged that a natural outcome of learning is assessment. And when the process of evaluation has been completed, two groups of students become discernible, those who have succeeded and those who have failed. In a book entitled *Other People's Children. What happens to those in the bottom 50% academically?* (2018), Barnaby Lenon offers an in-depth and well-documented analysis of academic failure in the British school system and he argues in favour of better funded and more efficient vocational schools to cater for those 50%. Improved technical skills, he argues, will give students better job opportunities in the economy, especially with regard to an expected after-Brexit shortage of skilled labour. Yet such an analysis does not take into account what André Antibi (2003) has named 'the macabre constant', i.e. the inevitable 30 to 50% rate of failure that is generated by the evaluation process itself. This is the question we are going to address in this chapter.

1   Introduction

Research has shown that 'too many children start primary school at the age of five without the basic skills they need to cope' (Lenon, 2018, p. 13). The skills children should master at the end of the "Early Years Foundation Stage (EYFS)". have been defined as follows (Lenon, 2018, p. 13):
- Listen to, understand and follow instructions
- Use the past present and future tenses correctly
- Talk about their own and other's feelings
- Read and understand simple sentences
- Count and carry out simple addition and subtraction

> This is assessed at the end of reception year, when most children are aged five, through the Early Years Foundation Stage Profile. It seems that in 2016, 31% of children in England began primary school without this good level of early development, 46% of those on free school meals. (Lenon, 2018, p. 13)

> Children who do not achieve the expected standard of early language
> and communication at age five are over four times more likely to be
> below the normal target level of reading at age five than those who did.
> (Lenon, 2018, p. 15)

Some low achievement is thus blamed on low income and its consequences
on the quality of parenting. "Parents from lower income homes speak less to
their children, have a more limited vocabulary, are less likely to help them learn
to read or count, are less likely to own books" (Lenon, 2018, p. 14).[1] Such observations are accurate and they seem to perfectly describe reality as experienced
by teachers, parents and students. They are confirmed by scientific research
based on academic knowledge and figures collected through empirical studies.

Yet little thought is given to the *standards* of evaluation themselves and to
their *social context*. Who has chosen the items of the EYFS list? Under what
authority? Have they been decided upon in an impressionistic way by a few
educationalists or have there been empirical studies to define them? Are they
free from ideological influence? An item such as "talk about their own and
other's feelings" is clearly linked to our zeitgeist: exchange about emotions and
feelings is probably given more value nowadays than a few decades ago when
more intellectual capacities would perhaps have been paramount.

Specialists in education are no doubt aware of the link between exposure
to rich and meaningful conversation at home and academic achievement
and they must know that items such as use the past present and future tenses
correctly and read and understand simple sentences will separate students
according to social class. In that case, evaluation becomes a sort of self-fulfill-
ing prophecy which results in identifying children from lower income homes.[2]
Gearing them toward vocational careers can then be construed as a way of
maintaining them in their social class.

In this chapter, I am not advocating a fairer EYFS list. Its items are in line
with society and produce generally accepted results even if they are ethically
dubious. If they were modified to favour working-class children, chances are
the failure/success ratio would remain the same, with more middle-class children in the failing group. The fact is that any evaluation will produce failure
because failure is part of the meaning of evaluation. It is this question that I
am going to address in this text.

I was an English teacher for many years in secondary schools in France and
abroad and I also taught French as a foreign language to adults in Germany.
Later I undertook a PhD in Computational Linguistics and I eventually became
a Senior Lecturer at the English department of Strasbourg University and then

a professor in Rheims. I mainly taught linguistics, philosophy of language and didactics. I was also involved in the setting up of multilingual self-study language centres in France and abroad and I became the head of two such language centres, first *SPIRAL*[3] in Strasbourg and then the *Maison des Langues* in Rheims. I quickly noticed that the evaluation of self-studying students could not be done in the usual way and this helped me look at evaluation in a whole new way, particularly with regard to my experience in French secondary schools (see Frath, 2019, 2020).

Teachers know that if all of their students have good grades on a regular basis, they will be considered too *nice*; conversely, if they consistently give marks below average, they will be considered too 'strict'. A "good" assessment thus divides the class into three groups: the "good", the "average" and the "bad" (whatever polite understatements are used to name them). Some students will certainly move to an adjacent group, but the structure will remain. About a third of students are thus condemned to failure regardless of educational conditions: whatever the level of the class, the quality of teaching, the subjects taught, failure will happen.

This unvarying proportion of failure has been called "the macabre constant" by André Antibi, a mathematics inspector in the Toulouse regional educational area, in his eponymous book published in 2003. Yet up to now, very few researchers have taken this obvious feature of evaluation into account. Most conferences and publications ignore it completely. Books about education sometimes mention it but they do not often perceive its centrality. This general blindness is disturbing and I will endeavour to explore its causes.

Docimologists have identified various biases affecting marking; educationalists have studied its damaging effects on children's well-being and learning; others have observed evaluative practices from a historical perspective; others still have established typologies. Most authors end up making suggestions for improvement, and indeed some suggestions are from time to time officially accepted and put into practice in schools.

However, no proposal has so far succeeded in really improving the situation: failure remains. The reason is that all evaluations are finally caught up by the macabre constant: there inevitably comes a time when the desire or the need to sort and eliminate comes about. For a significant change to really take place, it will be necessary to become aware of the central role of the macabre constant.

I shall begin with general considerations on assessment and grading and then proceed to offer a humanistic framework in which various assessment methods can be given their full measure.

2   Typology of Evaluation

Researchers have introduced a distinction between *summative* and *formative* assessment. The first is exemplified by the traditional written test given at the end of a teaching period and its purpose is to check whether learning has been achieved. It produces a global mark which allows students to appreciate what they have been taught and to see their rank relative to the other students in the same class. Summative assessment generates the macabre constant.

A variant of summative evaluation is a certificate examination. It is an exam based on a programme set up outside school, an example being the baccalaureate. A key difference is that certificate assessment is anonymous and takes place outside the classroom. It therefore does not produce the macabre constant and there is theoretically no limit to success. However, when all students succeed, the social value of the exam falls rapidly and this often means the end of its implementation. This is what happened in France to the *Certificat d'études primaires* (primary school certificate), an exam which used to be taken by all fourteen-year olds. It was dropped a few decades ago when its success rate practically reached 100%. The baccalaureate with its 90% rate of success over two years is now being gradually disposed of. A percentage of failure is therefore desirable to ensure the social value of the exam.

As for formative evaluation, its aim is to give students indications on their learning achievements and to help them overcome difficulties by means of a personalized work programme. Formative assessment takes place in a dialogue between student and teacher and it does not concern the class and the institution: there is no official mention of it in institutional documents such as reports. Students sum up formative evaluation as follows: 'we get marks but they do not count'.

Assessment should not be harmful. Pierre Merle (2018, p. 27) says studies have shown that benevolent assessment actually increases academic performance because it generates a feeling of confidence conducive to better learning. Formative and benevolent assessments are therefore extremely positive. Ultimately, however, they will be caught up by the macabre constant and a mark that '*counts*' will eventually be mentioned in reports. It is hoped that assessments that do not "count" will lead to better ones that do, but if the final assessment is summative, it will inevitably generate the macabre constant. Benevolent assessments then live under the threat of *malicious* assessment which will bring about a certain proportion of failure.

Another problem is that evaluation says nothing about what should happen to the students who have failed. Teachers claim to seek everyone's success but we all know that this will not happen. Schools may sometimes set up remediation courses, but they know perfectly well that they will only be marginally effective and will not eliminate failure.

3   A Historical Perspective

France has been plagued by a marking system which rates students on a numerical scale from 0 (very bad) to 20 (excellent), with 10 as the pivotal limit between failure and success. Pierre Merle (2018, chapter 2) explains that it was originally conceived in the 16th century by the Jesuits in the schools they had created to train an intellectual and religious elite, *the soldiers of God*. It ensured competition between three groups of students, the *optimi*, who were rewarded, the *dubii*, who were encouraged and the *inepti*, who were eventually excluded. This marking system was later adopted in schools at large and it was institutionalized in the 19th century when competitive examinations for the Grandes Écoles and teacher training schools (Écoles Normales) were introduced. From there, it percolated into primary and secondary education until it became the default system.

Yet there has been an alternative to macabre evaluation, and that is skills assessment. It was first established by Jean-Baptiste de la Salle in the Christian Schools he set up to teach and educate working class children at the end of the 17th century. According to Merle (2018, pp. 59–60), Christian Schools replaced the selective and permanent rivalry of the Jesuit model by a personal progression. Students start in the order of *beginners* and they try to reach the orders of *advanced* and *perfect*. The transition to a higher level is based on a form of global assessment against a list of pre-defined skills. Merle points out that this is a foreshadowing of modern-day frameworks of reference such as the Common European Framework of Reference for Languages (CEFRL) produced within the Council of Europe.[4] As classes were not formed according to age criteria, students could stay in a given level until they managed to enter the next or dropped out.

4   How Macabre Constant Strikes back with Skill Assessments

In France and most other countries in Europe, language learning is evaluated against the CEFRL. The skills to be acquired are expressed in terms of ability descriptors describing actions. At a given level, students should be able to *do* this or that, like write a postcard, understand a movie, write a report, etc.

Grammatical knowledge of irregular verbs and conjugation for example is not specifically measured. Teachers then implement educational activities to help students acquire these skills. In its first version, published in 2001, the *Framework* did not foster any particular methodology; it rather advocated eclecticism and recommended periodic consultations of the descriptors. Later, the Council of Europe suggested that task-based approaches were more in line with the *Framework* than most other methods.

Newly acquired skills can be evaluated at the end of a learning period by intuitively checking whether learners are capable of performing the tasks mentioned by the descriptors. However, such an evaluation does not produce marks and therefore has little institutional value. Written exams and certifications are then introduced. They often consist of lists of items to which the candidate should respond. Answers are often evaluated in binary terms (right or wrong, ability demonstrated or not). This is where the macabre constant strikes back. If some items are passed by all the students or on the contrary if all fail, exam designers will consider that the items are not sufficiently *discriminating*. They will then modify them until a dispersal of results is obtained. A *good* question will then separate the candidates into two groups, those who fail and those who succeed.

Philippe Perrenoud (1989) is right when he says that the hierarchy of skills produced by exams is an artefact of the evaluation methodology. There are certainly differences in skills among learners, he says, but they are increased by the assessment process. Perrenoud considers that evaluation should rather be geared toward the *reduction* of differences. The CEFRL could allow such a feat because it assesses what the learners *can* do and not than what they *cannot*; and yet the quest for the discriminating effect lessens that opportunity.

Preparation of language certification at university is another example of the macabre use of skills assessment. Universities quite often decide to impose a minimum level in languages, usually English, which students must reach at the end of a given cycle, say B2 at Bachelor's degree level. Evaluation is often achieved through an external certification such as CLES, TOEFL or TOEIC.[5] Teachers naturally want to prepare their students for the exam, especially since the results will allow comparisons between classes and therefore between them. The learning content is then formatted by the final assessment. This phenomenon is known as the *washback effect*.

Preparation is often quite tedious both for teachers and students. Students tend to drag their feet in order to demoralise teachers and lower their expectations. The *optimi* do not need to learn anything more than what they already know. The *inepti* are not motivated, because they have always been in the macabre group and they do not see why this should change now; they simply hope to minimize damage at the time of certification by revising the records. Only the *dubii* may be keen on making some progress. Instead of seeking excellence and linguistic diversity, universities are content with low-level mono-lingualism (English only), with no ambition other than training for certification in classes where the washback effect has reduced class-room learning to a joyless activity.[6]

A famous French writer, Paul Valéry, had harsh words about diplomas in a 1935 conference.

> The diploma is a mortal enemy of culture. As soon as some action is submitted to control, the deep aim of the controlled person is no longer the action itself but the anticipation of control and of the means to defeat it. If the aim of teaching is no longer the education of the mind but the acquisition of a diploma, the object of studying turns into a minimal requirement.[7]

Certification as it is now certainly only measures a minimal requirement.

5   Semiotic & Anthropological Causes of the Macabre Constant

Why do we have this taste for sorting and exclusion? Why do we not see the macabre constant? There is a semiotic reason: there can be no success without failure. Many words in a language work in pairs: *Small/large, indoor/outdoor, rich/poor,* etc. They structure our understanding of the environment and society. There would be no sense in talking about the *inside* if there were no *outside*; if there were no *poor*, there would be no *rich* either; *small* has no meaning without *large*. What would everyone's success mean? Nothing at all. Success would literally make no sense without its counterpart, failure. Schools systems often claim they want to eradicate failure. They forget that for some to succeed, others must fail.[8]

This semiotic structure of success and failure is in line with our anthropological nature. We live in extraordinarily unequal societies. Parents want their children to succeed in life, i.e. to get jobs that will provide them with sufficient income and which are prestigious enough to secure as high a social status as possible. It is better to be a doctor, a teacher, a CEO or a lawyer than, say, a chimneysweep or a cleaner. To achieve this, middle-class parents get involved in their children's education. They worry about schools and the level of their class. They do their best to bring their failing off-springs to success by helping them at home or by giving them private tuition.

Working-class parents want the best for their children too but when problems arise, they are frequently at a loss. Quite often they do not know what to do and they do not feel they can have a grip on the school system. They remember their own failure as children and they become fatalistic: school is not for "people like us". This may lead either to passive submission to the social order or to violence and petty criminality. In the best of cases such parents engage in political militancy, usually on the left, hoping to help bring about a fairer society. The success/failure hierarchy produced in schools reflects social class structure and this is why the macabre constant is etched in the stone of our common values. It is with this in mind that I will now try to make some humanistic proposals.

6   Humanistic Proposals

Two questions should be asked before engaging in evaluation: for what purpose, and what should be done with failed students? Institutional assessment is carried out following a ritual calendar at the end of term, semester, year or cycle. Failing students are usually offered remediation and indeed it often happens that some manage to make progress. However, if all got good results by means of remediation, the level of expectation would be raised in order to recreate the macabre constant.

Most failed students usually move on to higher classes where they go on failing, thereby ensuring *ad infinitum* the value of success for those who succeed. Their failure is enshrined in the evaluation system. They have no alternative. It is therefore not surprising that many adults, remembering their difficult education, maintain that they are hopeless at English, Math or French; some even claim it as an element of their personality.

The French Ministry for Education often organises nationwide assessments. The objective is to take stock of students' levels in order to help teachers adjust their lessons. But as tests are based on '*discriminating*' items, they necessarily generate the macabre constant. At any rate, if all students succeeded, tests would have no value at all; teachers would see them as a waste of time and would refuse to carry them out. Their sole role is then to confirm students in their relative positions. Any general improvement would be annihilated the following year by an increase in the level of expectation.

Now what could we do? Let us look at the options available: 1) No evaluation at all, 2) Evaluation against a framework of reference, 3) Macabre evaluation. I will first examine evaluation in primary schools and then evaluation of languages in secondary and higher education.

Macabre assessments should in any case be banned from primary schools. We could let children work at their own pace and wager on their natural curiosity and desire to learn. Teachers are aware of these two features of children's psyche, and they also know they can fluctuate depending on the children's family history, their empathy for their teachers, their interest in the subjects, their maturity, pair-influence, and so on. It would not be unreasonable to suppose that what they did not learn during this term they may learn in the next.

At any rate, macabre marking does not improve results and locks the children into an institutionalized perception of their level. Teachers could refer to syllabi which spell out the skills they should aim for at each stage. They could then conduct intuitive assessments using descriptors and discuss results with parents. They could also carry out formal assessments which should remain individual and results should only be communicated to parents. The last year of primary education could be devoted to the preparation of a stocktaking assessment to help students and parents make an informed choice of curriculum in secondary schools.

Macabre evaluations could also be removed very easily in the first cycle of secondary schools (known as collèges, i.e. the equivalent of comprehensive schools in Britain). Assessment could be regularly made against the CEFRL, either intuitively using the descriptors or through online tests or tests designed on site. No specific level should be required. Levels achieved in the understanding and production of oral and written language could simply be written down on a regular basis in a Portfolio, i.e. a document where best work and results are stored. Progress made, or the lack of it, would then become visible.

A student stagnating at a given level might then be motivated to provide additional work targeted toward the skills which need to be improved. This would require the use of a self-study set up, which would have to be installed. Most collège school-leavers apply for admission in a lycée, i.e. the equivalent of either grammar, technical or vocational schools. If these schools required a particular language level, say B2 in English and B1 in German, chances are students would take this as an external motivation and they might put in some extra-work to reach the required level.

Students should also be given another chance in another language. If they failed their first year of English for example, they could be offered to study another language in the following year, and they could eventually go back to English when they have gained confidence and learned the methods of success. Schools might also want to introduce inter-comprehension, an efficient method of learning to *understand*, not speak, a series of languages belonging to the same phylum, e.g. Romance or Germanic languages.[9] Inter-comprehension would allow students to acquire partial skills that can be used in real life and within the job market.

The same policy could be continued in the second cycle of secondary schools (lycées) and Portfolio-type evaluation could be complemented with external certifications, all the more useful since international universities usually require a certain level of proficiency in the language of tuition, quite often English. Of course, there would still be a certain ratio of failure, but at least it would not have been generated by the evaluation system. At university, the language situation is more diverse and a wider variety of assessments can be carried out. Students in Foreign Language and Literature Departments, those who want to become teachers or translators for example, can certainly be assessed by macabre exams: they need to reach a high level of excellence to be well prepared for their future careers. Competition may very well increase the amount of work done by the *optimi* and *dubii* and it will eliminate the *inepti*, making sure graduates will reach the market with the required knowledge and skills.

Most students specialize in subjects other than languages (Science, Medicine, Law etc.) and will still need languages in their future careers. They are known as non-specialist students. English is usually compulsory while other languages are optional. Non-specialist students only need to reach a certain level set by the institution, say B2 in English at Bachelor's degree level and B1 in one or two other languages. Skills assessment against a framework of reference does not rest on the macabre constant and so all non-specialist students could theoretically succeed. Yet university stake-holders, be they students, teachers or administration, are so used to macabre evaluations that they find it abnormal when practically all students pass. As the head of language centres, I had to explain again and again the philosophy of the evaluation we had adopted in our language centres.

Promoting non-macabre evaluation is an uphill struggle. Most universities simply do not understand what is at stake. They are content with an intermediate level in English when they could encourage students to do their best in English and promote voluntary multilingualism. A diagnostic assessment at the beginning of the first year could help identify three groups of students: those who already have the required level in English (say B2), those who are not far from it and those who are very far from it. The first group could then deepen their knowledge and skills and try to reach C1, even C2; they could also work on their second language, usually German or Spanish, or learn another one altogether. The second group could first work to reach level B2, then follow the same path as the previous group. The last group should focus on the compulsory level. Internal or external certification could then give an institutional value to the level achieved in the compulsory language.[10]

Students could easily be encouraged to learn more languages than just English. In the languages centres I used to head, we offered about twenty languages. Hundreds, thousands of students were happy to voluntarily learn Japanese, Norwegian or Bulgarian on their free time in our learning setups. Most of them did so without institutional recognition because the university did not know how to evaluate optional voluntary learning: they had not foreseen the possibility. After a period of hard lobbying, I eventually managed to have the levels inscribed in what is known as the *Supplément au diplôme,* a document which comes with the diploma.

To assess the students' levels of achievement, we experimented with the Portfolio, a completely relevant way of using the CEFRL (see Frath, 2004). It is particularly suitable for languages *chosen* by students, i.e. not compulsory. When a student has voluntarily spent several hours a week in a self-study language centre to learn for example Japanese in their free time, it is very inappropriate to impose a macabre exam which will inevitably be unrelated to the actual learning accomplished by the student. Failure is then more than likely, followed by the giving up of learning. This is why we designed a *declarative evaluation* of actual work accomplished. Students submit their Portfolio to a jury composed of a teacher and a speaker of the language learned. They claim to have reached a certain level in a given language, say A1 in reading Japanese, and they prove it by showing and using their Portfolio. The jury then takes a binary decision: no, the level is not (yet) reached, or yes, the level has been reached, in which case it issues a certificate which is later listed in the *Supplément au diplôme.*

7   Why Evaluate?

Let us go back to the two questions asked at the beginning of this chapter:
1.   Why evaluate?
2.   What to do with failed students?

We should ask ourselves the first question mainly to stop us from thoughtlessly engaging in conventional macabre evaluation. Do we want to exercise pressure on the students, to make them work harder, to eliminate the less successful? Then macabre evaluations are just what we need. Do we want to check if students have attained a certain level defined by the institution? Skills assessment against an external framework of reference is then perfect. Do we want to give an institutional value to free voluntary work? The Portfolio is the answer. And quite often evaluation is not needed at all because students are just interested in learning something for its own sake and do not necessarily need or want an official recognition of it.

As for the second question, students should always know what will happen to them after evaluation. If they study to become teachers or doctors, they must accept that the less talented will be eliminated and this is done with the help of macabre evaluation. In all other cases, we should wager on the students' willingness to learn. If they are not willing now, maybe we can wait and give them another chance later; if unwillingness perseveres, nothing can be done in any case. We can also offer alternatives: failure in history does not necessarily mean failure in geography; remediation is also quite efficient, especially in a self-study environment. Also, we should be aware that the school is a machine which inflicts "symbolic violence'"(Bourdieu, 1979) on "other people's children" (Lenon, 2018) in order to preserve the existence of social classes. We can either accept it or regret it; it is for the voters to decide in a democracy. The trouble is real issues are often blurred, even distorted by clever self-serving arguments and sheer ignorance.

8   Review

The macabre constant is at the heart of most evaluation systems. Most stake-holders, be they the institution, the students, the parents, the teachers and many educationalists, are not aware of its limitations and the damage it can inflict on learning. I have tried to explore its semiotic, anthropological and social foundations in this chapter. For anthropologist André Leroi-Gourhan (1965, p. 20), much of what we do originates in a *twilight state of mind;* we are not really aware of our motivations, sometimes because we are reluctant to recognize the evilness of what we do. Indeed, it is almost impossible to face an assessment system that ruins the life of so many school children. It is to be hoped that the exposure of the macabre constant will ultimately help make it untenable as the default means of evaluation and that schools and universities will eventually integrate it in a more effective, diverse and humanistic evalua-tion system.

Notes

1   Bernstein made a similar distinction between working-class *restricted code* and middle-class *elaborate code* (Bernstein, 1975).

2   This may be considered as part of the 'symbolic violence' inflicted upon the lower-classes, according to Pierre Bourdieu (Bourdieu, 1979; Bourdieu & Passeron, 1970).

3   http://spiral.unistra.fr/

4   The CEFRL defines six levels of competency (beginners: A1, A2; intermediate: B1, B2; advanced: C1, C2) in five skills: reading, writing, listening, speaking, conversation. Evaluation is achieved against a list of descriptors, also known as can-do statements, such as *I can write a postcard* (A1 in writing), "I can understand a film without subtitles" (C2 in listening), "I can participate in a conversation about a subject that I am familiar with" (B2 in conversation).

5   The CLES (Certificat de compétences en langue dans l'enseignement supérieur) is a French officially accredited certification; the TOEFL (test of English as a foreign language) and the TOEIC (test of English for international communication) are the two most widely used American certifications.

6   Many colleagues will certainly disagree with this description of class-room work. Yet, when I once came under attack on that subject at a conference about language teaching at university, I was eventually saved by students in the audience who concurred with me.

7   Valéry (1936/2011): "Le diplôme est l'ennemi mortel de la culture"; "Dès qu'une action est soumise à un contrôle, le but profond de celui qui agit n'est plus l'action même, mais il conçoit d'abord la prévision du contrôle, la mise en échec des moyens de contrôle"; "Le but de l'enseignement n'étant plus la formation de l'esprit, mais l'acquisition du diplôme, c'est le minimum exigible qui devient l'objectif des études".

8   The semiotic aspect of evaluation is explored in Frath (2012a).

9   See for example Castagne (2004), Capucho (2008), Capucho and Pelsmaekers (2008).

10 See Frath (2012b) for the use of the CEFRL in universities.

References

Antibi, A. (2003). *La constante macabre*. Math'Adore.

Bernstein, B. (1975). *Class, codes and control* (Vol. 3). Routledge.

Bourdieu, P. (1979). *La distinction: critique sociale du jugement*. Les Éditions de Minuit.

Bourdieu, P., & Passeron, J. (1970). *La reproduction: Éléments d'une théorie du système d'enseignement*. Les Éditions de Minuit, coll. "Le sens commun".

Capucho, F. (2008). L'intercompréhension est-elle une mode? Du linguiste citoyen au citoyen plurilingue. *Revue Pratiques, 139/140*, 238–250. https://doi.org/10.4000/pratiques.1252

Capucho, F., & Pelsmaekers, K. (2008). Au-delà des familles de langues: le projet Eu&I. *Les langues modernes, 102*(1), 75–80.

Castagne, E. (Ed.). (2004). *Intercompréhension et inférences*. Presses universitaires de Reims.

Frath, P. (2004, September 9–11). *Introducing the Cercles European Language Portfolio into a self-study multilingual resource centre* [Paper]. 8th CERCLE conference.

Frath, P. (2012a). Can illiteracy be eradicated? *Education Today, 62*(4) 3–8.

Frath, P. (2012b). Évaluation des étudiants non-spécialistes en langues à l'aide du CECRL. *Les Langues Modernes, 1*, 56–64.

Frath, P. (2019). Évaluation et 'constance macabre'. *Les langues modernes, 4*, 31–39.

Frath, P. (2020). Constance de la 'constante macabre'. *Études et didactique des langues, 33*. http://edl-ple.simplesite.com/438385497

Lenon, B. (2018). *Other people's children: What happens to those in the bottom 50% academically?* John Catt Education.

Leroi-Gourhan, A. (1965). *Le geste et la parole. La mémoire et les rythmes.* Albin Michel.

Merle, P. (2018). *Les pratiques d'évaluation scolaire. Historique, difficultés, perspectives.* PUF.

Perrenoud, P. (1989). La triple fabrication de l'échec scolaire. *Psychologie française, 34*(4), 237–245.

Valéry, P. (2011). *Le bilan de l'intelligence.* http://descolarisation.org/pdf/le-bilan-de-lintelligence.pdf (Original work published 1936)

CHAPTER 10

Third Generation Doctorates

The Practitioner Model

Rosemary Sage

The European Commission (EC) asked the UK College of Teachers (TCOT) to lead an international group evolving a policy for professional development of education in a career record. The present industrial age has machines taking over routines with traditional jobs disappearing. This requires educational redirection, targeting personal, practical abilities, as employers value these as much as qualifications for 'smarter' new work roles. We must improve communication, cooperation and collaboration to solve inequality, rapid people movements, multi-cultural communities and ecological degradation threatening existence. Doctorates are the highest educational achievements, with research on practice the goal of traditional models. However, the Carnegie Foundation for the Advancement of Teaching has lobbied for research *within* practice – sponsoring practitioner models in American universities, as they show greater impact on policy and practice. Focusing on pedagogy over traditional research, Germany has re-conceptualised the PhD to be career-training for high positions. To a lesser extent, UK Research Councils have tackled this from 1992, with Professional Doctorates, but these are criticised for limited research knowledge and practitioner focus. There is a need for highly-educated practitioners, as well as researchers, to meet demands for greater knowledge and competencies. The role of PhDs in research occupations differs markedly from the quality assurance one of professional qualifications in other fields. The EC project piloted a practitioner doctorate at TCOT (2011–16) and the University of Buckingham (2017–19). Data presents the implementation. The Practitioner doctorate is taught to the same research, design and analytic standards as other models. However, focus is on participant innovative work rather than a research dissertation displaying linear theories in designs answering questions that may not apply to life contexts (Sage, 2017). This surely must be the future.

© KONINKLIJKE BRILL NV, LEIDEN, 2022 | DOI:10.1163/9789004506466_013

1   Background

This section outlines the context for doctoral degrees to understand the relevance of a practitioner model for the 21st century. Although doctorates have traditionally focused on developing new knowledge, from posing questions and using abstract theories in a range of research methods to gain answers, this approach has had limited workplace impact. In response, professional doctorates established research on practice, but again effects are limited. Recently, practitioner models have facilitated innovative, participant practice – reviewing, reflecting and refining this for future directions. The model has gained international popularity – showing positive workplace improvements. Benefits are discussed for participants in the process and the organisations in which they work. The 21st century is not only characterized by knowledge, but by plural societies and networks now less centralized locally and globally. Careers are more diverse and communities less stable. A *practitioner approach* (Level 8) accounting for political, economic and social issues enables leaders to acquire high-level knowledge and expertise to solve complex issues, like cultural people differences and community segregation.

2   A History of Doctorates

At Humboldt University (Berlin, Germany), 19th century reforms demanded a dissertation reporting research for awarding Doctor of Philosophy (PhD) in Sciences and Humanities (Rashdall, 1964). Reforms produced *knowledge theories*, so that foreign students, particularly from the United States (US), came to Germany to obtain a PhD. Yale University (US) started a doctoral programme in 1861. The degree spread to Canada in 1900 and the United Kingdom (UK) in 1917 (Simpson, 1983). This attracted criticism, as from 1860 the University of London had awarded Doctor of Science (DSc) and Doctor of Literature (DLit) upon thesis submission containing original work, but with no research training requirement. Older degrees of Doctors of Divinity (DD), Music (DMus), Civil Law (DCL) and Medicine (MD) also existed. Apart from honorary degrees, these doctorates are rare today.

Humboldt reforms transformed both Faculties of Philosophy of Arts and Sciences from a lower order into one equal to Law and Medicine. European universities followed, with many having the triple structure of Bachelor-Licentiate-Doctor instead of Bachelor-Master-Doctor (Pedersen, 1997). Today, a Masters is a base-line qualification, with a doctorate increasingly required for senior positions, as a hall-mark of the highest level of knowledge and expertise (Wilkinson, 2005).

In the UK, applicants are admitted to doctoral programmes case-by-case, but usually an Upper Second-Class Honours and Postgraduate Master's degree are required, but variations occur. At the University of Oxford "the one essential condition of being accepted is evidence of previous academic excellence and future potential" (2014, p. 2). Students in many UK universities complete an *Advanced Post-Graduate* (APG) level, when producing a study plan and literature review defended before an academic audience. This is reached after 1–2 years and includes research methods. If not meeting requirements, students may submit for an MPhil degree. Those entering a PhD programme with an MPhil can by-pass APG requirements (Wilkinson, 2005). UK PhDs are distinct from other doctorates, like DLitt (*Letters*) or DSc (*Science*), granted for research excellence.

3   Progression from PhDs

Professional doctorates (D Prof/Prof D) have been introduced and regarded as the same level as a PhD, but are specific and titled for an occupation, like Engineer, Teacher or Psychologist. These second-generational models mostly combine a taught component and professional qualification, with smaller research projects, as well as a 40–60,000 word thesis making it collectively equivalent to a PhD.

4   Third Millennium Doctoral Development

Since 1970s, academics have questioned doctoral models based on *linear* theories codifying and applying abstract ideas, often in ways not translating to real situations. These views are found in Taylor's (2011) paper: *Reform the PhD or Close It Down*. Experts have criticised Professional Doctorates geared to research *on* rather than *within* practice. Academics view both First Generation Research and Second Generation Professional Doctorates as developing MODEL 1 Knowledge – produced objectively and generated from a specific research design collecting data to answer a question based on established theoretical constructs. Considered by practitioners to be remote from reality, there has been a move towards MODEL 2 Knowledge, created and used by practitioners *within* their work remit (Maxwell & Shanahan, 2001).

The model has a constructionist stance (Schon, 1987; Deutsch, 2013) with research and practice existing in a spiral, observant, reflective relationship, leading to new knowledge for informing present and future practice. This idea was pursued by Dr Kim Orton (2017, 2019), when Academic Development Officer, at the UK College of Teachers. Data on teachers for 70,000 world-wide students, showed that few could reflect effectively *within* practice, so affecting ability to educate an increasingly diverse society for potential and personal needs. The US Carnegie Foundation for the Advancement of Teaching (CFAT) has sponsored practitioner models in American universities, focusing on pedagogy developments over traditional research. Germany is re-conceptualising the PhD to be career-training outside academia for high positions. To less extent, the UK Research Councils have tackled the issue since 1992, with the Eng D (engineering and other professional doctorates), but reports criticise limited research knowledge and lack of practitioner focus (Taylor, 2011).

There is need for high-level educated practitioners as well as researchers to meet demands of the new industrial world. The role of PhDs in research occupations differs markedly from the quality assurance one of professional qualifications in other fields. The Practitioner Doctorate is taught to the same research, design and analytic standards as other models. However, the focus is on participant innovative work rather than a research dissertation displaying linear theories in research designs answering questions that may not apply to reality.

5   The UK Practitioner Model

The practitioner model was developed and sponsored by the European Commission at the London College of Teachers, involving 7 European partnerships (PEEP 2011–16). The submission record begins with an academic CV and a 4,000+ word career review, detailing a theme for selecting evidence under 4 internationally agreed professional criteria: acquisition and application of knowledge, continual professional development, mobility and partnerships.

A literature review demonstrates research and practice knowledge of the chosen topic, evaluating how data develops this in work roles. Evidence, according to 20 International Standard Classification of Education (ISCED) Level 8 criteria, has witness statements to verify events, with feedback on achievements.

A final, reflective statement shows how this has contributed to policy, practice and professional development. The submission is around 100,000 words, including visual and auditory material if appropriate. A 300 word hard-copy summary accompanies the e-portfolio.

Reviews of doctorates on social media commented on this approach as less open to abuse, with evidence of them being bought from unscrupulous institutions and websites.

UNESCO states that programmes classified at ISCED Level 8 are referred to variously, such as PhD, DPhil, D. Lit, DSc, LL.D, Doctorate or similar terms. For comparability, the term doctorate or equivalent refers to ISCED Level 8 (Kouptsov, 1994). The practitioner model was implemented at the University of Buckingham (2017–19), following ISCED criteria based on the PEEP research model.

6   Research and Professional vs Practitioner Doctorates

Research/Professional graduates add to an original body of knowledge for academic careers, but a Practitioner Doctorate contributes by applying existing information to solve real problems.

How are they similar?
– Highest degree in the field.
– Require coursework, residencies and submission of research work.
– Prepare for teaching college level courses.
– Culminate in title of 'Doctor', following international standards (ISCED) for collecting reliable, valid, ethical evidence at Level 8.

How do they differ?
– A Practitioner Doctorate prepares for professional leadership of policy and practice. This is not the primary goal of other models, which aim to verify a theoretical stance
– The practitioner model is about proving oneself as a professional by demonstrating impact of workplace innovations, unlike other models
– It does this by communicating, cooperating and collaborating with colleagues and other stakeholders through partnerships and mobility to maintain and sustain improvements, which are not criteria of others
– Research/professional doctorates focus on developing new primary knowledge with a *practitioner* concentrating on career application
– A PhD presents a *range* of research methods in *statistically significant* studies (the professional route does not require this to the same extent), but a *practitioner* one emphasizes qualitative methods – surveys, interviews and case studies – more suitable for real situations, but following research principles in construction and implementation.

Comment: A *practitioner* programme focuses exclusively on the value of applicable, practical research and relevant field studies arising from participant work. It requires them to prove themselves personally and professionally at the highest level for leading others. Holistic approaches to research/development driving innovation, find new ways to respond in our increasingly integrative, digital working environments – understanding political, economic and social influences on education/training. While Research, Professional and Practitioner Doctorates each have unique benefits, they are all considered internationally to be at the apex of their discipline. Each has elite scholars, requiring research/development, analysis and scholarship, to help people *write the book* in their specialism.

7   Review of the Practitioner Doctoral Process

Doctoral candidates are motivated to contribute to academic and practice communities and further their development. Increasingly, high positions require doctorates. Research suggests significant benefits to society for high-level study with knowledge and expertise acquired, but over-qualified workers are less satisfied and productive if not given roles of influence (Sage, 2017). Fiske (2011) explains that only 20% of life-science PhD students end up getting research roles (*pre-2000 data*). A 2015 study[1] found that for every 200 PhD people only 7 obtain a permanent academic post. Practitioner Doctorates are considered essential for the New Industrial Age and likely to become the major career path because of a personal emphasis.

Freeman (2010), like others, shows how the Practitioner Doctorate challenges tradition:
– Geared to practitioner needs with development projects, resulting in organisational/professional change to policy and/or practice
– Work-based research & development influence all stakeholders
– Focus on society problems – encourages inter-discipline collaboration
– Participants are leading practitioners with ability to make changes
– Model rooted in similar academic traditions to other doctorates, requiring up-to-date literature & specialist experience, but showing application and impact – not the primary goal of other approaches
– Participants build a customised, self-managed programme, based on work, assessed materials & projects, in an *achievement record*
– Applies to any field & promotes inter-disciplinary engagement
– Study schools, with input from practitioners & academics, seminars & participant presentations, are supported by online courses & personal supervision by experienced expert in the field of study
– Results show that high-level policy & actions are outcomes, leading to significant changes in organisations & communities of practice

The PEEP pilot and university evaluations show benefits from 52 respondents (see Appendix):

- Structures participant activities in a customised, self-managed programme in a workplace, which impacts on all stakeholders
- Assists articulation of theoretical ideas – evaluating these for practice and wider benefits that can be continually monitored
- Provides framework for a career from observation & reflection processes adopted which influence everyone in the workplace
- Improves quality and practical outcomes, sustaining and maintaining them through work-place communication to benefit all stakeholders
- Long-term impact on candidate professional practice & of colleagues
- Potential for creating system changes, with participants in leading positions with influence to make improvements from their research
- Produces creative, observant, reflective, interpretative leaders from MODEL 2 Knowledge & understanding from reviewing own practice
- Develops *process* rather than abstract *product* knowledge to assist understanding of real problems from a greater knowledge of context & behaviour of politics & people
- Targets political, economic, social & contextual issues to explain situations, as background for integrating influences with informed, practical wisdom for local & global adequacy in "making maps that work" (Leston, 2004)
- Focuses on mobility & partnerships, enabling awareness of international practice for preparing effective global orientation

TABLE 10.1   Response ranking to PD model above a 95% confidence level (N = 52)

Rank order response % confidence level

1.	Opportunity to research own practice for greater workplace impact and personal satisfaction	100%
2.	Focus on proving oneself personally and professionally to ensure workplace impact	98%
3.	The holistic model reviews issues for improved personal development and problem solutions	97%
4.	Emphasis on mobility and partnerships builds lasting connections and extends understanding	96%
5.	Greater confidence in decision-making evolves from a *process* not *product* approach	95%

8　Comments from Participants

8.1　*Visiting Experts to Study Schools*
- Study schools were really great – very high standards – very pleasant. I have met a lot of nice and very interesting people.
- Excellent participants and staff – a really first-class programme with the highest standards.
- A top-notch programme showing awareness of world needs with unique opportunities for participants regarding partnerships and mobility.

8.2　*Participants: The Peep Pilot and University of Buckingham*
- In the past learning has been done to me – now I'm doing it myself.
- I love the fact that I am custom-building a programme to suit my circumstances.
- The team are key and exceptional – from their book publications and study school inputs I have made innovations to teaching that have had real impact on students and colleagues.
- I have been waiting for such a course all my life! It is bang on the money.
- This observation and reflective approach to learning should start in primary education – I have enjoyed hearing from two of the team about their research in Japan to develop the 21st century citizen – Inspirational stuff. Hansei – here we come.
- The inter-discipline backgrounds of the staff team and course participants have opened my eyes to all sorts of new possibilities.
- This is what communication, collaboration and creativity is about.
- I find the whole experience of this practitioner approach inspirational.
- When the course is over I know I am going to miss the kicks this doctorate has given me.
- I can ring my tutors anytime (and do!). They are always there to pour oil on troubled waters.
- The philosophy and structure of the practitioner model is perfect. It is changing how I observe and reflect, review and refine my actions not only at work but in my life in general.
- The online courses are wonderful – just what is needed.
- I have learnt much about observation and intercultural issues, my information-processing and judgement have improved.

8.3　*Issues*
- One respondent found *formal* and *informal* evidence difficult to grasp (*formal* refers to abilities acquired at work and *informal*, those developed

outside. As example: a respondent volunteered in a Child Development Centre, learning about special needs to enhance a teaching role).
- One respondent felt a need for more programme face-to-face experiences, other than the 2 annual study schools and personal tutor contact. The ISCED criteria for evidence need guidance.

9   Review

Studies at doctoral level originally developed to promote research and push frontiers of knowledge to assist progress. Doctors have been employed traditionally in universities, teaching and researching specialist subjects to inspire, motivate and inform others. Academic research is often sponsored by organizations wishing to use new knowledge to improve status and global position. Recently, *Practitioner Doctorates* have been promoted for those seeking high positions, developing potential for personal, professional satisfaction as well as improving workplace policy and practice. This review is produced on a small data set but echoes opinions of other international programmes.

The PEEP project (2011–16), using an e-Portfolio to track careers, was piloted to produce a professional record appropriate for someone achieving high-level knowledge at doctoral Level 8, implementing work in innovative, beneficial ways to enhance policy and practice. This showcases participant knowledge, understanding, attitudes and competence in a broader, more holistic way than through a traditional research report. The aim is to support and advance education/training standards, by providing opportunities for practitioners to improve work-place performance.

The model emphasizes *mobility* and *partnerships* to enable sharing of information and understanding within and across nations. It appeals to people from many education/training fields. Participants from schools, colleges and universities, as well as commercial and industrial backgrounds are attracted to this model. Medical practitioners, bankers, economists, psychologists, therapists and engineers, plus different educationists, provide rich input for course participants to share experiences.

Examples of submissions include: a study of 10,000 children to evaluate spiritual development; the power of literature to enhance understanding; a model of reflection for teachers and learners; developing creativity in school activities; managing special needs in plural contexts; how ethics are implemented in training/practice; how a programme to develop values is established; how an academic residency in schools enhances learning and teaching; how training is developing now machines are changing industrial jobs; trials of a model for workplace adult learning; using the new protocol teaching system to design learning; developing competence-based learning for sport/industry. These are project examples that are ongoing and mentioned as outstanding in OFSTED reports.

The New Industrial Age (NIA: 4), with routines taken over by intelligent machines, requires professions to meet needs for improved communication, thinking and creativity in a world of environmental degradation undermining survival. Doctorates are increasingly the norm for leaders to better manage consequences of actions. When you realize a theory or model has limitations for solving problems, this marks a huge step forward in thinking. It is vital to know what cannot be simulated, made-up or imagined. At this point, one can open one's mind to more complex, infinite issues. Judgements can then not be limited by precedent. Education needs this thinking level as it wrestles with preparing populations for global engagement.

The *Magistrates in the Community* (MIC) and *Prison Me No Way* (PMNW) national projects find young people unable to think about consequences of their actions and relate easily to other people. Many learners fail to achieve personal, practical and academic competencies needed for jobs and feel disenfranchised in society. A Practitioner Doctorate develops '*smart*' leaders, who have acquired the academic, practical and reflective processes for solving today's problems – working towards a more equal society with everyone able to learn and contribute effectively. Such a model marks a new direction in studies, in keeping with a changing world. This is not to dismiss other doctorates that are appropriate for different goals, but suggests the importance of practitioner ones to meet *real needs* effectively.

Discussions with other Practitioner Doctorate leads confirm the importance of programmes being managed by academics with strong practical backgrounds and international research credibility. Staff need awareness of all doctorate models, with extensive teaching and examining experience both nationally and internationally to acquire global understanding. Those using the approach become passionate about it because of the significant impact observed at both a personal and professional level.

Four books showcase practitioner results from the PEEP programme to date: *Paradoxes in Education; The Robots are Here: Learning to Live with Them* and *Speechless: Understanding Educational Issues and Teaching with Technology.* All these texts have positive, international reviews putting the model on the map, with invites to join international research groups to further knowledge and practice. The practitioner model is an inspiration to those engaged with it and grows a pace in forward-thinking communities.

Acknowledgement

Project Title: Policy for Educator Evidence in Portfolios (PEEP) No: 521454-LLP-1-2011-1-UK-KA1. Sub-programme or KA1: Policy Co-operation and Innovation: A Review of Implementation.

Note

1   https://www.ncbi.nlm.nih.gov/pubmed/28922403

References

de Ridder-Symoens, H. (2003). *A history of the university in Europe: Universities of the Middle Ages*. Cambridge University Press.

Deutsch, D. (2013, October 22). A constructor theory. *Edge*.

Dinham, S., & Scott, C. (2001). The experience of disseminating the results of doctoral research. *Journal of Further and Higher Education, 25*(1), 45–55.

Fiske, P. (2011). What is a PhD really worth? *Nature, 472*(7343), 381.

Freeman, R. (2010, December 16). Doctoral degrees: The disposable academic. *The Economist*.

Kouptsov, O. (Ed.). (1994). *The doctorate in the European region*. CEPES Studies on Higher Education. UNESCO.

Leston, S. (2004). Conceptualising the practitioner doctorate. *Studies in Higher Education, 29*(5).

Maxwell, T., & Shanahan, P. (2001). Professional doctoral education in Australia and New Zealand. In B. Green, T. Mansur, & P. Shanahan (Eds.), *Doctoral education and professional practice for the next generation*. Kardoorair.

Orton, K. (2017). Evaluating communicative approaches in education. In R. Sage (Ed.), *Paradoxes in education* (pp. 209–233). Sense.

Orton, K. (2019). Reflective practice [Blog post]. http://www.educationblog.buckingham.ac.uk/2019/11/reflective-practice

Pedersen, O. (1997). *The first universities:* Studium generale *and the origins of university education in Europe*. Cambridge University Press.

Policy for Educator Evidence in Portfolios (PEEP Project Title: Policy for Educator Evidence in Portfolios. Project Number: 521454-LLP-1-2011-1-UK-KA1-KA1ECETB. Grant Agreement: 2011 – 4133/008 – Sub-programme or KA: Key Activity One: Policy Co-operation and Innovation.

Quality Assurance Agency for Higher Education. (2001). *The framework for higher education in England, Wales and Northern Ireland*.

Rashdall, H. (1964). *The universities of Europe in the Middle Ages*. Oxford Univesity Press.

Rosenberg, R. (1962). Eugene Schuyler's doctor of philosophy degree: A theory concerning the dissertation. *Journal of Higher Education, 33*(7), 381–386.

Russell, B. (1935). *The praise of idleness and other essays*. Norton.

Sage, R. (2017). Teacher training issues. In R. Sage (Ed.), *Paradoxes in education* (pp. 21–45). Sense.

Sage, R., & Orton, K. (2017). Theories informing teaching for success abilities. In R. Sage (Ed.), *Paradoxes in education* (pp. 45–69). Sense.

Schon, D. (1987). *The reflective practitioner*. Jossey-Bass.

Seddon, T. (2001). What is 'Doctor' in doctor education? In B. Green, T. Mansur, & P. Shanahan (Eds.), *Doctoral education and professional practice for the next generation*. Kardoorair.

Simpson, R. (1983). *How the PhD came to Britain: A century of struggle for postgraduate education*. The Society for Research into Higher Education.

Taylor, M. (2011). Reform the PhD or close it down. *Nature, 472*(7343), 259–260.

University of Oxford. (2014). http://www.ox.ac.uk/admissions/postgraduate_courses/index.html

Wilkinson, D. (2005). *The essential guide to postgraduate study*. Sage.

Wisker, G. (2005). *The good supervisor: Supervising postgraduate and undergraduate research for doctoral theses and dissertations*. Palgrave Macmillan.

Appendix: Questionnaire for Analysing a Practitioner Doctorate (PD)

Information from this questionnaire will be used to consider the further development of the PD model and evaluate issues that might affect effective implementation. Thank you for your cooperation.

Name ... (made anonymous).

1.   List reason/s why you chose a PD model rather than a Research or Professional one.

   a.   I feel that it is more aligned to the real world

   b.   You have more opportunity to apply knowledge gained and observe/measure outcomes

   c.   In my opinion traditional PhD's do not fully cover the complex human condition and can be narrow in their remit. I changed from a (traditional doctorate) as it had a very positivist approach which I felt was too restrictive

   d.   Education & development of people needs a holistic approach which this format allows.

e.   The structure of the program enables participants to balance their day to day life whilst also developing themselves and subsequently improving education and/or development.

2.   What are your personal & professional expectations from PD studies?

Personal (for yourself) to expand my knowledge on the how and why adults learn and then use this for more altruistic reasons i.e. working with charities in getting the less privileged back into the work place – specifically ex-military, young offenders, disabled and baby boomer generation.

Professional (for the job) The program has already opened doors for me in that I am currently working at board level in developing a reciprocal mentorship program for an organisation that have over 200 affiliated training centres around the world, training 350,000 people per year. I am also in discussions (again at board level) with a large college in the UK who have just bought a vocational training company on assisting with the formation and operationalisation of their vision. I am also in initial discussions with the board of a charity in the UK on establishing a communication program which will address the inherent difficulties of dialogue between generational divides and those that have suffered severe trauma.

All of these partnerships are being conducted in my own time and away from my normal daily duties for my current employer.

My medium to long term aspirations are to 'give up my day job' and to further pursue my studies and (hopefully) enable them to become 'my day job'.

3.   *What has gone well with your studies?*

The whole process has helped me be more reflective – although it is still something that I am not great at. I have found it fascinating and thoroughly enjoyable learning and developing myself. If I take a moment and reflect back to when I started the program, although I have been successful in my project set-up's it was more from experience and intuition. I now have the confidence that what I do has a strong academic foundation. Also, the more I have read, the more I want to learn. When I first started the program I had a rough general idea on my areas of interest but although the general direction is the same, my true interests have changed slightly in that I am fascinated by career development and mentoring/coaching and the (in my opinion) important roles that they need to take in the future development of our workforce.

4.   *What are the problems arising from your studies?*

Time!! I have an extremely busy job and have seriously struggled in keeping up with my submission requirements. The program allows up to 6 years to complete which has enabled me to take a breather now and then. Initially there was a lack of clarity and focus but the "fog" that the whole cohort were experiencing at the time slowly started to clear. This was explained to us at the time and to be honest (at the time) I thought that it was a poor excuse but on reflection, the program leaders were correct in their assertions that doctoral level knowledge shouldn't necessarily be prescribed but rather a journey of discovery for the individual.

5. What has been the impact of PD work for ...?

Yourself – It has opened my eyes on possibilities and shown me where my passions lie.

Work Colleagues – I would hope that they have seen subtle changes in my demeanour and communication in that I now attempt to listen more using active listening skills. I am still nowhere near where I want to be as I am still a 'solution provider' rather than a collaborative facilitator – but I am determined to continue on my journey.

Work Role – I work for one of the largest organisations in the world and my specific area of the business is extremely operationally minded which has proved to be challenging when trying to introduce a more holistic approach to workforce development. I have had some success in establishing career development activities within the workforce, particularly with new hire graduates but getting senior management buy-in has been challenging.

6. *What would improve your present programme?*

The structure and format is excellent and THE reason that I started the program. One area that could be improved is by increasing the use of technology for communications and documenting evidence. Perhaps a Centre of Excellence Portal where ideas can be shared? From the last study school this was mentioned but I'm not sure that it is set up as yet? We do have Moodle as a centralised communication portal but it is notoriously non-intuitive, at least it is to a 'baby boomer' like myself.

Any other comments:
From the Executive summary given above I would categorically say that the programme is doing exactly what it says on the tin. At least for me it is.

PART 3

Social Issues of Justice

∵

Introduction to Part 3

Rosemary Sage and Riccarda Matteucci

Education is valued worldwide to prepare learners for life and work. Issues surrounding it are constantly shifting to accommodate societal changes. What is acquired in education largely determines the person they will become. If pushed to be the best they can be, students will then cope with life and shine in their careers. If constantly bullied, disrespected, ignored and unheard, these negative attitudes can reflect onto others in future. An empathetic education is more important now than ever before. Problems arise daily and each new generation must be able to solve them. One cannot do so without being taught correctly. Education plays a key role in developing *social aspects* of how learning is given and received. Race, poverty, disability, culture, inequality and interpersonal tensions should not be barriers to a better education, but in plural societies they are obstacles to overcome, with students affected by problems caused. What they learn in classrooms is a reflection of what the real world is presenting as their future. For these reasons, the classroom should be a space for all learners to grow and thrive, according to their interests, potential and needs and not a place of judgment and harassment. Inequality is a big challenge in educational diversity today and the one-size-fits-all philosophy for learning and assessment does not meet the needs of many students.

Amid the sleaze, corruption, lack of integrity and respect that envelops many aspects of modern life, the importance of social values has never been so vital to encourage in educational institutions.

Chapter 11: Academic Integrity discusses the important social value of honesty in a review of world research that has studied cheating strategies. Certainly, these activities have become a common and serious aspect of learning in an increasingly competitive world. They show the necessity of a values education.

Chapter 12: Prioritising Values demonstrates how they are being developed in a school setting. Although the core values will be similar across institutions, the way they are implemented will be different according to the context.

Chapter 13: Sociological Aspects of Educational Robots presents robotic approaches to curb undesirable behaviour, outlining their novel, engaging appeal. They illustrate the importance of an objective but sympathetic approach to ameliorating problems.

Chapter 14: Additional Learning Needs introduces a neglected social value – the management of communicative issues of students with hearing difficulties.

© KONINKLIJKE BRILL NV, LEIDEN, 2022 | DOI:10.1163/9789004506466_014

Additional learning needs include *physical, mental, emotional and social problems* that might hinder formal learning. The requirements of deaf and hearing impaired students have been specifically chosen to signal their problems. The pandemic has thrown up compulsory mask-wearing as robbing hearing-impaired individuals of lip-reading and facial expressions necessary for understanding. This is an example of social injustice as lobbyists have noted!

1   Reflections From Part 3

Values enable an individual to become their best version but this depends on both *internal* and *external* communicative competencies to reflect deeply and understand how to develop the *good* rather than the *bad* side of human nature. The malaise of academic integrity that exists points to a failure to instil ethical values in informal and formal learning experiences. The proliferation of *Essay Mills*, where students can buy assignments and academic theses, is something that governments are now trying to legislate against, as this debases qualifications. A lack of personal internal dialogue is demonstrated, that fails to consider the consequences of actions. The escalating of bullying behaviour, endured by students and staff, also reflects a lack of self-talk, reflection and respect for others. Robots are a way to assist acceptable behaviour and the authors point out how they magically change the emotional environment, bringing about miles of smiles! Communicative and social competencies are facilitated with robot activities, to produce well-rounded individuals who can listen and respond appropriately. The issue of *listening* is introduced and discussed, to illustrate the additional learning requirements of students with hearing problems, as an example of *physical, mental, emotional and social* needs. This group are exceptional listeners but need time to absorb information, so the non-verbal aspects of learning must be enhanced for them. Language and communication problems have been particularly heightened by on-line teaching approaches during the 2020 pandemic, as they have deprived students of paralinguistic support. This illustrates social justice and equality issues and the importance of dealing with these sympathetically.

CHAPTER 11

Academic Integrity

Research from World Studies

Irene Glendinning

Abstract

Most recent research into academic integrity has focused on higher education (HE). Often the research is framed negatively around academic dishonesty in assessment that results in examination misconduct, inappropriate collusion and other forms of cheating. Another approach to this subject concerns how poor academic writing skills lead to plagiarism. Much of my own research has centred around the way universities and national policies-makers are responding to different forms of student cheating. However, a recent global study that I led for the USA-based Council for Higher Education Accreditation's International Quality Group (CHEA/CIQG) demonstrates that if we wish to reduce academic misconduct by HE students, we must first understand and address corruption and malpractice at all levels of education, by students, but also by teachers, managers, institutional leaders and external agents (Glendinning et al., 2019). This chapter will draw on findings from my own research that explore educational practices in different countries. I will argue for the benefits of adopting a holistic approach in engendering academic integrity throughout education. In addition to the obvious benefits to academic standards, fostering responsible, honest conduct via education can help to promote a gradual transformation to society, from being unfair and corrupt towards practices that are trustworthy and reliable, potentially influencing inappropriate cultural issues in industry, commerce, government, family and wider society

1 Introduction

Research into academic integrity, plagiarism and academic writing skills typically focuses on higher education. Researchers are often university librarians and specialists in academic writing skills, intent on improving students' referencing, paraphrasing and use of literature and other information sources (e.g. Borg, 2009; Pecorari, 2013). These people are on the front line of skills development in many universities. Another angle for research into academic integrity is from teachers specialising in English as a second language (L2) (Pecorari &

Petrić, 2014). L2 teachers and other specialists often conduct very useful comparative research into students in different learning settings (Davis, 2011; Robinson-Pant, 2009). Subject specialists sometimes become involved in research in this field after becoming concerned or exasperated by student (mis)conduct, such as plagiarism in computer source-code (Joy et al., 2013).

2   Summary of My Research

My own research interests in this field started with attempts to understand and find ways to reduce plagiarism in higher education, focusing on bachelor and taught master's degree students. Plagiarism remains the most common type of academic integrity violation in most parts of the world, not just affecting students, but also professionals and academics everywhere (Glendinning, 2013; Foltýnek et al., 2018; Glendinning et al., 2020). Most student plagiarism results from lack of skills and knowledge of how and when to acknowledge the work of other people (Borg, 2009; Pecorari, 2013). Only in a minority of cases is plagiarism an intentional act, to gain unfair advantage – perhaps due to laziness, poor time-management or fear of failure. However, teaching academic writing skills to students is problematic if teachers themselves do not fully understand the rules.

After leading an Erasmus research project to explore national and HE institutional policies for plagiarism in the 27 European Union countries (IPPHEAE 2010–15), I concluded that very few countries in Europe had developed any national or institutional policies for plagiarism or academic misconduct. The exceptions to this rule at that time were the UK, Sweden and Austria; in these three countries there was clear evidence of a national consciousness about the threats to quality and standards from academic misconduct in general and the need to put in place measures in response. Although even in the best equipped countries, not every institution was fully engaged in this process and more action was needed both nationally and institutionally (Glendinning, 2016).

This initial research illuminated other differences, such as the prevalence of cheating in examinations where that was the main type of assessment, for example in France (Mazodier et al., 2012). There was also evidence of essay mills and use of ghost writers in many countries. Bribery and other forms of corruption, such as nepotism and favouritism, were discussed by participants from countries, including Bulgaria, Romania and Poland.

The success of the IPPHEAE project led to a range of exciting opportunities to extend the research, both geographically and in scope. The Council of

Europe (CoE) funded two surveys, first into five former Balkans countries and Albania (Foltýnek et al., 2018), then exploring the situation in Armenia, Azerbaijan, Georgia, Kazakhstan and Turkey (Glendinning et al., 2020). Through the three projects, we surveyed 38 countries in total between 2010 and 2018. In the CoE research we explored all forms of academic misconduct in higher education, not just plagiarism, and, in the light of the revelations from IPPHEAE, we did not confine our research to misconduct by bachelor and master's students. This research was conducted by my team from Coventry University, UK, in conjunction with a team from Mendel University in Brno, that had been a partner in the IPPHEAE project.

In parallel with the CoE research, two Coventry colleagues and I undertook a global project for the USA-based Council for HE Accreditation's International Quality Group (CHEA/CIQG). This time we were surveying quality assurance and accreditation bodies throughout the world to explore their responses to different HE forms of corruption, building on a published report that I contributed to, on the same topic (CIQG & IIEP, 2016). We investigated corruption in higher education oversight, governance, the teaching role, recruitment and admissions, assessment, credentials, research and academic publishing. It was a massive undertaking that we completed in just one year (Glendinning et al., 2019). It was also a great wake-up call for my own appreciation of how embedded corruption is in education, but also in society in general, in every country (Transparency International, 2013, 2019) and what is being done to address this. This project certainly broadened my view of the world in many unexpected ways, some positive surprises, such as national academic integrity initiatives in Georgia and Kazakhstan, as well as the negatives.

Very little of the evidence about HE corruption – defined as a deliberate attempt to unfairly gain or confer advantage, often by disadvantaging others – was available in academic publications. The vast majority of the evidence came from investigative journalism, press and media, through anti-corruption organisations, such as Dissernet in Russia (Rostovtsev, 2015), ORCA (2017) and ACA/AKK in Kosovo, work by NGOs and international bodies such as Transparency international (2013, 2019) and IIEP/UNESCO and voluntary organisations such as Retraction Watch and the Committee on Publication Ethics (COPE).

Most of the 69 AQABs that responded to the CIQG survey were either unaware of corruption involving HE providers under their remit or said it was not part of their responsibility. This does raise the question, of who should take responsibility for rooting out corrupt practices in higher education that have a direct impact on quality and standards. CIQG followed up on our research with a Key Actions report targeting AQABs (CHEA/CIQG, 2019).

3   The Nature of Corruption in Higher Education

There is not space here to describe the full extent of corruption we found, but I have included some interesting examples to give readers a flavour. We included mention of corruption in admissions to USA athletics programmes in the CIQG research, but new evidence has come to light since involving bogus admission of non-athletes to these programmes at elite USA universities, including Georgetown, Yale and Berkeley, after payment of bribes or donations or through favouritism (BBC News, 2019; Jashnik, 2020). Staying in North America, in 2017 Canadian Broadcasting Corporation reported that "hundreds of Canadians have fake degrees", in an article about diploma mills and fake universities (Szeto & Vellani, 2017). A Pakistan-based company called Axact is associated with a very long list of fake universities and schools (CBC, 2017), all in the business of issuing bogus credentials. To counter this threat of fake credentials, secure digital services to verify qualifications are now available in many countries and increasingly internationally connected (Daniel, 2018).

It emerged that less than one third of HE institutions in India have been subject to external quality assurance or accreditation, with the majority of providers having no oversight at all (Glendinning et al., 2019, p. 30). Also in India, a scandal erupted about cheating in pharmaceutical research and education, implicating the director of the Institute, 46 students and 14 academics (Times of India, 2018).

In Russia the Dissernet group has been checking PhD dissertations (*hence their name*) and discovered thousands of 100% plagiarised theses resulting in unearned doctorates awarded legitimately by highly prestigious universities. The same supervisory teams, mostly highly respected professors, some serve on accreditation and quality assurance panels, were found to be responsible for up to fifty plagiarised dissertations (Rostovtsev, 2015). Dissernet found that many of the students with heavily plagiarised doctorates are now university rectors. Further details of corrupt practices in HE in Russia have been published by many other authors (for example, Dubrovsky, 2017; Denisova-Schmidt et al., 2016).

We found that the UK was far from clean on corruption. The undeclared conflict of interest arising from the Vice-Chancellor of the University of Bath being a member of the committee deciding her own generous remuneration package was reported in the Guardian newspaper (Adams, 2017). A BBC Panorama programme exposed the admissions scandals at private UK HE providers, which had resulted in students gaining access to student loans, including falsified qualifications created by recruitment agents and an impersonator sitting an IELTS test for the student (Watson, 2017). Another news report found evidence of fraud and malpractice in admissions involving 19 UK HE *alternative providers* (Grove, 2018). In a BBC radio broadcast an investigative journalist reported on how the contract cheating industry is affecting UK HE providers – both supply and demand sides of the industry (Crowthorne, 2017).

Covert video recording made by brave volunteers exposed two professors at the University of Ghana, who were asking journalists, posing as would-be students, for sexual favours in return for university admission (BBC News, 2020). Several other reports from different countries have focused on sexual harassment of either staff or students (Atuhaire, 2018; Pillay, 2018; BBC News, 2018; Turner, 2018).

Kenya is heavily implicated in fake degrees (Maina, 2015) and the global commercial contract cheating market, supplying services to anglophone countries, with many essay mills and workers seeing the contract cheating industry as a mainstay of Kenyan economy, with a headline claiming the country supplies "University Coursework for 115,000 Cheating British Students Every Year" (Simons, 2019).

The good news is that action is being taken in some countries to counter identified threats to academic integrity, quality and standards, as well as in some cases, dignity and personal safety. In Australia, guidance has been produced for HE providers on measures to counter sexual harassment by the quality and standards body TEQSA. In common with UK's QAA, TEQSA have created guidance for the HE sector on addressing contract cheating (QAA, 2020; TEQSA, 2017). Republic of Ireland, New Zealand and Australia have recently introduced legislation banning essay mills, including proscribing the advertising of contract cheating services.

4   Corruption and Cheating Relating to School

I know from my own experience as a teacher and mother that children are often rewarded for "*research*" that is simply a plagiarised or downloaded essay or report, computer programming code or illegal use of copyrighted pictures. If students are not told this is wrong at an early stage, it is not surprising they are confused when they enter university.

During my career I have taught many teachers (*secondary and higher education*) who were completely oblivious about the need to acknowledge and/or use quotation marks for work that was not their own. Established practice in the classroom is not likely to be seen as corrupt or unacceptable by children. I am reminded of an interview I conducted with a teacher in Armenia, where the question prompts from me awakened my interviewee to the normality of corruption in that society. She realised that what she thought was perfectly acceptable behaviour. In this case, one member of a family or social circle, working in a university, was helping another by ensuring their son or daughter passed a difficult examination or gained admission, by pulling strings, which was actually a serious form of corruption (Glendinning et al., 2020, p. 20).

Some examples of corruption that we uncovered directly implicated schools, such as the bizarre example of a rather large head teacher in Burundi caught and photographed sitting a public examination on behalf of a pupil (BBC News, 2018); leaking of questions and answers to public closed-book exams before the exam in the UK (e.g. Busby, 2017). We came across reports of parents, or the family doctor, equipping children with ear buds, microphones and cameras before taking examinations (Glendinning et al., 2020, p. 18), so they can communicate answers to their children during the test. In Hubei province, China, there was outrage from an estimated 2000 students and parents when authorities cracked down on cheating in the Gaokao (university entrance examination), with sentiments expressed such as "There is no fairness if you do not let us cheat" (Moore, 2013).

By its very nature, contract cheating is one of the most difficult types of cheating to detect and prove, even using the lesser burden of proof, balance of probabilities, that normally applies in educational settings. The vast global scale and ephemeral nature of the highly lucrative commercial side of contract cheating makes it difficult to legislate against. However, there has been some success in challenging promotion of such services by third parties, including UK Essays advertising on the London Underground (QAA, 2018; ASA, 2018). It was shocking, even for seasoned researchers into cheating like me, when the "EduBirdie scandal" erupted, whereby YouTube celebrities were targeting school children, encouraging them to make use of a cheating service instead of doing the work themselves (Jeffreys & Main, 2018). A web site listing and reviewing 881 essay mills for use by UK students (UK Top Writers, n.d.) includes work for GCSE, NVQs and A levels, in a list of the services provided.

I recall an incident when I was about 8 or 9 years old and in the Brownies. Janice and I, my best friend who lived next door, proudly showed our homework from the previous week to Brown Owl. We had been told to darn a hole in a sock for our sewing badges, but another brownie completely overshadowed our pathetic efforts with a very professional darn that looked like delicate woven cloth. On closer questioning by Brown Owl, the girl admitted that her mother had done it. I do not know whether she was allowed to use this towards her badge, but I do remember the sense of injustice we felt at the time. Ironically, had the other girl's mother been rather less adept at darning, the cheating would not have been noticed.

The acceptance of the situation I mentioned earlier with contract cheating in Kenya may be perpetuated indefinitely by continuing systematic cheating affecting early years education, where it was reported that 'teachers and (secondary school) candidates work together to beat the system' by teachers 'selling exam and marking papers' and other cheating practices, including use of mobile phones in exams (Spooner, 2018). Toleration of this kind of practice results in the normalisation of the cheating ethic in wider society.

In all these examples, young children have been encouraged or helped to cheat by adults that they respect and depend on for learning about standards and values for their future life. What sort of example does that set them for life? Does it really matter? I would argue strongly that of course it matters. Education must provide the blueprint for good citizenship. Not all school-leavers go on to HE so by the time they leave school, irrespective of their immediate destination, at that point in their lives they need to have their moral compass pointing in the right direction.

Most of the examples presented date to before 2020. COVID-19 created new risks and threats to educational integrity and new opportunities for those making money from cheating, especially essay mills, often disguised as tutoring or proof-reading services, praying on the insecurity that students of all ages were experiencing. Several such companies tried to increase custom by offering COVID-19 discounts and special offers (Lancaster, 2020, p. 10).

Where planned exams did go ahead, switching to remote delivery at very short notice, there were new opportunities for students to cheat, particularly where examiners were inexperienced or ill-equipped to monitor student conduct on-line. Closed-book examinations based on rote learning are particularly problematic with remote delivery, because answers can be easily looked up or otherwise acquired and pasted into the answer paper.

The lockdowns caused existing inequalities to be magnified. Most students studying internationally went home to different time-zones around the world, sometimes suffering poor, cramped working and study conditions and inadequate access to technology. More affluent students had highly educated family members on hand to help them complete their assessments. The instructions to students on how to behave in this new situation may not always have been clear.

A massive increase in student cheating was reported in some HE providers in 2020, for example students in Queensland, Australia have been required to resit their exams in person after 'academic honesty had been compromised', when 'colluding and plagiarising in exams ... increased four-fold', with the move to on-line assessment in the first semester of 2020 (Garcia, 2020). In response to similar problems, Quality and Qualifications Ireland (QQI, 2020) has created useful guidance on assessment and academic integrity for all levels of education, specifically learning lessons from the situation we all faced in 2020.

In the UK the cancellation of public examinations (particularly GCSE, Scottish Highers, A-Levels) in 2020 caused chaos, that will continue to reverberate for many years. After some confusion and U-turns, teachers' predicted grades became the final ones, without any moderation. This was to counter the disadvantage to under-represented students that became apparent caused by the algorithm used to normalise and moderate teachers' predictions. Inevitably, some predictions were over-generous, leading to massive grade inflation, but it is impossible to know how many students would have exceeded their teacher's expectations had they taken the examinations.

By-passing any form of assessment by unfair means is not just about an undeserved grade and cheating fellow students. The student has also by-passed the learning experience associated with completing that task or examination. The underpinning knowledge and skills for any future learning that depends on the missed assessment will be absent, which potentially sets the student on a career of academic dishonesty.

Whether we are thinking about horrendous forms of corruption, such as bribery, extortion or sexual harassment, or just minor cut-and-paste plagiarism to pad out an essay, we need to find ways of breaking this cycle of cheating, steering young people in the right direction, by ensuring that they understand what is acceptable behaviour, by them and other people they may encounter, and why. If they make mistakes in the course of their learning, the policies, systems and procedures need to be sufficiently robust to ensure the failings are detected, suitable redress is applied to negate the unfair advantage and the offending student is supported and guided to ensure it does not happen again.

5   Academic Integrity in Schools

Throughout the research I have contributed to in this field, there have been calls from participants for students to be taught about plagiarism and related topics much earlier in their education. Better preparation at secondary school or earlier would certainly equip young people to challenge corrupt practices they encounter in HE, but also in work and social settings. However, it can be difficult, and sometimes dangerous, to challenge accepted customs and practice, in any context. We cannot expect young people or their teachers to take the initiative without some form of support.

Most secondary schools do not have procedures and policies for either detecting or managing cases of cheating by pupils, although some US schools

do seem to take this more seriously. Exploring what happens in HE would help, but considerable work would be needed to adapt strategies developed there for use in primary or secondary education. We need to think through the practicalities of what guidance and education is needed for pupils, by finding answers to these questions:
– What is the right age & setting to teach children about academic integrity?
– How should it be framed?
– What should be taught?
– Who should teach it?
– Could space be found to include this topic in the crowded curriculum?
– How could head teachers and teachers be convinced that this is relevant?

I do not have the answers to all these questions, although I have some ideas on where to begin. In my view it should not be taught as a separate topic, it should be an integrated element of moral and social skills for education and life. Starting in early education, even pre-school, children already need to know about concepts and behaviours such as honesty, fairness, sharing, ownership and saying 'thank you'. Educational integrity is about developing these themes gradually, throughout the student journey, between 3–18 years. Conversations must include concepts, such as: ways of questioning the reliability of information, identifying 'fake news' and poor scholarship; learning methods for acknowledging ownership and understanding copyright; developing skills to critique and build an argument; exploring ethical dilemmas and increasingly complex decision-making. Involving parents of younger children in delivering this content would make it particularly powerful for generating positive influences for societal and family values. Constructing this curriculum and designing associated policies and procedures, would be a very worthwhile collaborative research project, cutting across educational levels.

To make any progress on changes of this nature, there needs to be a convincing argument made to why this topic should be added to the curriculum – unless policy-makers for education and head teachers are on-side, nothing will happen. This chapter provides some of the necessary evidence to build that case.

Raising awareness in regulatory bodies responsible for schools may be a good starting point for encouraging the necessary changes. Organisations equivalent to Ofcom and Ofsted in the UK, should be alerted to the need to take action to tackle corruption and cheating in schools, in order to ensure standards and quality are upheld. These organisations should be able to influence and provide the necessary leverage (directly or indirectly) to mandate the introduction of a strategy for educational integrity in schools and colleges, in the same way it has been championed by quality bodies responsible for higher education in UK, Australia and Montenegro, for example.

In parallel with the influence from quality and standards bodies, I believe we need work with school leaders in every part of the world to ensure they are educated about integrity in education and the value of instilling good practice from an early age. This could be done through head-teachers' associations. It would help if head-teachers were made aware of the types of academic dishonesty currently handled by HE providers, including accidental plagiarism through ignorance. In some parts of the world head teachers will argue that there are more pressing issues than misconduct and plagiarism. Others will complain about lack of time to add yet another subject to a very tight timetable, especially if it is seen as non-essential.

A very relevant document, created by Muriel Poisson of IIEP/UNESCO (2009), sets out guidelines on creating and applying codes of conduct for teachers. Although the guide is aimed at education in developing countries, it does have relevance globally 'to increase the professionalization' (Poisson, 2009, p. 13) of everyone involved in the education of children. Embedding educational integrity in teacher training, both for new teachers and in-service retraining, is a critical element of a strategy for encouraging change. There is certainly a need for training any teachers tasked with delivering this topic in the classroom.

It would be useful to interview teachers and some pupils in schools that already claim to have policies that cover these subjects. This would provide very useful intelligence about what is taught, how it is delivered, to which year groups and how well it is absorbed and understood by the pupils.

6   Review

Although some of the available evidence presented here came from journalism rather than peer-reviewed publications, it is clear that the malaise of academic dishonesty, which HE globally has been grappling with for some time, also applies to an extent to secondary education. It could even be argued that the root of the whole problem lies in failure to instill ethical values in children, both by parents and in early-years education. Responsible adults, particularly parents and teachers, are often found to have assisted or condoned attempts by young people to gain an unfair advantage in their studies and assessments. This implies that this problem can only be resolved by fundamental change, affecting all levels of education, which will not be quick or easy. I have shared my initial thoughts and a few ideas for how to start addressing this problem. This under-researched area is very complex; the extent and causes vary in nature at different levels of education and in different parts of the world. However, this phenomenon is certainly ripe for exploring in more detail. I am convinced that the rewards from even small successes will be worth the efforts made.

References

ACA/AKK. (n.d.). Anti Corruption Agency, Kosovo. http://www.akk-ks.org/en/Home

Adams, R. (2017, November 24). Could Bath University's vice-chancellor's latest pay controversy be her last? *The Guardian.* https://www.theguardian.com/education/2017/nov/24/could-bath-university-vice-chancellors-latest-pay-controversy-be-her-last

ASA. (2018, March 21). *ASA ruling on all answers Ltd t/a UK essays.* https://www.asa.org.uk/rulings/all-answers-ltd-a17-394574.html

Atuhaire, P. (2018, March 14). Uganda's Makerere University: 'My lecturer tried to rape me'. *BBC News.* https://www.bbc.co.uk/news/world-africa-43287621x

BBC News. (2018, November 28). *The Nigerian rape survivor helping others to report sexual violence* [Video]. https://www.bbc.co.uk/news/av/world-africa-46359669

BBC News. (2019, March 13). *Felicity Huffman: Desperate Housewives star charged in exam cheat plot.* https://www.bbc.co.uk/news/world-us-canada-47543036

BBC News. (2020, February 18). *University of Ghana lecturers suspended after 'sex-for-grades' exposé.* https://www.bbc.com/news/world-africa-51546271

Borg, E. (2009). Local plagiarisms. *Assessment & Evaluation of Higher Education, 34*(4), 415–426.

Busby, E. (2017, June 20). Exam board Edexcel launches investigation into alleged leak of economics A-level paper. *Times Educational Supplement.* https://www.tes.com/news/exam-board-edexcel-launches-investigation-alleged-leak-economics-level-paper

CBC. (2017, September 17). *List of schools linked to Axact.* http://www.cbc.ca/marketplace/blog/list-of-schools-linked-to-axact

CHEA/CIQG. (2019). *Combatting academic corruption and enhancing integrity: Inventory of key questions for quality assurance and accreditation organizations.* https://www.chea.org/combatting-academic-corruption-and-enhancing-integrity-inventory-key-questions-quality-assurance

CIQG & IIEP. (2016). *Advisory statement for effective international practice combatting corruption and enhancing integrity: A contemporary challenge for the quality and credibility of higher education.* IIEP/UNESCO and CHEA/CIQG. http://unesdoc.unesco.org/images/0024/002494/249460E.pdf

COPE. (n.d.). Committee on Publication Ethics. http://publicationethics.org/

Coughlan, S. (2015, April 23). Exam board investigates question leak. *BBC News.*
https://www.bbc.co.uk/news/education-32438570

Crowthorne, E. (2017, April 9). Degrees of fraud [Audio documentary]. *BBC Radio 4.*
http://www.bbc.co.uk/programmes/b08kv5fd

Daniel, J. (2018). *Innovating in an age of uncertainty.* CHEA/CIQG. https://www.chea.org/
sites/default/files/pdf/Daniel.pdf

Davis, M. (2011, June 9). *Differing perceptions of international postgraduate students and
tutors regarding plagiarism policies and practice* [Workshop]. ASKe Oxford Brookes
University.

Denisova-Schmidt, E., Huber, M., & Leontyeva, E. (2016). On the development of students' attitudes towards corruption and cheating in Russian universities. *European
Journal of Higher Education, 6*(2). http://dx.doi.org/10.1080/21568235.2016.1154477

Dubrovsky, D. (2017). Escape from freedom: The Russian academic community & the
problem of academic rights & freedoms. *Interdisciplinary Political Studies, 3*(1), 177–
199.

Foltýnek, T., Dlabolová, D., Glendinning, I., Lancaster, T., & Linkeschová, D. (2018).
*ETINED – Council of Europe Platform on Ethics, Transparency and Integrity in Educa-
tion, volume 5: South East European Project on Policies for Academic Integrity
Council of Europe.* https://book.coe.int/usd/en/education-policy/7531-etined-
council-of-europe-platform-on-ethics-transparency-and-integrity-in-education-
volume-5-south-east-european-project-on-policies-for-academic-integrity.html

Garcia, J. (2020, September 30). QUT reports four times more cheating as exams go online. *Brisbane Times.* https://www.brisbanetimes.com.au/national/queensland/qut-
reports-four-times-more-cheating-as-exams-go-online-20200930-p56om3.html

Glendinning, I. (2013). *Comparison of policies for academic integrity in higher education
across the European Union.* http://www.plagiarism.cz/ippheae/

Glendinning, I. (2016). European perspectives of academic integrity. In T. Bretag (Ed.),
Handbook of academic integrity (pp. 55–74). Springer. https://doi.org/10.1007/978-
981-287-098-8_3

Glendinning, I., Foltýnek, T., Dlabolová, D., Jana Dannhoferová, J., Králíková, V., Michal-
ska, A., Orim, S.-M., & Turčínek, P. (2020). Project on academic integrity in Armenia,
Azerbaijan, Georgia, Kazakhstan and Turkey, Council of Europe.
http://www.plagiarism.cz/paickt

Glendinning, I., Orim, S.-M., & King, A. (2019). *Policies and actions of accreditation and
quality assurance bodies to counter corruption in higher education.* CHEA/CIQG.
https://www.chea.org/sites/default/files/pdf/CHEA_Corruption-Report-Final-
underlines.pdf

Golubeva, M., & Kanina, V. (2017). *ETINED – Council of Europe Platform on Ethics, Transparency & Integrity in Education, Volume 4: Codes of conduct for teachers in Europe: A
background study.* http://etico.iiep.unesco.org/en/resource/etined-council-europe-
platform-ethics-transparency-and-integrity-education-volume-4-codes

Grove, J. (2018, April 25). Academic fraud is a 'real challenge' to UK's quality assurance. *Times Higher Education.* https://www.timeshighereducation.com/news/academic-fraud-real-challenge-uks-quality-assurance

HEFCE. (2017, November 20). *Enquiry concerned with governance surrounding senior pay at University of Bath.* Higher Education Funding Council for England. http://www.hefce.ac.uk/reg/staffpay/bath/

IPPHEAE. (2010–2015). *Project results: National reports on plagiarism policies in 27 different European countries.* http://www.plagiarism.cz/ippheae/

Jashnik, S. (2020, September 23). U of California Admissions Blasted by Auditor. *Inside Higher Education.* https://www.insidehighered.com/admissions/article/2020/09/23/audit-blasts-admissions-university-california#.X2uGYAXGtnE.twitter

Jeffreys, B., & Main, E. (2018, May 1). The YouTube stars being paid to sell cheating. *BBC News,* https://www.bbc.co.uk/news/education-43956001

Joy, M. S, Sinclair, J. E., Boyatt, R., Yau, J. Y.-K., & Cosma, G. (2013). Student perspectives on source-code plagiarism. *International Journal for Educational Integrity, 9*(1). http://www.ojs.unisa.edu.au/index.php/IJEI/article/view/844

Lancaster, T. (2020, April 23). Assessing with integrity – The role of technology – Webinar slides [Blog post]. http://thomaslancaster.co.uk/blog/assessing-with-integrity-the-role-of-technology-webinar-slides/

Lancaster, T., & Clarke, R. (2016). Contract cheating: The outsourcing of assessed student work. In T. Bretag (Ed.), *Handbook of academic integrity* (pp. 639–654). Springer. https://doi.org/10.1007/978-981-287-098-8_17

Maina, S. B. (2015, February 1). Certificates of doom: How universities and colleges sell diplomas and clean up degrees. *Nation* [Kenya]. https://nation.africa/kenya/news/how-universities-and-colleges-sell-diplomas-and-clean-up-degrees-1064942?view=htmlamp

Mazodier, M., Foucault, M., Blemont, P., & Kesler, S. (2012, April). *La fraude aux examens dans l'enseignement supérieur: Rapport à monsieur le minister de l'Enseignement supérieur et de la Recherche.* Rapport no. 2012-027. Inspection générale de l'administration de l'Éducation nationale et de la Recherche. https://cache.media.enseignementsup-recherche.gouv.fr/file/2012/94/1/2012-027_rapport_217941.pdf

Moore, M. (2013, June 20). Riot after Chinese teachers try to stop pupils cheating. *The Telegraph.* https://www.telegraph.co.uk/news/worldnews/asia/china/10132391/Riot-after-Chinese-teachers-try-to-stop-pupils-cheating.html

ORCA. (2017). *The academic integrity of the managing staff of the University of Prishtina.* http://orca-ks.org/wp-content/uploads/2017/02/ORCA-Raporti-Komplet-English.pdf

QAA. (2018). *QAA complaint on 'misleading' essay mill upheld by ASA.* https://www.qaa.ac.uk/news-events/news/qaa-complaint-on-misleading-essay-mill-upheld-by-asa

QAA. (2020). *Contracting to cheat in higher education: How to address essay mills and contract cheating* (2nd ed.). https://www.qaa.ac.uk/docs/qaa/guidance/contracting-to-cheat-in-higher-education-2nd-edition.pdf

QQI. (2020). *The impact of COVID-19: Modifications to TLA in Irish further education training & HE.* https://www.qqi.ie/News/Pages/Irish-Further-and-Higher-Education-and-Training-Sectors-step-up-during-Lockdown.aspx

Pecorari, D. (2013). *Teaching to avoid plagiarism: How to promote good source use.* Oxford University Press.

Pecorari, D., & Petrić, B. (2014). Plagiarism in second-language writing. *Language Teaching, 47*(3), 269–302. doi:10.1017/S0261444814000056

Pillay, K. (2018, July 10). Students attack lecturers. *The Witness.* https://m.news24.com/SouthAfrica/News/students-attack-lecturers-20180709

Poisson, M. (2009). *Guidelines for the design and effective use of teacher codes of conduct.* IIEP-UNESCO. http://teachercodes.iiep.unesco.org/teachercodes/guidelines/Guidelines.pdf

Rostovtsev, A. (2015). Some observations on the subject of dissertation fraud in Russia. *HERB: Higher Education in Russia and Beyond, 3*(5), 17–18. https://herb.hse.ru/data/2015/09/22/1075563638/HERB_05_view.pdf

Simons, J. W. (2019, August 23). Inside the African essay factories that churn out university coursework for 115,000 cheating British students every year. *Daily Mail.* https://www.dailymail.co.uk/news/article-7290333/cInside-African-essay-factories-producing-essays-cheating-UK-students.html

Spooner, M. (2018, July 16). Why Kenyan students are cheating in their exams and what can be done. *The Conversation.* https://theconversation.com/why-kenyan-students-are-cheating-in-their-exams-and-what-can-be-done-99409

Szeto, E., & Vellani, N. (2017, September 10). 'All of us can be harmed': Investigation reveals hundreds of Canadians have phoney degrees. *CBC News.* http://www.cbc.ca/news/business/diploma-mills-marketplace-fake-degrees-1.4279513?cmp=rss&utm_source=Academica+Top+Ten&utm_campaign=b0c50b7056-EMAIL_CAMPAIGN_2017_09_11&utm_medium=email&utm_term=0_b4928536cf-b0c50b7056-51904845

TEQSA. (2017). *Good practice note on contract cheating.* http://www.teqsa.gov.au/sites/default/files/media-release-Good-Practice-Note-contract-cheating-oct17.pdf

Times of India. (2018, May 23). *46 students, 14 teaching staff held for running cheating nexus in pharma institute.* https://timesofindia.indiatimes.com/city/dehradun/46-students-14-teaching-staff-held-for-running-cheating-nexus-in-pharma-institute/articleshow/64278201.cms

Transparency International. (2013, October). *Global corruption report on education.* https://www.transparency.org/gcr_education

Transparency International. (2019). *Corruption perceptions index.* https://www.transparency.org/en/cpi/2019/results

Turner, C. (2018, March 31). Female teachers are being sexually harassed by pupils and groped by colleagues. *Daily Telegraph.* https://www.telegraph.co.uk/news/2018/03/31/female-teachers-sexually-harassed-pupils-groped-colleagues-figures/

UK Top Writers. (n.d). https://uktopwriters.com/best-essay-writing-services

Watson, R. (2017, November 13). Student loan scandal [Video]. *BBC Panorama.* Retrieved September 30, 2020, from http://www.bbc.co.uk/programmes/b09g5l1c

CHAPTER 12

Prioritising Values to Prepare for Life

Susan James

Abstract

Most schools identify a set of values. These labels are referenced in promotional material giving prospective parents a sense of what is important to the school for teaching personal, practical and academic abilities. The implication is that values will be adopted by students to make them more rounded individuals able to understand the consequence of actions. For many parents, a more holistic education is the reason why they choose to send their children to a particular school, with values resonating with them for preparing children for future lives? If so, how does a school ensure values are embedded and embraced, rather than rest superficially as nothing more than words upon a page?

1 Introduction

In 1854, The Manchester District Schools for Orphans & Necessitous Children of Warehouseman & Clerks was instituted. A committee of Manchester benevolent men were determined to provide education for orphans, offspring of warehousemen and clerks "founded and conducted on the most liberal principles and be open for the reception of children of both sexes". In October 1854, donations were sought from Warehousemen and Clerks. In 1884, Cheadle Hulme School was named, moving to its current site for educating 244 pupils, including 193 orphans. The School states their 5 principle values below.

2 Attributes

The school's history is a rich source of examples with each value displayed within teacher and pupil activities. The emotional development research of Erikson (1963) showed that these attributes are rooted in communicative development, producing ideas, feelings and behaviour, for sharing, reviewing and refining in cooperation with others. For example, in 1915 CHS offered itself as a hospital and 1,402 soldiers, injured in World War 1, were treated there. During this battle, CHS sacrificed 2 acres of play-space for farmland, providing the community with meat and vegetables. School students were the workers to grow food, showing communicative, cooperative and collaborative spirit.

Values, demonstrating thought, empathy and care for others, with ability to adapt to challenging situations, are clearly evident. Since 1885, the School has grown from 6 to 1500 pupils. Currently, its Transformational Bursary Scheme, actively seeks *looked-after children*, who might benefit from the privileges of a funded education. To remind them of their foundation, School community members (present & past) are referred to as *Waconionans*, or informally as *Wacs* or *Old Wacs*, thus recalling the warehousemen and clerks who founded the School. Underlying CHS values are pillars of: Active, Altruism and Academic. Pupils, in keeping with the liberal arts foundation, are required to access and embrace a range of experiences contributing to their education (Baker, 1955; Richardson, 2005).

3   What Are Values?

Values are a motivational force. They inform attitudes and guide behaviour, developed and shaped through interactions with others. The main caregiver transmits values within child rearing practices, acting as models observed from verbal and non-verbal behaviours. However, values are an abstract concept, applied in situations as desirable behaviour. A value system is a vital part of personal development. Understanding this as a motivational, behavioural guide, is gained after entering primary school. Pupils then have the capacity to comprehend complex perspectives and intentions, assuming adequate learning opportunities and the language and thinking to process and perform. During adolescence teenagers seek a sense of greater *I* identity, for construction of self (Erikson, 1950, 1963).

4   Values as Beliefs

Values are part of our belief system. *The World Values Survey* (2019) highlights their key role in economic development, democracy, gender equality and effective national governance, as well as how we interact with others. Whilst there are universal values, different communities prioritise some over others. The interplay between a person and their context is part of shaping their value system, in terms of prioritisation at a given point. Values are not entirely fixed and change according to the contexts in which we function. Boer and Boehnke (2015) point out the significance of values, which "play a central role in human development" (p. 129).

5   Changes in Values

Alteration in values occurs after a series of temporary shifts, which accumulate to then mark a moment of permanent change. This arises from a significant environmental change and desire to be aligned with dominant thinking (e.g. a pupil moving to secondary school and wanting to fit in, or an immigrant to assimilate). This highlights the importance of explicit values that students are expected to embrace and follow. The Duke of Edinburgh Award Scheme was created for these reasons. Whilst arming young people with practical abilities, it expects them to focus on their personal communicative development, to think at higher levels for problem solving and survival, as well as connect with others to share and broaden ideas. Thus, pupils are given core values to guide development. For example, teamwork is reliant on trust, integrity and ability to communicate, connect, cooperate and collaborate.

Srivastava and colleagues (2003) investigated *stability* versus *plasticity* of traits. They found little evidence of person stability. Most traits develop further after age 30, with a similar trajectory suggested for values. There is need for further research, but this suggests that environmental factors play a large part in influencing a person's value system. Sheldon (2005) found that values alter after students enter secondary school. Value development concludes in late adolescence, with evidence of change within school settings. This highlights the status of a school value system that is more dominant than peer gang culture.

A pupil's wider context impacts on capacity to embrace school values, which the Contextual Safeguarding Network (2020) is built around. Environment factors, like a dominant peer group or forceful family are important. In addition, some youngsters have a dispositional resistance to change, so there is less likelihood of an alteration in values because of an inbuilt trait. This considers the impact of a *setting* on value development. However, thinking changes beyond peer group influence. For example, introduction of technology (mobile phone/social media use) becomes relevant to a caregiver, because of a child's use of a device. It is brought closer to life, impacting on their value system and attempts to influence a dependent.

6   Values as Guides

Values are an essential part of our existence, guiding behaviours and directing desires, actions and interactions. Communication and relationships are core processes in their development. Therefore, values are an integration of communication and culture. Theories of development are interlinked with societal values and circumstantial changes. Personal values are part of our identity and a complex cognitive process. Ontogenetic and phylogenetic developmental perspectives enable understanding of values as central individual as well as cultural constructs, which are dynamic, multi-layered and complex. Values are not fixed and are responsible for the dynamic interplay with self and others.

7 Subjective and Objective Values

Subjective values come from reason and are strongly influenced by background and cultural family beliefs. *Objective values* evolve from a source of authority like school. Morality is informed by either subjective or objective values or both. Morality reasons are informed by our subjective values and, in turn, by empathy and experience, resulting from communicative exchanges. Empathy arises from experiences of communicating and sharing the human condition and depends on narrative language and thinking to work through ideas. Morality matures as we age and our communication develops to be able to think, reason and understand the consequences of actions. The cultivation of communication is vital to understanding values and how they operate. Developing values must take into account whether students have the subjective values to cope with objective ones. What Does Research Say about Future Work and School Values? Society is entering a period of rapid change, known as the *Fourth Industrial Revolution.*

> It began at the turn of this century and builds on the digital revolution. It is characterised by a more ubiquitous and mobile internet, by smaller and more powerful sensors that have become cheaper and by artificial intelligence and machine learning. (Schwab, 2016, p. 7)

Millennials already change jobs on average every 2 years and it is estimated that 65% of primary school children will learn in ways not currently existing (Sage, 2017). The McKinsey Global Institute (Manyika, 2018) predicts that robots will replace 40–75 million jobs by 2025. Both *The Future of Jobs* report (World Economic Forum, 2018) and *The Future of Employment* (Frey & Osborne, 2013), have looked at workplaces and agree a need for radical educational changes. The Industrial Revolution (*like the present one*) occurred because new technologies were not asset risks to political powers. Whilst both revolutions might appear disadvantageous for the least skilled, eventually everyone benefits. An

example is T-Ford, as advancements in car manufacturing made it affordable
for the average person.

The Future of Jobs report (World Economic Forum, 2018) identifies 4 dominant drivers for the Fourth Industrial Revolution: "ubiquitous high speed
mobile internet; artificial intelligence; widespread adoption of big data analytics and cloud technology" (p. VII) and states they will be responsible for key
changes in business growth. The report adopts a holistic approach, accounting for factors beyond the business world. Positive trends are advances in
cloud technology and expansion of education. Negative influences involve an
increase of cyber threats, government policy shifts, an ageing society and climate change effects, with wider contexts impacting on the job market.

The report indicates that "75 million jobs might be displaced, while 133
million new roles may occur concurrently" (p. 8). Both reports agree that the
human work-force must adapt as machines take over routine roles. Human
labour has a unique skill set that cannot yet be matched by computers. However, it is likely in the future that technologies will be able to enter human
complex cognitive domains. (Goldin & Katz, 2008).

In education, algorithms will increasingly serve as tutors, using information about pupils and courses to provide teaching and assessment strategies to
serve individual needs. Data analysis will predict results and advise for training
and occupations. Historical progress has been about mechanisation of manual
tasks, but now technology will contribute to cognitive ones, allowing humans
to focus on world problems. Tasks requiring creativity, social and practical
intelligences are reported as roles least affected by intelligent machines.

8   Life Changes Affecting Schools

Changes mark a potential alteration in more than jobs. There will be a change
in our way of feeling and being. The impact on mental health of young people is
not to be underestimated. In 2011, the *Morbidity and Mortality Weekly Report* published results showing that over 30% of people in the USA do not have enough
sleep. Similar results were reported in The UK Observer in 2012. The Walter Reed
Army Institute of Research (2008) measured impact of sleep lack. It reduces
emotional intelligence, empathy, quality of relationships, thinking and impulse
control. *Time famine* (Perlow, 1999) expresses the idea that people feel starved
of time. Increased work demands leave little opportunity for family or one self.

Adults are not only under unprecedented levels of pressure. Schools face
a big challenge, with increasing numbers of students reported having stress,

anxiety and depression. One in eight 5–19-year-olds have increased mental health issues (Mental Health of Children and Young People, 2017). Those with a lifetime condition first experience symptoms at age 14 years and 28% of pre-school children have problems impacting on psychological development (Sabates & Dex, 2013). In 2014, half a million+ UK children recorded as unhappy (Children's Society, 2014). About 1 in 5, 15-year-olds self-harm (World Health Organization, 2018). The term *snowflakes* appeared in the Collins' Dictionary (2016) – "Young adults, of the 2010s, viewed as being less resilient and more prone to taking offence than previous generations".

9   What are Qualities and Values for Success?

In 2016, The World Economic Forum identified 10 skills for success in 2020:
– Complex problem solving
– Critical thinking
– Creativity
– People Management
– Co-ordinating with others
– Emotional intelligence
– Judgement and decision making
– Service orientation
– Negotiation
– Complex flexibility

The Foundation for Jacobson Resonance identified skills in demand for 2020:
– Analytical thinking and innovation
– Active learning and learning strategies
  Creativity, originality and initiative
– Technology design and programming
– Critical thinking and analysts
– Complex problem-solving
– Leadership and social influence
– Emotional intelligence
– Reasoning, problem solution and ideation
– Systems analysis and evaluation

The Royal Society of Arts (2003) developed a 21st Century Secondary Curriculum, *Opening Minds,* with 5 essential competencies.

10   Relations, Citizenship, Learning, Managing

In *The Fourth Industrial Revolution*, Klaus Schwab (2016) comments that change is not the *what* and *how* of doing things but also *who* we are, *so* integrating skills and values. Citizens must prepare appropriate abilities, but need a mind-set allowing them to flourish.

> The big challenge for most societies will be how to absorb and accommodate the new modernity whilst still embracing the nourishing aspects of our traditional value system. (Schwab, 2016)

From day one, schools bring young people together; they create connections and promote communication, community, learning and understanding. Technology advances are seen as being in conflict with or threat to social, communicative competencies and building of relationships. For example, in 2010, Konrath, O'Brien and Hsing found a 40% decline in empathy amongst students compared to pre-2000. This study shows results of a community in which managing communicative experiences, dealing with different audience types and finding ways to connect, is declining. Turkle (2015) found that 44% of teenagers remain connected to devices during other activities, like eating and playing sport. He mentions studies proving that two people in conversation will be impacted by a phone presence within peripheral vision. It changes talk and connectedness.

Relationship with mobile devices and social media mean less listening, eye-contact and reading body language. Key non-verbal competencies are not practised or mastered as formally (Castells, 2014). As an advocate of mindfulness and reflection, Schwab's (2016) *Human Connection* is potent. He references writers who chime with my experience of children and students. Carr (2010, p. 101) says:

> The Net is by design an interruption system, a machine geared for dividing attention. Frequent interruptions scatter our thoughts, weaken our memories and make us tense and anxious. The more complex the train of thought we're involved in, the greater the impairment the distractions cause.

It would be unreasonable for phones to be removed from children. However, schools must promote self-regulation. Students need to ensure that technology, like mobile use, is supported by values-based guidance and rooted in thought for others and contributions to society. Social and emotional intelligence mark us apart from machines and at the heart of education. Pace of life and immediacy of information has huge implications for well-being. Reflection helps us stop, recall, analyse, progress and review lessons learned. Pico Iyer (2014), quoted by Schwab, captures this idea,

> In an age of acceleration, nothing can be more exhilarating than going slow. And in age of distraction, nothing is so luxurious as paying attention. And in an age of constant movement, nothing is so urgent as sitting still. (p. 102)

He advocates nurturing and applying 4 types of intelligence:
– *Contextual*: anticipate trends and become more connected across networks
– *Emotional*: self-awareness, self-regulation, motivation, empathy, social skills (*within communication – recognition of audience needs*, Sage, 2000)
– *Inspired*: (Latin, *spriare,* to breathe)-continuous search for meaning & purpose
– *Physical*: nourishment and support of a healthy body and mind

Schwab takes a holistic approach to education, in terms of mind, heart, soul and body. He recognises that success of collective futures, rests not with technology advances but how we can adapt: "In the end, it comes down to people, culture and values".

> Let us together shape a future that works for all by putting people first, empowering them and constantly reminding ourselves that all of these new technologies are first and foremost tools made by people for people. (p. 114)

The school challenge is how to develop these qualities when the curriculum places most emphasis on exam results. Human qualities for success derive from communicative competence. How does a school embed values and know they are embraced? How will they be introduced? It should consider how to measure success.

11 How Does a School Embed Their Values

Work competencies plus well-being are required for society to function. Well-being is seen as synonymous with *happiness*, occurring spontaneously or through luck. *Eudomania*, the Greek word, is sometimes translated as *happiness*, but more accurately aligned to *virtue*. Controlling wellbeing, thorough action (*doing good*) and thinking, is viewed as a means to happiness.

Ancient and modern thinkers agree that balance and calm is attainable through our actions and attitudes. Thus, education of pupils, beyond knowledge and skills, is vital for success from instilling core values. If resilience value is promoted and rewarded; if a student knows this helped them overcome difficulty, then the work-force will better navigate the future? Education, developing self-understanding and well-being, is life preparation. The Personal, Social and Health Education Association (PSHE) supports teaching on well-being and MindEd is a free online training tool. *Worth It* is the only external training providing mental health and well-being from a positive standpoint. Guidance is useful, but a school must engage and often regards this topic as non-essential. If well-being and core values create adaptable, resilient students, then a programme must be a whole school priority.

> Very little is needed to make a happy life; it is all within yourself, in your way of thinking. (Marcus Aurelias, Roman Emperor)

To evidence integrity, endeavour, compassion, contribution and resilience values, a pupil must show how ownership impacts on life. Metacognition and reflection, take time and practice to develop, requiring high priority. For pupils to review, lesson-tasks must be altered to prioritise the 10 workplace skills. Therefore, staff must be convinced that the status quo needs change to achieve this *new bliss*. It does not dismiss knowledge. Lennon (2017) says successful UK state schools demonstrate this:

> If we teach pupils to think critically about ... the causes of the Second World War, this does not mean they can think critically about climate change or alternative energy options. Critical thinking processes are tied to background knowledge. (p. 143)

Hirsch's study (1987) found students from two different colleges showed marked differences in understanding a passage from Ulysees, Grant and Lee. Richmond students were inferior to Virginia – lacking understanding of the American Civil War. He formulated *cultural literacy*, to show comprehension requires not just letter decoding but a rich cultural background. Sage (2000, 2017; Sage & Matteucci, 2019) shows, from UK studies, how *general knowledge* is vital for developing *inference* and *coherence* in connected language.

In 2019, having identified future needs, Cheadle Hulme School reshaped PSHE provision in *The Waconinan Programme*, with 5 main areas: *Relationships, Physical and Mental Health, Future Self, Citizenship and Study Skills*. It adapted the Eurodoc Report, 2018, ensuring Early Career Researchers (ECRs)

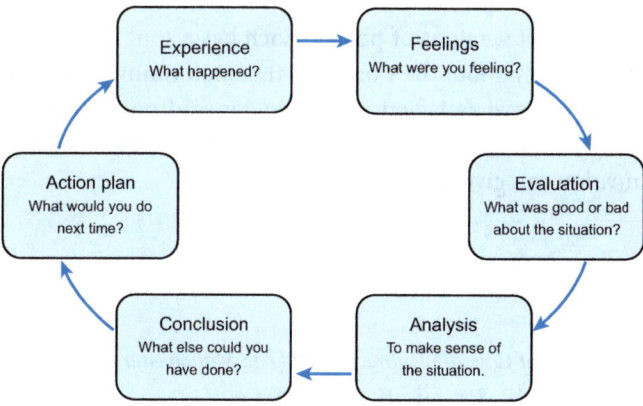

FIGURE 12.1   Adaption of Gibbs model

build a work portfolio that records evidence (formal and non-formal) with reflective comments. ECRs follow STAR principles: Situation, Task, Action and Result. This provides evidence of pupil awareness and mastery from applying their value system in daily life. The School uses a Gibbs model (1988), acknowledging situational experiences and feelings – providing reflection and evaluation to link learning and practice. It connects head, heart and mind, giving chance to know *self* in a balanced, holistic way.

12   Review

Humans want to evolve, progress and achieve gratification. Technological advancement is now at unprecedented levels. We can be optimistic about new job opportunities and the way intelligent machines enhance lives. That said, there is potential for detrimental impact on well-being. We must urgently review provision and prepare young people for their futures. There is need for re- and upskilling those already working. Imparting knowledge remains a vital part of what schools can and should do to enhance and increase cultural literacy. However, education must facilitate abilities for life and jobs. Communication competence, social and emotional intelligence, critical and creative thinking, flexibility and self-awareness bring confidence to ensure high levels of productivity and well-being. Informal and formal talk is essential for connection, cognition and coping. With technology taking over taking, we must be aware of how to promote speaking and give it greater priority in formal learning. These values need to be lived and breathed in all school experiences, as part of the culture.

Many have argued over centuries, that humans have choices about how they react to life. We are more than the sum total of our physical, working selves.

Education must build the best versions of people. Each has a soul, desire and capability to think more deeply about the world and their community. The aim must be for everyone to achieve satisfaction, well-being, and peace. Awareness of the power of *self* to manage, embrace and flourish in endeavours is the greatest gift that education can give to learners.

References

Baker, G. J. M. (1955). *A history of Cheadle Hulme School (The Manchester Warehousemen and Clerks' Orphan Schools) 1855–1955.* H. Rawson & Co.

Boer, D., & Boehnke, K. (2015). *A handbook of value: Perspectives from economics, neuroscience, philosophy, psychology and sociology.* Oxford University Press.

Carr, N. (2010). *The shallows: How the internet is changing the way we think, read and remember.* Atlantic Books.

Castells, M. (2014, September 8). The impact of the internet on society: A global perspective. *MIT Technology Review.* https://www.technologyreview.com/2014/09/08/171458/the-impact-of-the-internet-on-society-a-global-perspective/

Children's Society. (2014). *Children's Society report.*

Contextual Safeguarding Network. (2010). *Principles.* icsnetwork.org.uk

Department for Education. (2011). *Teachers' standards: Guidance for school leaders school staff and governing bodies.* https://assets.publishing.service.gov.uk/government/uploads/system/uploads/attachment_data/file/1007716/Teachers__Standards_2021_update.pdf

Erikson, E. (1963). *Childhood and society.* W.W. Norton.

Frey, C. B., & Osborne, M. A. (2013, September 17). *The future of employment: How susceptible are jobs to computerisation?* [Paper]. Oxford Martin School, University of Oxford. https://www.oxfordmartin.ox.ac.uk/downloads/academic/The_Future_of_Employment.pdf

Gibbs, G. (1988). *Learning by doing: A guide to teaching and learning methods.* Further Education Unit.

Goldin, C., & Katz, L. F. (2008). *The race between education and technology.* Harvard University Press.

Hirsch, E. D. (1987). *Cultural literacy: What every American needs to know.* Houghton Mifflin.

Iyer, P. (2014). *The art of stillness: Adventures in going nowhere.* Simon & Schuster.

Konrath, S., O'Brien, E., & Hsing, C. (2010). Changes in dispositional empathy in American college students over time: A meta-analysis. *Personality and Social Psychology Review, 15*(2), 180–198.

Lennon, B. (2017). *Much promise: Successful schools in England.* John Catt Educational Ltd.

Manyika, J. (2018). *AI, automation, and the future of work: Ten things to solve for.* McKinsey Global Institute. https://www.mckinsey.com/~/media/McKinsey/ Featured%20Insights/Future%20of%20Organizations/AI%20automation% 20and%20the%20future%20of%20work%20Ten%20things%20to%20solve% 20for/MGI-Briefing-Note-AI-automation-and-the-future-of-work_June2018.pdf

Perlow, L. (1999). The time famine: Towards a sociology of work time. *Administrative Science Quarterly, 44*(1), 57–81.

Richardson, M. (2005). *Heads and tales: The 150 year story of Cheadle Hulme School.* Cheadle Hulme School.

Sabates, R., & Dex, S. (2013). The impact of multiple risk factors on young children's cognitive and behavioural development. *Children & Society, 29*(2), 95–108. https://doi.org/10.1111/chso.12024

Sage, R. (2000). *Class talk: Successful learning through effective communication.* Blooms-bury.

Sage, R. (Ed.). (2017). *Paradoxes in Education.* Sense.

Sage, R., & Matteucci, R. (2019). *The robots are here.* University of Buckingham Press.

Schon, D. (1984). *The reflective practitioner: How professionals think in action.* Ingram.

Schwab, K. (2016, January 14). *The Fourth Industrial Revolution: What it means, and how to respond.* World Economic Forum. https://www.weforum.org/agenda/2016/01/ the-fourth-industrial-revolution-what-it-means-and-how-to-respond/

Sheldon, K. M. (2005). Positive value change during college: Normative trends and individual differences. *Journal of Research on Personality, 39*, 209–223. http://web.missouri.edu/~sheldonk/pdfarticles/JRP05.pdf

Srivastava, S., John, O. P., Gosling, S. D., & Potter, J. (2003). Development of person-ality in early and middle adulthood: Set like plaster or persistent change? *Journal of Personality & Social Psychology, 84*(5), 1041–1053. https://doi.org/10.1037/0022-3514.84.5.1041

Turkle, S. (2015). *Reclaiming conversations: The power of talk in a digital age.* Penguin.

World Economic Forum. (2016, January). *The future of jobs: Employment, skills and workforce strategy for the Fourth Industrial Revolution.* https://www3.weforum.org/ docs/WEF_Future_of_Jobs.pdf

World Economic Forum. (2018). *Insight report: The future of jobs report 2018.* https://www3.weforum.org/docs/WEF_Future_of_Jobs_2018.pdf

World Health Organization. (2018). *Health behaviour in school-aged children: HBSC report.*

World Values Survey. (2019). *WVS Wave 7 (2017–20).* https://www.worldvaluessurvey.org/ WVSDocumentationWV5.jsp

CHAPTER 13

Sociological Aspects of Educational Robotics

Stefano Cobello and Elena Milli

Abstract

The following reflections result from almost 10 years of practical activity in schools (*mainly primary*) in the field of Educational Robotics. These experiences have allowed us to understand how Educational Robotics, in small groups, can be excellent school practice for the development of social competencies and pro-social attitudes. Over the years, teacher insights and activities have become the basis for studies and projects, co-funded by the Erasmus Plus Programme of the European Commission, in different fields and age groups. For example, the project PEARL – Emotional Empathetic Proximal Learning Educational Environment (2018-1-1TO2-KA201-048515) – addresses early childhood and develops an educational model based on the feelings that arise in children age 3–6 years, while playing together with a learning robot (http://pearl-project.org). Also, the Policy Reform Project, Robots versus Bullying (612872-EPP-1-2019-1-EN-EPPKA3-PI-FORWARD) focuses on the promotion of social competencies and the prevention of bullying, with educational robotic activities for school pupils age 5–11 years (www.roboticsbullying.net). The observations made during educational robotic activities in groups and the dialogues with teachers have given rise to a series of reflections on the sociological value of robotics. The activity of educational robotics in groups, due to the dynamics, brings in social, pedagogical and educational aspects that are seldom considered or discussed.

1   Background

The sociological aspects of Educational Robotics are those that characterise the relationship between the child and society around him. By *society* we mean the classmates, teachers, caretakers, family and even the social structure itself, including the future perspectives of the child and parent choices, as well as the environment in which they were born and reared. The introduction of a tool, like robotics in education, at home or school, is one aspect of playful entertainment or something functional for a certain teaching model. It also becomes a structural element for the social growth of the child.

The facilitative aspects, due to the characteristics of robots, emerge in individual and group behavioural processes, reshaping the whole educational function of the environment – the tools, roles and approach to growth itself. To give an example, we might think that by introducing the *Chutes and Ladders* game in a class, once the game is over, the play itself ends. On the other hand, when we bring a small robot into a group, because it is a dynamic object with its own autonomy, it becomes an active subject in the fantastic and imaginative reality of children. In other words, the experience lived with the robot, does not end with the simple act of playing, but continues its work of "*education*", through the imaginative dynamics that the robot stimulates in each child and the whole peer group. Even when placed back in its box, the robot waits to live again, because in their imagination and fantasy the children are waiting for the new game, activity and purpose to be invented and which materializes in a new educational process as a small social reality of living actors. The robot, in fact, can represent for children a neutral element on which fantasies, stereotypes, experiences, etc. can be projected. The game is enriched through the interaction and collaboration of children and the robot transforms from a simple machine into a robot-saviour, discoverer and cook, to become a kind of projection of a child's ego that makes dreams come true.

2   The Importance of Roles

One sociological aspect to be taken into consideration is that of *roles*. Within the group, working/playing with educational robotics, all children acquire and play a role. Acquiring a role, for a child, is not a simple thing, it means having a distinctive position in the *micro-society* of the game that extends into the real macro-society. The attribution of a role in a playgroup context facilitates the inclusion of everyone, even those who are shy or have difficulties, since in the dynamics of robotics each group member has a task, therefore this attribution puts everyone on the same level. The role is also an element of acceptance by the group and of commitment to others. This is linked to the rules and function of the game itself, since in the distribution of tasks related to the use of the robot, each child has a responsibility towards the others and the goal of the game. From the role played in the group, a child can learn to be part of it and identify how they can help others. The role is not only the one that can be imagined with the robot and the game, but, once assigned by the teacher or by the group, it continues in the classroom, with friends and institutions represented initially by teachers and parents.

Therefore, we can see a generalization in society of the role played in the classroom. This process occurs naturally for the child, within a playful, educational context in which they can take on different roles. In fact, the role given or acquired, within the group working with robots, is never static but can be repeated or changed, becoming itself a learning model of how the child can relate to the society in which they live.

The contribution and importance of the role played by the individual pupil (initially attributed by the teacher, after explaining the group function and importance of this for achieving the common goal) is increasingly enriched by the collective choices to attain the activity goal. Choices, when made individually, lead to sole success, while group choices become a collective achievement. When these choices are made independently and lead to failure or non-achievement of the objective, they are attributable to individual failure. Thus, they have a strong effect on the growth of self-esteem in a child, compared to when failure occurs due to group choices.

In the latter case, robots eliminate individual stress and frustration, while facilitating the repetition of the game to achieve success. The group becomes a social corpus, with which to face difficulties and learn from each other. This aspect, identified many times by us, has been called the *Proximal Learning Environment*. This is an evolution of Vygotsky's (1978) proximal learning zone. It is a transmission of knowledge, responsibilities, roles & intuitions in groups, where peer education becomes a collective, evolutionary learning process.

3   Respect for Rules

The second sociological aspect to underline is the respect for rules. Inevitably, the robot needs rules to work properly, which are determined by the role and functions of the game and, above all, the objectives or goals to be achieved. Chaos neither allows the game to be played nor to real the goals. It does not create the *group dynamics* previously mentioned. The phase of sharing rules is fundamental for robotic activities. Very soon in the process, children learn to establish and respect order, not only because programming requires them to follow a precise sequence, but also as this is indispensable both to enjoy the game and achieve the set goals.

Therefore, the use of the robot in groups becomes a metaphor for behaviour in society, in terms of following the conventional rules. Teamwork, itself, stimulates abilities like collaboration, positive communication and mutual help. In cooperating for a common goal, children learn to put the needs of the group before their own and this is the basis of pro-social behaviour. This learning takes place playfully and naturally, developing attitudes of listening to each other. Attributes of empathy and proactivity are strengthened without external intervention, but thanks to the dynamics that are established between participants. These educational and pedagogical dynamics develop naturally in the game. They are enhanced by the use of robotics, both for the remarkable fascination that children feel for this toy and the symbolic value that it has for them. Therefore, they are involved in play-learning dynamics, thanks to the robot, with interactivity providing immediate feedback for their actions. Also, the robot creates a safe space in which to experience their limits. The robot is both an extension of the child's intentions (by carrying out action programmes) and an external, separate element. This double principle means that when the robot reaches the desired goal, it is the child (and group) who wins. However, when there is a mistake, it is the robot that is responsible.

This emotional freedom to act, try and perhaps make a mistake, means that through group educational robotics, children can express their potential freely and cultivate positive, helpful relationships with others. The robot also performs a psychological function, strengthening the process of building self-esteem and because it does not put blame for errors on an individual or group, it psychologically discharges the stress of performance onto the tool/game and not the children.

4   The Dimension of Time

The working/playing with the robot has its own times, which are not those of the school, teacher and pupil's imagination. They are times that pass between the moments in which the strategy is elaborated and the game activity developed and concretized. These are the times of the robot that do not finish with the game end. This continues in the imagination of the child creating expectations, enthusiasm and dynamism in the natural learning environment, whether at school or home.

Therefore, another element of reflection is one linking educational robotics and *the dimension of time*. The time in the game, with the educational robot, acquires another dimension, compared to the time of school and home life. We can affirm that time, as it is considered in daily reality, is neither uniform nor correct, because everyone relates in a psychologically different way with it.

Time, in educational robotics, becomes very fast – paradoxically faster as the robot is slow. Therefore, we could say that it becomes inversely proportional to the function of the game with the robot, because the objective justifies time invested and so is never boring. It is always active and participatory, but above all dynamic. This game/time dimension develops partially in reality but above all in the child's imagination. Sometimes, in child fantasy, the playtime with the robot lasts entire days.

On several occasions, we noticed that children spend much time *standing still,* elaborating the strategy, dedicating more time to this moment than in playing with the robot. It happened that at the end of the preparation and game activity, the children did not realize that so much time had been spent in the educational and pedagogical development space. They were never fully aware of this, in contrast to their teacher. Time is not a minor factor in robotic playing, because it becomes a regulator of the game, a space for each actor in the group and an integral part of the ongoing metacognitive process.

There is a time for rules and activities and for development of child imagination. Therefore, the robot can be extremely educational because it needs the contribution and patience of all participants, requires cooperation, allows mistakes to be made without guilt and is ready to repeat the proposed operations endlessly.

5   The Role of Teacher

Another important socio-psychological aspect is the role of the teacher. This role extends from a supplier or provider of knowledge to a supporter for the rules and parts played in activities. The teacher is initially a guide, but soon takes a step back and becomes a facilitator, i.e. an attentive accompanying person in the process of learning and growth that takes place in the group. As a facilitator, the teacher embodies a closer, more reachable adult model for children. Therefore, they learn from an open, curious and non-judgmental attitude to relate less anxiously or critically to novelties and unknowns.

The teacher also carries out the support function, according to those aspects and parameters that must be shared, so that each pupil knows why they have been given a role and the importance it has in the group. This "attributed role" reinforces self-esteem, the awareness and importance of play in the group and class. It inevitably enriches the role of the individual in society, at home and with family. When a child returns home, after an educational robotics activity, they simply replicate the one previously assimilated in the group, proudly emphasizing this to parents, because it represents a role as an adult. It is the child who wants to grow up in a positive way by embracing behaviours and models that are functional to learning and holistic education, but above all to their role in society. This is why educational robotics has a vital sociological function.

6   Why Choose Educational Robotics?

Why have we chosen educational robotics, rather than other tools, such as tablets, smartphones or video games? Without wanting to belittle activities and research, in the field of digital learning, our experience has helped us identify how group educational robotics is effective to learn from and with others and develop social skills from the early years of schooling. From observations we noticed how, after early childhood, playing alone with a robot becomes boring. It then loses its education function, intended as an exchange of information and knowledge, which happens naturally when the robot is used in a group. Educational robotics in groups has 3 dynamic processes:

– *Peer education* – in which respect for roles, times, others and shared rules are basic. This process can be seen as a moment in which the child understands his own skills. They then make these available to others by learning to communicate and reflect on their own limits and ability to ask for help when necessary. Peer education encourages communicative and relational processes that enable children to grow knowledge, attitudes and skills.
– *Proximal learning environment* – as the set of meanings and competencies that emerge within a group, to develop strategies and activities to achieve goals. These are cooperation, empathy, solidarity and mutual support processes.
– *Development of mathematical and scientific competencies* – that are linked to the intrinsic dynamics of the robot itself. These need an elementary, medium and advanced form of coding, adapting to age and personal learning style.

The social value of coding linked to robotics should be highlighted, because it is not only an approach to science and motivation to learn this discipline, but also a form of group valorisation, through the dynamics of shared learning. Coding activities structure the mind and consequently the behaviour of those involved. They can be compared to chess, as strongly based on rules, reflection, review, commitment and challenge, but these elements are experienced individually and not in a group, thus missing all the educational value linked to the game and the educational dynamics among peers.

Therefore, unlike pure coding, educational robotics fosters a part of our neuropsychological and relational development system not based on the sometimes strongly alienating individualism, which can grow through other technology tools related to ICT (smartphones, tablets, etc.). The use of these tends to be promoted to improve the speed of thought and calculation, forgetting how important it is to increase awareness, socialization, elaboration and metabolisation of the learning processes. Coding, in group educational robotics (programming of robot actions) becomes a social, shared exploit.

The result of a decision is taken in agreement with others; the effect of discussion brings common objectives and strategies to be adopted. It is an opportunity for experimenting in leadership and communication styles and is the product of the union of several viewpoints and ways of thinking. Therefore, coding in group educational robotics is not only an abstract task that assists computational thinking, but also takes the form of mediated reproduction, adapted to child development. This is what happens in daily reality, when the resolution of a problem situation takes place within a complex social matrix, involving heterogeneous people, elements, conditions and variables.

7   Metacognitive Processes

Perhaps the most significant aspect of learning, related to group educational robotics, is that of *metacognitive processes*. These refer to the ability to identify methods, strategies and techniques functional to learning, as well as managing the emotions involved in the growth process. The robot represents a stimulus to reach the objective, established by the group, which fits naturally into a process of peer and self-learning through trial and error. The child becomes an active protagonist of their learning, since it is they who identifies the best strategies to programme the robot to reach the goal.

Having to share these decisions with the group means that the child becomes aware of the reasons for these choices and begins not only to think about them but also to find the words to communicate them, developing self-awareness and an active, competent and autonomous role. We have observed how educational robotics develops pupil metacognitive competencies, with awareness of *what, why* and *when* they are doing tasks. Therefore, children learn about what is appropriate for specific conditions.

In developing a desire for learning (also linked to metacognition) the educational robot is functional to this objective, because all the processes it can mediate are developed on several levels. The basic level is that of attraction towards the toy and discovery of its programming. At this captivating, *"notionistic"* level of learning, robotics is used individually to often stop the metacognitive processes, limited only to aspects of self-directed awareness. Educational robotics, used in the group, reaches further levels.

–   Relationships with others – group elaboration of the structure of action, beginning the dynamics of role experimentation and definition of social rules within cooperative interaction.

- Affective expression, self-regulation and creativity – through which every-thing is developed.

Through these dynamics, pupils bring into play knowledge and skills of which they were unaware. In the process of sociological development, educational robotics is a multi-level and multi-dynamic tool because part of the activity takes place in the real world, but most of it develops in the inner realm of creativity, fantasy and imagination. This is why the robot has great value for the development of the creative processes that form personal competencies. The metacognitive objective of educational robotics group activities is for children to take over the activity itself, to set their own objectives – modifying and reworking them. This creates new paths by experimenting with roles – *putting themselves into play.*

8 The Smile

The idea of getting involved and experimenting introduces the last relevant aspect in educational robotics – the *smile*. We have observed, during educational robotic lessons, how learning takes place through a *smile*, as the appearance of the robot instantly changes the emotional climate of the class. This predisposes pupils to certain affectivity towards the toy and their classmates. This propensity to smile becomes a facilitator of learning. It is not only linked to the playful aspect of the toy-robot, but to the already identified lack of judgement of activities. Success is for the group and the individual, with any failure experienced due to the robot.

Children are free to learn by trial and error, because the robot becomes a transfer of responsibility that never judges. We have observed the development of these educational feelings that grow while playing with the robot in groups. They are evident in the tone of voice, desire to participate, smile, laughter and ability to accept error as a natural process of learning and of life, in a serene, jovial way. Moreover, the robot allows the repetition of an action, as many times as needed or wanted, without leaving a memory trace of mistakes and imperfections.

9 Review

In reviewing the use of educational robotics, the approach clearly assists the holistic development of children, which is essential for their ability to adapt,

cope and become resilient in a rapidly changing and increasingly technological world. We could say that the robot is a creator of a process of perfecting the
game and the skills of the playing team. The educational robot thus becomes
the personification of a living fable (*tableau vivant*), where children can face
the experiences of life in a sort of metaphorical space, without the dramas of
failure and performance, because the robot is always a winner.

References

Bandura, A. (1977). *Social learning theory*. Prentice-Hall.

Benitti, F. (2012). Exploring the educational potential of robotics in schools: A systematic review. *Computers & Education, 58*(3), 978–998.

Boda, G. (2006). *L'educazione tra pari: linee guida e percorsi operativi*. Franco Angeli.

Cornoldi, C. (1995). *Metacognizione e apprendimento*. Il Mulino.

Mecacci, L. (2017). *Lev Vygotskij. Sviluppo, educazione e patologia della mente*. Giunti.

Sarbin, T., & Allen, V. (1968). Role theory. In G. Lindzey & E. Aronson (Eds.), *Handbook
of social psychology, Vol. 1: Reading* (pp. 488–567). Addison-Wesley.

Vygotsky, L. (1978). *Mind in society: The development of higher psychological processes*.
Harvard University Press.

CHAPTER 14

Additional Learning Needs

Hearing Development

Gloria McGregor

Abstract

Having lived with hearing loss (HL) for over thirty years, I understand the problems faced and the importance of early intervention for a child or an adult. Any disability brings many challenges and when you look for them – achievements to celebrate! This is particularly true, I think, of hidden disabilities such as mental problems and hearing loss. Communication is central to life and being unable to do this effectively makes a significant difference. Hearing loss impacts on all social and work areas and can be very stressful. Hearing loss affects not only the individual concerned but to a greater or lesser extent everyone with whom they interact. Some consequences of hearing loss can be a sense of isolation, lack of confidence and self-esteem and feelings of inadequacy in most situations. This is especially true for work or learning environments and even social situations. It is difficult for both adults and children! Today, there are many challenges with the advent of online learning for most students. A hearing loss can greatly affect the situation both in the classroom and with online learning. Challenges facing those with hearing loss, at present, when people are wearing masks, are great. To lip-read, the face must be visible. Lip-reading aids language development and helps to resolve stress and emotional issues and to develop confidence in the learning situation thus fulfilling students' potential.

1   Introduction

The World Health Organization Website URL Deafness and hearing loss 1 March 2020 key facts has the following information.
- Text extract from page 1 "Over 5% of the world's population – or 466 million people – has disabling hearing loss (432 million adults and 34 million children). It is estimated that by 2050 over 900 million people – or one in every ten people – will have disabling hearing loss" (1 March 2020).

– Millions of people across the world live with disabling hearing loss. The vast majority live in low- and middle-income countries where they often do not have access to appropriate ear and hearing care services. Without suitable interventions, hearing loss poses a significant challenge in the lives of those affected. Many causes of hearing loss can be prevented through public health measures. Through rehabilitation, education and empowerment, people with hearing loss can reach their full potential.
– Raising awareness and improving access to services at the primary level can help to reduce the prevalence and adverse impact of hearing loss.

Many factors cause hearing loss. According to the WHO 2016 pdf file, *Childhood Hearing Loss Now Here's How* – they are as detailed below:
– Page 4 – Genetic factors at 40%
    – Conditions at the time of birth: premature; low birth weight; lack of oxygen & neonatal jaundice
    – Infections: Rubella in pregnancy; child meningitis, mumps & measles may lead to complications.
    – Diseases of the ear: Common ear problems
    – Noise: Prolonged loud noise can cause ear damage
    – Medicines: some medicines used in pregnancy
– Page 6 "They also suggest that 60% of hearing loss in children under 15 years is preventable. This could be prevented by immunization, good hygiene and improving prenatal care and care of newborns".
– Page 7 "Early intervention for children with hearing loss is strongly recommended."
    According to information received from UK *Action on Hearing Loss,* based on population data from 2018 (*the latest data available from the Office of National Statistics* [ONS]).
    – *There are 12 million adults with hearing loss greater than 25 dB – equivalent to 1 in 5 adults.*
    – *By 2035, estimates suggest around 14.2 million adults will have hearing loss greater than 25 dB.*
    – *50,000 UK children have hearing loss. About half are born with it and the rest lose hearing in childhood.*
    Action on Hearing Loss does not record child data. The Consortium for Research in Deaf Education (CRIDE) produce annual surveys of Local Authority Specialist Educational Services for deaf children. Data includes children with hearing loss in each local authority. The latest UK wide report available indicates at least 53,954 deaf children across the UK in 2019.
    – *An estimated 900,000 people have severe or profound hearing loss*

This depends on how severe or profound hearing loss is defined. The closest statistic Action on Hearing Loss has for this is 'currently there are 1.2 million adults in the UK with hearing loss greater than 65 dB'.

– *At least 24,000 people use British Sign Language (BSL) as their main language.* This figure is outdated and it is widely acknowledged that it underestimates the total number of people who use sign language. Unfortunately, estimates of the population who use BSL vary considerably depending on how data to determine the figure was collected. It is estimated that there are 151,000 UK people using BSL and of these, 87,000 are Deaf.

– *More than 40% 50+ year olds have hearing loss, rising to more than 70% for 70+ year olds.*

The *information in italics* can be found on the RNID website in the Fact and Figures section.[1] This data will change as updated information becomes available.

Much useful information about childhood deafness and ideas for support can be found on the National Deaf Children's Society (NDCS) website.

2   Effects of Stress Levels

Research shows that stress can cause increased levels of cortisol to be produced. While in the short term this can be useful, increased cortisol harms learning (Sage, 2000). If it is increased over a sustained period, it can have damaging effects on health. This is particularly true for children and babies in the womb. If it is regularly too high, problems like increased blood pressure, kidney, digestive function and increased blood sugar may occur. In infancy, high levels impact on brain development, memory, attention, language problems, increased anxiety and heightened emotions. Today, many factors affect stress levels of pregnancy, but if care is given these can be reduced for mother and child.

Some toxic medicines, chemicals and air pollution may cause problems for the developing child. From exposure, even in foetal development, the child may develop asthma or increased risk of birth defects. Many childhood illnesses can cause problems, including hearing loss, and could be prevented by immunization. Raising awareness is essential if we are to avoid hearing loss and support those when it still occurs. Wherever they live, children need to access support for their development. There is no universal sign language. I shall now focus on what can be done in the UK, but it will be relevant in any other country. Research indicates that resources and strategies are similar all over the world.

3   Hearing is Critical to Communication & Learning Development

Following the publication of the CRIDE Report, the head teacher, Peter Gale, of the Mary Hare School for the Deaf (centre of excellence) shared his views:

> Teaching units for deaf children keep closing. The data from the CRIDE report is deeply worrying. Deafness is a low incidence disability which all too often ends up being an insurmountable barrier to a good education and good mental health. For deaf children to excel, all the key ingredients – good acoustics, learning in small groups and specialist staff, need to be in place. There needs to be a range of provision, but whatever that provision is, it needs to take away the barriers to learning and fulfilment. The closure of units means that deaf children will be even more isolated, and I believe that a deaf peer group can be vital if we are to secure a positive self-image. I believe that specialist schools have a place in this and that LAs should use schools like mine as part of their spectrum of provision. I see too many pupils seeking to join Mary Hare in Years 8, 9 and 10 telling me that they were isolated, unhappy and critically that they could not hear well enough in their previous provision. The ideal of inclusion – every child in their local school – should not trump the voice of young people and their families. To end on a note of hope – deafness need not be a barrier to learning and to good grades and bright futures.

I am sure we would all agree with this!

4   Impact of Hearing Loss in Children

This depends, to some extent, on whether children are brought up with the Deaf community where they will be exposed to sign language from the beginning. If born to deaf parents, children will become part of the Deaf Culture and learn sign language. This enables effective communication between signers in both home and Deaf Community environments. On a Level 1 BSL course, there was a pediatric nurse teaching sign language to mothers and babies. Baby sign language helps communication, allowing the non-verbal child to express needs before knowing how to use words. This was not just for deaf children but for all, to aid better communication. One hearing grandchild could sign as a baby, and this was credited with leading to smoother interactions, fewer frustrations and communication through words.

Many deaf and hard-of-hearing children have hearing parents, so having a child with hearing loss may be emotionally difficult. Not all parents experience this, but it can be daunting to support a child with hearing loss. In the UK, there is a hearing test for babies before leaving hospital; then a review between 9 months–2.5 years and again at 4–5 before school entry. Even a small hearing loss affects ability to hear speech and acquire language. Hearing loss also affects ability to produce and monitor their own speech. (Some deaf persons have loud voices as they are speaking to hear themselves!)

Everybody is different and some cope well, but for many children with little hearing, it is difficult to learn the speech sounds (*phonemes*) in spoken language and how they work. If intervention does not occur early, hearing loss/ deafness, even if mild, can seriously affect spoken communication. This affects family and peers, the development of complex language use and many aspects of educational development. Without intervention and support in early years, children may not learn speech sounds or language and thus learn at a slower pace. Consequences of not being able to express ideas/needs/moods etc. may have a lasting effect on expectations and life quality. Children with hearing loss may not be able to follow complex instructions; be excluded from conversations and interactions for making friends; and unable to interact fully. They may feel left out; have few friends; be unhappy and even be bullied.

Exclusion from social interactions or reluctance to join group activities, for fear of making themselves look foolish, may lead to them being socially withdrawn and further unhappiness. They may not fully understand what is taught or discussed, so have no idea what to do. Also, they may misbehave or become quiet and invisible, so their learning suffers. This could indicate learning disability, but *may* be due to hearing loss, which is not always obvious as speech appears near normal. Sometimes, classrooms are noisy which is unhelpful. Mishearing or not hearing what is said can lead to confusion and frustration and poor achievement, so the position of the child in class is crucial and modification is needed. When working with adults, I refer to the lip-reader's smile. This is non-committal, similar to that of the Mona Lisa, and can include nodding, that lip-readers use when they are not hearing. It is appropriate to respond in this way, which some children will also do. Listening and lip-reading in a large group and/or noisy environment is hard, tiring work.

5   What Can Be Done?

All children respond to parents and friends making noises and faces at them. Those with hearing loss are no exception. Even if not hearing much, they may pick up something and this stimulant requires a response – gurgle or smile. From these early interactions with natural gestures, all children learn sounds and actions and what will gain them attention. Hard of hearing children need these interactions as much as hearing ones. They will also begin to recognise signs of expressions, moods and lip patterns – the beginnings of lip-reading. Everybody is different. There is no one way to develop communication competencies – families must use what works best for them. The important thing is to enable a child to communicate with others, to give a sense of self-worth, confidence and inclusivity (belonging).

6   The Importance of Early Speech Perception (Auditory & Visual)

The following information was published by NDCS, available online and was last checked on 23/11/21:

> 1.1 Deaf children's language development can be significantly affected by their speech perception skills." (cf., for example, Levine et al., 2016, citing Werker & Hensch, 2015)

> 1.2 Speech-reading: To help deaf infants and young children to perceive speech and acquire spoken language, it is important that they are encouraged and supported to lip-read (speech-read) as well as to listen to speech. The best evidence from neuroscience shows that lip-reading is a natural and important part of acquiring spoken language for all children (and a normal part of speech perception for hearing adults). As the brain actively tried to integrate redundant auditory and visual speech information to make sense of spoken language – what can be termed *auditory-visual integration* or *auditory-visual speech perception*. 8 to 10 months of age for instance, hearing babies begin to focus their attention on a talker's mouth (Hillairet de Boisferon et al., 2016). Whereas it used to be assumed that deaf children should be helped to develop spoken language by primarily focusing on their listening and perhaps even restricting their visual attention to speech, deaf children's listening and spoken language skills are in fact more likely to be helped by enabling them to watch as well as listen to people speaking around them. (cf., for example, Levine et al., 2016; Nittrouer & Caldwell-Tarr, 2016; Strelnikov et al., 2016; Tomalski, 2015; Yeung & Werker, 2015)

This research reinforces the importance of using all cues to aid language development in young children and of the need for attention to lip-reading/visual skills.

7   The Importance of Lip-Reading

Learning to lip read, with a hearing aid, can improve communication and learning. Also, many assistive devices improve the level of hearing. Following a diagnosis, the medical consultant or audiologist makes recommendations for the best device for a child and support needed. Options include: a variety of Hearing Aids; cochlear implants; loop systems (*personal & for a room*); speech therapy; and class assistance – both face-to-face and online learning. Other support includes captions/subtitles on educational videos, plus increasing self-made ones with subtitles; speech to text software and notetaking facilities.

Even when school support structures are in place, some children will benefit from specialist placement. I remember a 12-year-old boy, with profound hearing loss, that I supported. He was popular and interacted well with hearing others, using an assistive device and teacher assistant, but found learning tiring, which slowed his progress. Sometimes, he forgot his loop system and could not manage without it in class. Arrangements had to be made not only to assist his hearing loss but to organise his learning. This was 20 years ago and hopefully there is more support now available. It did not seem right that he had only one assistive device for both home and school use. He was admitted to a school for the deaf and although sorry to see him go, we knew it was for the best.

Lip-reading can be effective. It worked for me and as a lip-reading teacher I have seen the benefits for others. Sign language incorporates some lip-reading. Most of the hearing world do not sign and often are not deaf aware. The ability to lip-read supports the sense of what is heard. This will depend on the level of hearing loss, but lip-reading is not just about watching mouths. Children, as noted, learn to lip-read from birth and if encouraged become skillful. Added to this, everybody uses nonverbal language in life. According to research by Professor Mehrabian (1971), when we communicate with others, our words make up only 7% of our total communication; 38% is our vocal dynamics and 55% our body language. When we converse with others, we transmit things about ourselves unknowingly – without saying a word! Obviously, this is missing when communicating online or by telephone.

As children develop lip-reading, language and communication, those they interact with need to be deaf aware. Both hearing and non-hearing children lip-read naturally but the latter become more effective as they need this to understand speech. They pay more attention to mouths and other clues than hearing children, who can understand speech regardless of seeing the person. When teaching children with hearing loss the need to develop language abilities is vital because these are basic to thinking and communicating. There are many paths to lip-reading acquisition and for a child with hearing loss every aspect of life is a language lesson. When learning phonics through the approach used, the need to focus on lip-reading is implicit and those working with hearing loss should ensure that they face the children; use clear speech and make their mouth visible, along with gestures and appropriate age/ability language.

If this is right for children with hearing loss, others will also benefit. These include those with learning difficulties and English as a second language. Some profoundly deaf people are such expert lip-readers others are not aware of deficits. Often the best way to develop language is through games. This is especially important where children do not speak in sentences or use language appropriately. I once worked with a 9-year-old popular boy who was good at sport. He had a moderate hearing loss and was in a mainstream school. I was assigned to develop his spoken language. When asked what he wanted for breakfast he would reply *toast* or point to something. I did no formal teaching, as we played language games – not specific to hearing loss so his sister could join us sometimes. Many of the games used extended vocabulary. Through these, he was encouraged to look at whoever was speaking to develop lip-reading. Parents required him to answer them in sentences all the time. After initial reluctance, he made amazing progress and at the end of year he was Level 4 language and did not need me anymore!

8   Competencies for Lip-Reading

Lip-reading is like a puzzle and the skills together enable effective *speech reading*, which is an accurate description.

   Lip reading abilities include:
- Using lip reading to make sense of what is heard/or through signing
- Recognition of word sounds (phonemes) – recall lip patterns for sounds/ words (imagine a voice if not heard)
- Note movements of lip, tongue and jaw as a person speaks to help recognition of sounds not heard.
- Note rhythm of the speaker and the stress used – this helps recognition of what has been said – "Hello, how are you?"
- Follow speech to get the gist of what has been said
- Use other clues to confirm/inform what has been lip read
- Clues include facial expression, mood, gestures-nodding, pointing, body language, posture-happy/dejected

All these help a lip-reader to follow conversation, but the most important piece of the jigsaw is CONTEXT. If the context/subject/topic is known, then the lip-reader can function more effectively. Other factors aid lip-reading – the environment and speakers. Frequently these are outside the lip-readers control but can enhance the lip-reading experience:

The Lip-reader needs to ...
- Know conversation is taking place
- Have hearing aids & assistive devices switched on
- Have a quiet place for conversation – there are often best places to sit to use a loop system
- Have reduced background noise, soft furnishings, carpet & wallpaper
- Have a good light so the speaker's face is not in darkness
- See speaker's face – near, not moving about or covering with hands
- Attend to what is being said
- Know the CONTEXT
- Relax – enjoy the experience

The Speaker needs to ...
- Gain the lip-readers attention
- Make sure loop system is on & working
- Find a quiet place for talk with soft furnishings, carpets & wallpaper
- Not stand with back to light, as face will be dark – face the lip-reader
- Make sure the lip-reader can see face – near, not moving or covering mouth. If possible, have short/or no moustache/beard
- Speak clearly but not over-enunciate – keep natural rhythm to assist meaning and speak a little louder but not shout
- Tell lip-reader the CONTEXT.
- Relax and enjoy the experience

These factors must be considered for a deaf/hard of hearing child in the classroom. Also, a buddy helps to keep them on track with what is happening/required and makes a valuable contribution to the learning process. Teaching assistants must enable the child to eventually complete work themselves. This is supported by the theories of Vygotsky. Hearing loss, in itself, is not a learning disability, as with the right support children make good progress.

Lip-reading is challenging and tiring. Parents and teachers should be aware and make allowances for this. It also poses problems, as it is not precise. Only 30–40% of what is said can be lip-read. Therefore, the lip-reader is required to make intelligent guesses based on all other clues noted. Children need reminding that everybody mishears at times. Deaf and hard of hearing people tend to take responsibility if they make mistakes! This can be explained to some extent by looking at the McGurk effect. This is when lip movements do not match what you hear – so is confusing. This will be the same for hearing children too. This can be a problem for online presentations, as sound and picture are often not well synchronised.

9   Lip-Reading Benefits

Learning to lip-read takes skill and effort and can be exhausting, but enables people to understand, appreciate and interact with others in the world around them. This is worth the effort and with support and deaf awareness of others, it can enable learners to be happy, successful, confident members of society fulfilling their potential and making valuable contributions.

10   Review: The Last Word

To be a good conversationalist involves not only speaking but listening. People with hearing loss are usually exceptional listeners. This may sound like a contradiction in terms, *but* they must concentrate, pay attention to detail and use every clue they can to follow a conversation. A big problem is the delay between hearing/following what is said and the brain processing it. This means it is harder to take part in conversation because much energy is needed to follow what others are saying! The results of this affect perception of the person with hearing loss. They are frequently noticeably quiet! Sometimes it is thought they are, stupid, rude, aloof or worse.

A person with hearing loss had this on their school report: "Is very dreamy and always copying the other children's work!" Why? Being profoundly deaf, this child had no idea what was required. Fortunately, intervention was sought, and the person is now a graduate. One only has to look around to find successful role models in all walks of life. One example is a deaf person given support throughout their secondary/tertiary education. This, together with dedication and determination means they have now become a highly respected musician. They not only teach music but work as a creative director initiating and managing worldwide music and arts projects. We must enable children to acquire the necessary skills, equipment, assistive devices, teaching and learning to make the most of their talents.

Also, teachers must be aware of intermittent hearing loss with their students. Rosemary Sage (1995) tells the story of when first starting teaching in a social priority inner city school and announced in the staff room that she thought 75% of her class had hearing difficulty. Everyone was disbelieving, but she called in the audiologist to test the pupils, who confirmed this percentage exactly. How we heat, cool and ventilate buildings exacerbates upper respiratory problems and children have narrow Eustachian tubes (drains from the middle ear) which easily are blocked to interfere with hearing. We must never assume that our audiences hear us adequately, so should check that our voice projection and volume are sufficient. In a plural society with many accents and Standard English not a requirement to teach in schools since the 1970s (deemed elitist), this means that processing language is more problematic. In *Class Talk* (Sage, 2000), studies show that understanding the teacher and communicating with adults was the students' main problem with learning. Such issues cannot be ignored and *can* be addressed if aware of them.

To conclude, the importance of providing more measures for the prevention of hearing loss is an area that is being developed. Where hearing loss has occurred, if there is early intervention and provision of required specialist support, people with hearing loss can achieve success, lead a full life using their skills in whatever field this takes them, enhance their own self-esteem and confidence, thus enabling them to contribute to their communities. There is a need to raise deaf awareness not only in schools but in all areas of life. Hard of hearing and Deaf people can do everything that hearing people can do except hear. Overcoming hearing loss is a very worthy aim for those who work with students of all ages. These attitudes and appropriate specialist provision could benefit people with other disabilities.[2]

Notes

1 https://rnid.org.uk/about-us/research-and-policy/facts-and-figures/
2 The Mary Hare School website – News & Films reproduced with permission from the school.

References

Alegria, J., & Lechat, J. (2005). *Phonological processing in deaf children: When lip-reading cues are incongruent*. Laboratoire de Pschychologie Experimentale, Université Libre de Bruxelles.

Baker, L., Clements, K., Gravenstede, L., Grey, V., Moore, G., & Prieto, K. (2010). *Deafness and language ... delay or disorder?* Division of Psychology and Language Science, Deafworks.

Campbell, R., & Mohammed, T. (2015). Speechreading for information gathering. *BATOD Magazine*.

Clason, D. (2018). *Emotional effects of untreated hearing loss*. Healthy Hearing. https://www.healthyhearing.com/report/50526-emotional-effects-linked-to-untreated-hearing-loss

Collinson, S. (2017). *Early years language and development in deaf children – A best evidence scoping review synthesis of key findings*. NATSIP. https://www.ndcs.org.uk/media/2568/natsip_paper_synthesis_of_key_findings.pdf

CRIDE: Consortium for Research into Deaf Education. (2019). *CRIDE report on 2018/2019 survey on educational provision for deaf children*. http://www.batod.org.uk reports

Davis, E. P., & Sandman, C. A. (2010). The timing of prenatal exposure to maternal cortisol and psychosocial stress is associated with human infant cognitive development. *Child Development, 81*(1), 131–148. doi:10.1111/j.1467-8624.2009.01385.x

Dobie, R. A., & Van Hemel, S. (2004). Hearing loss in children. In R. A. Dobie & S. Van Hemel (Eds.), *Hearing loss: Determining eligibility for Social Security benefits* (pp. 180–223). National Academies Press.

Erickson, L. C., & Newman, R. S. (2017). Influences of background noise on infants and children. *Current Directions in Psychological Science, 26*(5), 451–457. https://doi.org/10.1177/0963721417709087

Fox, N. (2012). *Sound advice: Lip-reading*. https://sound-advice

Gale, P. (2012). Best options. *BATOD Magazine*.

Gale, P. (2020). Teaching units for deaf children keep closing. Statement to Tower Hamlets Council. *British Deaf News*. https://www.britishdeafnews.co.uk

Gravenstede, L. (2014). Phonological awareness and deaf children. *BATOD Magazine*.

Gravenstede, L., & Clements, K. (2015, July). Specific language impairment and deaf children. *Bulletin*, 13–15.

Harris, M., & Moreno, C. (2006). Speech reading and learning to read: A comparison of 8-year-old profoundly deaf children with good and poor reading ability. *Journal of Deaf Studies and Deaf Education, 11*(2), 189–201. https://doi.org/10.1093/deafed/enj021

Harwicke, K. (2018, September). The use of visual phonics in an oral setting. *BATOD Magazine*.

Hillairet de Boisferon, A., Hansin Tift, A., Minar, N., & Lewkowicz, D. (2016). Selective attention to a talker's mouth in infancy: Role of audiovisual temporal synchrony and linguistic experience. *Developmental Science, 20*(3), 1–12.

Landrigan, P. J., Kimmel, C. A., Correa, A., & Eskenazi, B. (2004). Children's health and the environment: Public health issues and challenges for risk assessment. *Environmental Health Perspectives, 112*(2), 257–265. doi:10.1289/ehp.6115

Levine, D., Strother-Garcia, K., Golinkoff, R., & Hirsh-Pasek, K. (2016). Language development in the first year of life. *Otology & Neurotology, 37*(2), e56–e62.

Lewkowicz, D., & Hansen-Tift, A. (2020). *A new study found infants watch parents' lips to watch language.* The Ontario Institute for Studies in Education, University of Toronto.

McCracken, W., & Pettitt, B. (2011). *Complex needs, complex challenges: A report on research into the experiences of families with deaf children with additional complex needs.* National Deaf Children's Society. https://www.ndcs.org.uk/media/1825/complex_needs_and_complex_challenges_report.pdf

Mehrabian, A. (1971). *Silent messages.* Wadsworth.

Musselman, C. (2000). How do children who can't hear learn to read an alphabetic script? A review of the literature on reading and deafness. *Journal of Deaf Studies and Deaf Education, 5*(1), 9–31. doi:10.1093/deafed/5.1.9

National Scientific Council on the Developing Child. (2014, January). *Excessive stress disrupts the architecture of the developing brain.* Working Paper 3. https://developingchild.harvard.edu/resources/wp3/

NATSIP. (n.d.). Website. www.ndcs.org.uk

NDCS. (2015, July). *Buddy up!* A guide to setting up a peer support scheme for deaf pupils. National Deaf Children's Society. https://www.ndcs.org.uk/documents-and-resources/buddy-up/

NDCS. (2015, December). *Supporting the achievement of deaf children in primary schools: For teachers of children with hearing impairment.* National Deaf Children's Society. https://www.cumbria.gov.uk/elibrary/Content/Internet/537/3953/6769/6772/41739151147.pdf?timestamp=43303234

NDCS. (2016, March). *Creating good listening conditions for learning in education.* National Deaf Children's Society. https://www.ndcs.org.uk/media/1698/creating_good_listening_conditions_headteachers_property-managers_academy-trusts_las_2016.pdf

NDCS. (2017). *Early years language and development in deaf children – A best evidence scoping review. Synthesis of key findings.* Retrieved November 23, 2011, from https://www.ndcs.org.uk/media/2568/natsip_paper_synthesis_of_key_findings.pdf

NDCS. (n.d.). *Developing language and communication in 0–2's.* National Deaf Children's Society. https://www.ndcs.org.uk/information-and-support/language-and-communication/supporting-your-childs-learning/developing-language-and-communication-in-0-2s/

Newcombe, R. (2012, October 2). *Lip reading for deaf children.* Kids Development. http://www.kidsdevelopment.co.uk/lip-reading-for-deaf-children.html

NHS. (n.d.). *Hearing loss treatment.* https://www.nhs.uk/conditions/hearing-loss/treatment/

Nittrouer, S., & Caldwell-Tarr, A. (2016). Language and literacy skills in children with cochlear implants: Past and present findings. In N. Young & K. Iler Kirk (Eds.), *Pediatric cochlear implantation* (pp. 177–197). Springer. DOI:10.1007/978-1-4939-2788-3_11

Richardson, K., & White, L. (2005). Spoken language and deaf learners. *Sen, 50*.

Sage, R. (1995). *Unacknowledged issues in classrooms* [Unpublished paper]. RCSSD, University of London.

Sage, R. (2000). *Class talk: Successful learning through effective communication*. Blooms-bury.

Scottish Sensory Centre. (2005, December). *Factors which help or hinder lip-reading*. http://www.ssc.education.ed.ac.uk/courses/deaf/ddeco5d.html

Strelnikov, K., Marx, M., & Fraysse, B. (2014). PET-imaging of brain plasticity after coch-lear implantation. *Hearing Research, 322*.

Tomalski, P. (2015). Developmental trajectory of audiovisual speech integration in early infancy. A review of studies using the McGurk paradigm. *Journal of Psychology of Language and Communication, 19*, 77–100.

Victory, J. (2020, June). *How hearing loss affects school performance*. Healthy Hearing. https://www.healthyhearing.com/report/50526-emotional-effects-linked-to-untreated-hearing-loss

Vygotsky, L. S. (1997). The instrumental methods in psychology (R. van de Veer, Trans.). In R. W. Rieber & J. Wollock (Eds.), *The collected works of L S Vygotsky*. Plenum Press. (Original work published 1924–1934)

WHO. (2016). *Childhood hearing loss: Act now, here's how!* World Health Organization. https://apps.who.int/iris/handle/10665/204507. Extract reproduced with permission

WHO. (2020, March 1). *Deafness and hearing loss*. World Health Organization. https://www.who.int/news-room/fact-sheets/detail/deafnessk-and-hearing-loss

Yeung, H., & Werker, J. (2013). Lip movements affect infants' audiovisual speech per-ception. *Psychological Science, 24*(5).

PART 4

Technology in Education

∴

Introduction to Part 4

Rosemary Sage and Riccarda Matteucci

When a Stanford University professor offered a 2011 free online *Artificial Intelligence* course, he was staggered that it attracted 160,000 students in 190 countries. From a rapid explosion of massive open online courses (MOOCS) to widespread use of mobile devices, supporting various *"blended learning"* models (part online & institution based), technology is creating new challenges and opportunities for education. It is changing learning dynamics, especially the relationship between teachers and students. As educators rethink learning experiences, it will be important to also reshape spaces to support this evolution. Among growing trends are use of laptops, tablets and other mobile devices. These are used to substitute for handouts, books, paper and pens. They are transforming how instruction and learning take place. Teachers are replacing rote-learning models and creating more personalized, self-directed, real experiences for students. There is multi-device synchronization, with software supporting collaboration and virtual conversations *within* and *beyond* classrooms to create digital content – animations and videos.

Chapter 15: The Rise and Rise of Digital Learning shows that traditional teaching is being questioned as to whether it is effective, efficient time use in a digital age. Instead, pedagogy must be re-designed for online and blended delivery rather than attempting to replicate existing face-to-face models.

Chapter 16: Technology & COVID-19: Remote Learning & Flipped Classes describes how technology has turned education upside down. In traditional mode, teachers *speak* and students *listen* but this brings problems. Not all students learn in the same way or at similar speed with inevitably many left behind. Technology can provide more personalised learning but needs teachers to be trained to manage this effectively.

Chapter 17: Maker Faire: Opportunities for Innovators – the Maker Faire organization holds events around the world. It is a convention of do it yourself enthusiasts, started by the *MAKE* magazine in 2006. Participants come from a wide variety of interests, such as robotics, 3D printing, computers, arts and crafts and the hacker culture. Maker Faire demonstrates their importance in life long education.

Chapter 18: E-learning But Not Always E-Quality suggests that students with problems processing and producing quantities of talk and text are more numerous than realised. On-line presentations do not adjust to needs as is possible

© KONINKLIJKE BRILL NV, LEIDEN, 2022 | DOI:10.1163/9789004506466_019

in face-to-face learning. Information must be delivered in small chunks with strategies to grasp understanding.

Chapter 19: A Blueprint for Learning presents recommendations for future effective practice. The largest challenge is coping with student diversity with improved communication the key. Rapid people movements and inequalities are some of the big tests of the 21st century.

1   **Reflection from This Part**

E-learning is in its infancy but has the possibility of providing more person-alised learning. Teachers need training and support for this, with updated knowledge of information processing and production and how this develops and breaks down, so that learning can best be facilitated. The book highlights *communicative issues* as a common theme in all 4 parts and these must take priority for training educators, so that they know how to produce competen-cies in students for enhanced productivity and citizenship. Nations taking communication and relations seriously implement holistic development. Experts reinforce this as the way to cope with life and cultivate resilience and flexibility to survive changes. *The Communication Opportunity Group Strategy* (Leicester University) is a blended learning model winning awards in New York for its innovative approach and success in developing all-round competencies. The future is bright if we focus on communication matters, as this is a sure way to achieve greater equality. In order to achieve this means a shift from teacher-controlled learning to a situation where students are given more choices to develop their initiative and self-management. This means that teacher training needs to redirect for a role as facilitator rather than transmitter of knowledge.

CHAPTER 15

The Rise and Rise of Digital Learning in Higher Education

Peter Chatterton

Abstract

This chapter recounts my journey as a digital innovator in UK higher education (HE) from the early 2000s to 2020. During this period, I was fortunate to have worked *at the coalface* on digital innovation and change projects with over 50 higher education institutions and with the major UK government educational agencies e.g. Jisc, HEA, QAA, HEFCE, HEFCW, LFHE and Becta. Most projects benefited from substantial Government investments with a primary purpose to bring teaching, learning and assessment and the overall student experience into the digital age.

The rationale for telling my story is that there are important lessons to be learnt which universities need to embrace when shaping their ongoing responses to COVID-19. The most important is that it is far from simple to embed digital learning throughout the university whilst maintaining high-quality teaching and a satisfying experience for students. Just before starting this chapter, BBC News was interviewing student freshers, asking them, 'What is it like to have online lectures' and the Guardian newspaper had a headline: 'UK university staff: How are online lectures going?' Both rather imply that it is a simple matter of using web-conferencing technologies to replicate the lecture experience online.

I will show how this approach invariably fails, particularly as traditional lecturing is increasingly being questioned as to whether it is an effective and efficient use of tutor time in our digital age. Instead, pedagogic approaches need to be re-designed for online and blended delivery rather than attempting to replicate existing face-to-face models. The dilemma for institutions is that this can be a time-consuming process with many potential barriers in the way e.g. QA processes and insufficient resources, support and expertise. Additionally, many academics find it difficult to visualise *alternative* online tutoring and are intimidated by the barriers and the skills needed as well as finding techies difficult to communicate with. Experience has shown that change management and coaching approaches need to be adopted to motivate, inspire and support academics in rethinking and visualising how they teach, communicate and engage with students.

On the positive side, many academics recount how quickly they overcame their digital fears and how their experiences forced them to go back to basics and radically rethink their teaching methods and now believe they are providing a much-improved student learning experience. Furthermore, a general perception exists that digital learning is the poor cousin of face-to-face learning. However, it is not as clear cut as this as digital learning has several advantages. For example, certain personality types find online engagement easier than in face-to-face scenarios.

Furthermore, higher degrees of regular and ongoing student engagement can be achieved online not only between students and tutors but also with external experts, employers and alumni, which can be valuable in supporting student project work and developing student employability. It also prepares students for a *'new-normal'* of virtual working and clever universities will set students working with employers on project assignments to help research and shape how new-normal working will develop in different sectors.

This chapter will draw out lessons learnt from the UK Government-driven digital modernisation programme for higher education to describe what excellence looks like for digital learning and what institutions need to do to embed high-quality approaches throughout all faculties. It will sum up with the proposition that academics should adopt *future-proofing* approaches to flexible and agile curriculum design. This will allow curricula to be delivered fully online or in blended approaches, dependent upon changing needs and demands of students and employers and unforeseen external factors such as another COVID-19. The chapter gives a brief history of digital learning 2000–20; the distraction of MOOCS; the COVID-19 game-changer; lessons learnt from the UK government investment in digital learning; online teaching excellence; what institutions need to do to support academics in digital learning and technology futures. It also briefly describes my experiences and lessons learnt in supporting large numbers of academics during the lockdown period in rapidly converting their courses for online delivery.

1 A Brief History of Digital Learning: 2000–2020

My story started when I was a consultant to Ford of Europe. The corporation recognised that the *half-life* of degrees was dropping, so they established a programme to treble the throughput of their key professional staff on master's courses in e.g. automotive engineering design, manufacture and management and MBA courses. Many of these master's courses had been co-designed between Ford and its university partners. However, they realised that they could not afford to remove such large numbers of staff from the workplace to attend on-campus. They asked me to work with their UK education partners to *re-engineer* courses into a blended learning format to allow more flexible learning e.g. in the workplace and at home.

Little did I realise at the time that this experience would help inform and shape my work in higher education for many years to come and was a good example of how employers can positively influence university teaching and learning. We adopted a three-fold approach:

– Development of interactive multimedia learning materials;
– Use of video-conferencing and
– Development of an online learning system called VALE (Virtual Automotive Learning Environment)

This set the scene for the emergence of VLEs (Virtual Learning Environments) in the sector. A particular anecdote of this time highlights the need to rethink pedagogy for the online world. At one university, I worked closely with one of the senior academics to redesign a module. Students were asked to undertake a project assignment whilst they were back in the workplace. We made the design such that the students would submit their assignments online in three stages and at each stage they would receive feedback from the tutor and their peers, resulting in ongoing online engagement.

Following marking, I asked the tutor his perspectives on the experience and the response was: 'The quality and quantity of the student work was much higher than in previous years, but you made my life hell'. There was a pause and he then said: 'You made me engage a lot more with students which resulted in a much improved learning experience for them, but I don't have the time available to be able to sustain this', and he concluded: 'I need to reduce my lecturing time to help me engage with students more. Lectures are probably a poor use of my time in this age of online knowledge and learning resources'. This anecdote illustrates how *assessment for learning* approaches (e.g. greater use of formative assessment leading to dialogue and action on feedback) can enhance student learning and work very efficiently online. My story continues with two major projects.

The first was the setting up of the (virtual) Automotive College, funded by the Department of Trade and Industry (DTI) in the form of a partnership between HE, FE and industry. This was designed to collaboratively design, develop and deliver education programmes that meet the needs of employers, thus overcoming the much-aired complaint of employers that HE and FE do not provide them with the graduates they want. The *learning service* was focused on company manufacturing improvement and commenced with a company diagnostic followed by the delivery of a customised course. Company staff were then mentored as they implemented their improvements and a *before and after* evaluation was performed using industry defined performance indicators. This was a follow-on to an earlier DTI project to bring Japanese manufacturing expertise to the UK and was a good example of how industry, HE and FE can collaborate effectively, though considerable attention had to be paid to managing the very different cultures between HE, FE and industry.

One role was co-ordinating the development of e-content, where one of the cultural issues I had to address was that FE staff developed considerably better e-content than the HE staff who were not keen on being shown up!

The second major project was the three-year HEA/JISC national E-learning Benchmarking and Pathfinder programmes (2005–2008), designed as a response to the HEFCE strategy for e-learning with the intent of building capacity for e-learning in UK HE/FE institutions. My role was one of two lead consultants in the benchmarking programme and one of several Critical Friends in the Pathfinder programme. The idea was for universities and colleges to establish where they were with e-learning (*the benchmarking phase*) and then to implement approaches for scaling up its adoption (*the pathfinder phase*). In total, 77 institutions took part in the benchmarking programme and five different e-learning benchmarking methodologies were adopted (ELTI, eMM, MIT90s, OBHE/ACU and Pick & Mix). When we started working with universities, most were suspicious that they were signed up to a competitive ranking initiative but in most cases, we were able to convince institutions to engage in the collaborative and improvement-focused initiative. I mention this sector initiative as an example of how institutions can adopt benchmarking methodologies to help scale up digital learning.

From 2008 onwards, a multitude of Government-funded themed innovation and change programmes were implemented in the HE/FE sectors, each lasting between two and five years. Themes included assessment and feedback, digital literacy, shared services, flexible learning, students as change agents, student Edtech innovators, work-based learning and employer engagement as well as more general themes such as Centres for Excellence in Teaching and Learning.

The educational agencies funded institutions to *digitally modernise* with awards of anything between £10,000 and £5million as well as providing project support in the form of Critical Friends (I took this role in many of these themed programmes). This was indeed halcyon days for institutions and the programmes led to considerable innovation and major step-changes in knowledge and good practices in digital learning. The agencies also encouraged a high degree of collaboration between institutions, facilitated by the Critical Friends, which resulted in significant sharing of good practices.

2   The Distraction of MOOCS

I remember the period when I heard from many digital learning colleagues in universities complaining that their VCs were demanding that their universities rapidly get on the MOOC bandwagon without any clear reasons why except as a response to over-hyping them in the media. MOOCS have largely failed to deliver their original promises for democratic mass access to higher education and have declined from their heyday with low retention and enrolments and a failure to expand into the less well-developed countries.

The underpinning commercial model for *open* courses was always suspect and today, a few key providers (e.g. Coursera & Future Learn) offer low-cost largish-scale online courses but do not typically use the term MOOC, which is appropriate as they are mostly neither *massive* nor *open*. The audience for such courses tends to be those interested in CPD and I often wonder whether the term MOOC should be renamed to *Massive Open Online Communities*, targeted at professional communities of interest.

3 The COVID-19 Game-Changer

In 2020, as COVID-19 reared its ugly head, I was asked to mentor academics as they rapidly attempt to convert their courses for online delivery. Most had no or minimal involvement with the digital modernisation programmes. In fact, I found there to be the same relatively low level of knowledge about digital learning as I had experienced in the sector 15 years ago. This indicates that the sector has largely failed to learn from the UK Government digital modernisation programmes. When asked about their first attempts at online delivery, there were horror stories of 3-hour web-conferencing lectures, using technologies such as Teams, Zoom and Blackboard Collaborate, made even worse by many students located overseas with low-spec technology set-ups.

These were clearly not one-offs. The digital services director reported that pre-COVID-19 the number of simultaneous users of their web-conferencing system was typically 100, which increased to 6,000 as tutors started their online lectures. Having polled colleagues in several universities, my experiences seem to be commonplace, with universities struggling to adapt teaching for online delivery.

However, academics and their support staff have all been highly motivated and energised to provide students with a positive online learning experience though they did not have the time to redesign their curricula with pedagogy fully appropriate for online delivery. Colleagues and I advised that the most effective enhancements achievable in short timescales should focus in the following four areas:
– Facilitate high degrees of regular communications, engagement and community building
– Balance synchronous with asynchronous learning approaches

– Adopt *Assessment for Learning* approaches
– Adopt DIY approaches to content creation in many media

These areas are explored in more depth later in this chapter and it is stressed that the above is not a framework for excellent online pedagogy (*more about this later*), but what can best be achieved in a short time-scale, given that most academics had minimal experience with online delivery and that access to professional support staff was spread fairly thinly.

By recounting my journey in HE, it is apparent that digital learning is not simple and the landscape for institutionally embedding it is considerably broader than the technologies themselves. New pedagogic models need to be developed appropriate for online delivery. Furthermore, all those who are familiar with working in universities know that you cannot easily instruct academics to do something new, particularly if they are not motivated, resourced and incentivised.

Change management programmes that are designed for academic cultures need to be adopted to support digital learning. The landscape for *digital change* therefore encompasses technology, pedagogy and change management and many institutions have failed to understand the need for fully addressing all three of these. This is also reflected in how Government agencies have funded and supported *modernisation* in higher education, largely through Jisc (*technology background*), HEA (*academic staff & curriculum background*), LFHE (*leadership & management*) and QAA (*quality assurance*), though many of these agencies have now merged.

4   Lessons from UK Government Investment in Digital Learning

I have drawn out 5 key lessons from my experiences working with universities on programmes of digital modernisation in teaching, learning and assessment.

4.1   *Too Much Innovation and Insufficient Scaling-Up*
My major criticism of the UK Government's digital modernisation programme was too much focus on continual innovation and insufficient drive to scale-up/ institutionally embed the innovations. Academic innovators generally have minimal interest, incentive or expertise in facilitating uptake of their innovations and once one innovation project was finished, they would typically publish a paper and go on to apply for funding for a new innovation project (we referred to them as the 'usual suspects'). In collusion with these academics are the professional support staff e.g. the e-learning experts. Their careers, interests and skills similarly relate to continually innovating rather than in supporting

reluctant academics to adopt new digital learning approaches. Furthermore, universities generally have minimal systems, processes and resources in place to take innovations in teaching and learning and attempt to ramp them up into widespread practice.

4.2   *Too Much Choice and Information for Academics*

A continuing challenge for academics is that digital learning technologies are growing in numbers, features and complexity e.g. VLES, e-portfolios, web-conferencing, Cloud-based tools, social networking, wikis, blogs, digital story-telling, lecture-recording, online assessments, mind and concept mapping, online polling and surveying, screen-recording, interactive multimedia content, virtual worlds, simulators, podcasting, assistive technologies and so on. Academics face a bewildering choice of what to use not only from institutionally supported technologies but also the many, often free to use, online tools e.g. Facebook, though use of these are not always with the blessing of the university. The advent of low-cost mobile devices has brought more chaos. It is no longer good enough to design online learning that works only on desktop and laptop computers. Also, it must also work on mobile devices which brings new complications in terms of design, accessibility and usability. Academics are also presented with a large array of pedagogic techniques and approaches e.g. flipped lectures, action-learning, constructivist learning, collaborative learning, inquiry-based learning, reflective learning, authentic learning, assessment for learning, social learning, ipsative feedback, peer assessments, role-play gaming, simulations and APEL (Accreditation of Prior Experiential Learning). All this choice has led to a vast online resource of articles, papers, guides, books, conference proceedings, toolkits and knowledge bases that is overwhelming to newcomers to the area. Some of the educational agencies have attempted to distil all this information and choice into guides, but academics new to the area frequently tell me it is all *too much of a good thing*.

4.3   *Lack of Recognition and Resourcing for Teaching and Learning*

As a rule, universities do not sufficiently incentivise academics to be innovative in teaching and learning. Progression paths are normally aligned to research outputs and impact. Furthermore, the time and effort required to convert courses to online format are considerable and this is not recognised to a sufficient level.

4.4   *Real Change Takes Time*

Most of the innovation project timespans were from one to three years, though the HEFCE-funded CETL programmes lasted five years. These periods sound long, but real change across an entire institution takes many years to bed in.

The HE sector could learn from the automotive sector where the Government (DTI) persisted over a ten-year period in funding and supporting manufacturing improvement programmes for vehicle manufacturers and their SME supply chain companies, with great success.

4.5   *A Poisoned Chalice for Managers Rising Their Career Ladders*

Probably one of the most important questions to ask is why have not most senior managers in universities made digital learning a strategic priority? First, it must be recognised that digital learning is highly complex. It is a lot more than about technology – teaching, learning and assessment models must be redesigned and there are major institutional barriers to scaling-up across the whole institution. Because of this complexity, many senior managers were at sea with it all and perceived digital learning as a poisoned chalice on their career ladders.

5   Online Teaching Excellence – Can It Be Measured?

The UK Government thinks it knows what teaching excellence looks like and in 2017, introduced the Teaching Excellence Framework (TEF) supposedly to rebalance the relationship between teaching and research and to help students make informed choices concerning teaching quality and graduate outcomes. A series of institutional-based metrics are used encompassing e.g. student satisfaction (linked to the National Student Survey), retention and graduate outcomes.

An institution's rating is aligned to the level of fees it can charge and this indicates the Government's core intention towards marketization of higher education with increasing competition between universities. The metrics, as with all rating systems, encourage gaming of the system and do not measure something as intangible as teaching excellence, instead relying on e.g. student views and graduate-level employment rates, which are more influenced by social class. To be fair, the TEF is under review but many remain pessimistic that it will incentivise universities to focus primarily on the needs of business and further erode a valuable collaborative culture between universities.

Earlier, I mentioned the complexities of digital learning and the associated technologies and I certainly believe it cannot be reduced to a series of metrics. However, it can be described in the form of *principles* which provide a direction of travel without being prescriptive. Based on my experiences with the UK Government's digital modernisation programme, I have created seven key principles for moving courses online – they are not pedagogic models, but they help to shape how pedagogic models can be made more effective online.

5.1   *Facilitate Regular Communications, Engagement and Community Building*

This is probably one of the most important areas to focus on for online learning, recognising that students will be feeling isolated and without the ability to easily form relationships. My advice to academics is to build in regular ongoing engagement with and between students, helping to build an online community. This should commence with pre-induction and induction. Most importantly, engagement should be built in to learning activities. Many pedagogic models lend themselves to high degrees of engagement if carefully adapted for online delivery e.g. group work, flipped lectures, peer assessments, assessment for learning approaches (see below), constructivist learning such as collaborative building of knowledge bases. I have found that as academics adopt these ideas, they begin to realise that online learning has its advantages e.g. they are not restricted by the *tyranny* of timetabling/room booking systems and students who struggle with face-to-face communication can find it easier in the online world.

5.2   *Engage Outsiders*

Engaging outsiders such as employers, charities, professional and sector bodies, alumni and experts can be highly effective in supporting digital learning, particularly as they can be located anywhere in the world. For example, employers can support group work by setting students real-world challenges to address or knowledge bases to construct, requiring students to develop their critical thinking, problem-solving and research skills. Other possibilities include interdisciplinary group work with employers e.g. focusing on new sectors such as Industry 4.0 and projects involving schools and FE colleges. The automotive sector has taken this to a new level with the annual *Formula Student* competition, led by the IMechE, where final year automotive engineering students undertake a year-long team-based project to design and build a racing car in competition with other universities worldwide. Alumni can also be co-opted e.g. as student mentors. Engaging with outsiders can provide students with highly motivating and authentic learning experiences which broadens perspectives and horizons and contributes towards their personal and professional development, and hence their employability.

5.3   *Balance Synchronous with Asynchronous Approaches*

In the early days of COVID-19, many academics turned to web-conferencing to replicate their lectures online but most soon came to realise that this is not a sustainable approach and therefore started to develop asynchronous approaches where students can study at their own pace and in their own time.

This is particularly advantageous where students are in different time zones and where their technology set-ups are not so suited to synchronous learning. Asynchronous learning can comprise a multitude of approaches, e.g. watching/reading learning materials, quizzes and polls, asynchronous discussions, assignments, group work, peer assessment, reflective learning, constructivist learning etc. and VLEs can provide pathways and scheduling for these activities. There is one issue here though – students and the media deem *contact time* with academics as an important indicator of the quality of courses and associate this with face-to-face contact time e.g. in lectures, tutorials, labs rather than with asynchronous online learning.

5.4   *Adopt 'Assessment for Learning' Approaches*

Assessment for learning approaches encourage greater use of formative assessment together with dialogue and action on feedback. This approach is important in modular-based courses where summative assessment marking and feedback is delivered right at the end of modules, giving minimal opportunity for students and tutors to engage with, plan actions and follow-up on the feedback. Greater use of formative assessment can help distribute academic time across the module rather than bunched up at module-end for summative assessments. It is likely that academics will spend more time engaging with students and this is where course/module leaders need to re-evaluate how best tutors allocate their time and ask questions such as: Should lecturing time be reduced? Do we need so many summative assessments (i.e. one for every module)?

5.5   *Adopt DIY Approaches to Many-Media Content Creation*

Many academics have resisted the idea of creating digital content themselves except, for example, textual documents and PowerPoint slides. I believe the two main reasons have been fears about the skills and expertise required together with a belief that they cannot provide materials of sufficient *quality*. There are also concerns about ownership of their content. Taking the *quality* issue first, I encountered many times the belief that any content created needs to be *professional/broadcast* quality, with some arguing that this needs to be developed by professional media production companies. This confuses stylistic/presentation aspects with *substance* i.e. core academic content. My belief is that student expectations are such that they are wanting engaging academic content rather than something that tries to replicate a Hollywood film experience. It is also a totally unsustainable approach from a cost perspective.

On a positive note, I have found that it is not that hard to help academics overcome their fears about DIY content creation. There are some useful technology tools now available that support DIY approaches and once mastered, academics typically have the confidence to continue. For instance, screen recording allows you to take a PowerPoint file and record an audio narration and the result can be saved as a video which can then be uploaded to a VLE or YouTube.

This is a simple way to enhance existing content and, in many ways, is preferable to lecture-recording as the tutor can focus more easily on the content. It can be further enhanced using PowerPoint's features such as animations. Many tutors have adopted this technique as part of a *flipped lecture* approach, where they require students to watch the video before the lecture timeslot and then take an online test. The tutor then uses the lecture timeslot in a highly interactive way to engage students with the content, using the results of the test to focus on areas where students did not perform well.

5.6   *Longitudinal Approaches to Academic, Personal & Professional Development*

Modular-based courses are common and provide students with choice to customise their courses towards their topic preferences. The reality today is that many courses are just a series of modules each with their own academic team and summative assessments and not always linked into an overall coherent whole. When I first started working with universities it came as a big surprise that on these types of modular courses, student progress and assessment and feedback were generally not tracked nor supported throughout the course. In fact, it seemed that students would take one module, do an assignment and at the end of the module get their marks and feedback by which time everyone had had enough. Students would not want to enter into discussions on the feedback, never mind sharing ideas on how they plan to respond to the feedback and the tutors were exhausted from having had all their marking bunched into a short space of time. The students then went on to the next module where the tutors had no access to the feedback given to students on the prior module and hence resulting in minimal support for student academic, personal and professional development throughout the course.

Many academics would like to bring back a focus on course-level outcomes and assessment to balance the focus being largely on module-level assessments. This would enable course-level assessment to incorporate student personal and professional development as well as academic development for example, in the shape of student employability criteria and graduate attributes. This would be supported in a variety of ways such as by personal tutors who ideally engage with individual students throughout their courses.

Student's longitudinal progression can be supported digitally in several ways. An increasingly popular approach is for students to use e-portfolios to document, plan, review, evidence and reflect on their learning and progress as well as engaging with tutors and others, including employers. Students can also use their e-portfolios to showcase and evidence their learning as well as articulating the skills and expertise they develop, which can all greatly enhance their employment prospects. Many students are now using different media e.g. capturing audio and video testimonials to contribute to their e-portfolios. Many sectors (e.g. health) have been using e-portfolios for some while, not only in learning programmes but also as part of continuing professional development.

5.7   *Future-Proof Curricula Design*

Universities must recognise that the world has become unpredictable with unforeseen events as well as changing student and employer demands that will increasingly shape how learning programmes will be delivered including 100% online and blended approaches. Curriculum design needs to be such that delivery methods can be quickly and efficiently switched to suit prevailing circumstances. This can be referred to as *future-proofing* course design for flexible an agile delivery.

6   What Institutions Need to Do to Support Digital Learning

Previous sections highlighted how UK institutions have largely failed to fully implement digital learning across the entire institution despite generous UK Government funding being widely available for digital modernisation. Based on the lessons learnt from this period, here are some recommendations for institutions to more rapidly scale-up digital learning:

6.1   *Recognise and Address the Barriers*

Institutions need to recognise and address the complex barriers to implementing digital learning institution-wide and most importantly of all to recognise that it is fraught with cultural, tribal, structural, pedagogic, management, technical, commercial and behavioural constraints.

6.2   *Local Devolution – More Stick Than Carrot*

In my experience VCs and PVCs are reluctant to put pressure at a local level (i.e. faculties, schools, departments) to implement digital learning, particularly in the Russell Group universities where the power balances are skewed more locally. In fact, when I tried to influence one university to require faculties and schools to embrace digital learning more fully into their strategies and plans, the vc responded: 'I don't want to do that – I want them to feel excited about digital learning'. A recipe for business as usual!

The optimum approach is to require Deans and Heads of Schools/Departments to fully embed digital learning into their teaching, learning and assessment strategies and plans as well as requiring them to specify and evaluate (not too prescriptive) performance indicators. vcs/pvcs should then hold them to account to these plans and performance indicators. Now that covid-19 has happened, senior institutional managers need to recognise that they probably can use more *stick* than *carrot,* though such approaches must recognise limits to academic workloads and the availability of appropriate resources and support.

6.3   *Blending Physical and Virtual Learning Spaces*
covid-19 means that it can no longer be assumed that it will be possible to cram a lecture theatre or seminar room with students, but technologies can now allow these types of learning spaces to be seamlessly linked to the virtual world. Lectures and seminars can be delivered simultaneously face-to-face with virtual attendees. This does require sophisticated (and not cheap) digital and audio-visual technologies, but it can be achieved with good learning space and technical design.

6.4   *Curriculum Design/Review Processes*
The optimum timing for redesign of pedagogy to incorporate digital learning is at curriculum design/review stages and this needs to be a lot more than a tick-box exercise. Course teams should be required to participate in a partnership relationship with internal *change consultants/coaches* with the aim of reviewing/analysing their course and then designing enhancements that support digital learning as well as embracing other key requirements of the teaching, learning and assessment strategy such as student employability, graduate attributes and employer engagement.

6.5   *External Examining*
External examining aims to provide informed and impartial perspectives on academic standards, assessment processes and programme design which can be particularly important for sharing good practices and innovations between institutions. However, in my admittedly limited experience as an external examiner, my input was always asked for too late in the process when the curriculum design was mostly complete. I would therefore advocate for external examining processes to commence early in the curriculum design/review stages so that examiner recommendations can realistically be incorporated.

6.6   *Appropriate Resourcing and Support for Change*

Too often, institutions have expected academics to embrace digital learning without appropriate resources, often leaving them to design enhancements in their spare time. The most important issue for academics is having time allocated to their workloads together with training and development as part of CPD and access to a variety of support including technical and pedagogic.

6.7   *Balance Innovating with Institutional Embedding*

Institutions need to recognise that digital innovations need to be treated separately from scaling-up/institutionally embedding key innovations and each requires different support people with different skills, incentives and motivations. Scaling-up requires skills related to change management and/or coaching.

6.8   *Think What Consistency Means for the Student Experience*

Time after time, student surveys come up with the demand for *consistency* in responses focused, for example on digital learning. At a practical level, this could relate to course resources such as reading lists and learning materials to be made available in a consistent way (with consistently good usability and accessibility) as well as consistency in asynchronous and synchronous ways of engaging with academics. There is the irony that those academics who have pioneered digital learning have sometimes unwittingly given rise to poor student feedback in the National Students Survey as they have raised student expectations for quality digital learning but their colleagues on other course modules may not be good digital practitioners, hence students feeling aggrieved. I have even heard from some academic innovators that they have been criticised by colleagues for showing up their own poor digital skills! A word of caution though – although *consistency* is often requested, it needs care in how it is interpreted. Many academics will argue that inconsistent academic approaches are a cornerstone of a higher education, reflecting different personalities, expertise and contexts and students should be able to adapt to different approaches. I shall not go into this more except to say that balance is needed!

6.9   *Academic Recognition for Digital Teaching and Learning*

An often-heard complaint amongst academics is that academic careers and recognition are linked to research outputs and, since the days of the REF, the impact of research. This does not provide a great incentive to put time and effort into digital teaching and learning which can be considered ironic, given that students are paying fees and are being encouraged to make judgements on which university to go to, based on the quality of teaching and learning.

The TEF might help to change this state of affairs, though it is more likely that COVID-19 will be a significant influencing factor.

6.10 *Find Ways to Understand & Meet Student Expectations, Needs & Demands*

Universities are facing a COVID-19 crisis in relation to student expectations, needs and satisfaction. Evaluating these has traditionally been approached using surveys. I have never been convinced that these are that effective, particularly as students tend to be *over-surveyed*. Instead, new and more creative and engaging approaches are needed which involve students in ongoing dialogue and feedback about their experiences and which encourages them in a partnership approach with academics to improve their experiences.

6.11 *Learn from Other Sectors*

I mentioned earlier my experiences helping to set up and run the UK (virtual) Automotive College. This was funded by the DTI as part of its long-term manufacturing improvement programmes for UK-based vehicle manufactures and SME supply chains, which proved highly successful in reenergising the sector to world-class status. It is my belief that the HE sector has much to learn from these automotive manufacturing improvement programmes. For instance, lean approaches to manufacturing improvement could be adapted to rethink and re-design processes and systems associated with the student life-cycle journey right from the stage students first enquire about courses, through pre-induction and induction to learning and assessment, progression, engagement with employers, graduation and becoming an alumni. As well as redesigning processes and structures to be integrated and student-centric, underlying IT systems would also be redesigned to the *19times* approaches to data management, thereby paving the way to much enhanced data/learner analytics. The same lean thinking can also be applied to the curriculum design/review/accreditation life-cycle where integrated IT systems will help to shorten course development times.

7 Technology Futures

Let me qualify straightaway that I have always been wary of *futurists* who confidently predict technology outlooks. It is a mug's game, where too often a simplistic view is taken that does not embrace broader influences which shape how technologies are adopted such as human, behavioural and cultural factors, organisational constraints and so on. I hope I have been able to show in this chapter how such factors have constrained the widespread uptake of digital learning in universities, despite large amounts of Government funding and support in the UK and I suspect this will not change in the future. I will use this experience to put forward some viewpoints on technology futures.

7.1   *University IT Departments*

Drive and support for digital learning in universities has largely been provided by departments external to IT departments and named, for example, e-learning, blended learning, technology-enhanced learning, educational development units. Within such departments, a mixture of skills, backgrounds and expertise typically exits, including academic, technical, audio-visual and pedagogic expertise. To some, it is surprising that IT departments have not driven the digital learning agenda, however there are many reasons for this which relate to the background, education and attributes of IT people and the complexities of implementing digital learning. However, all this must change. As digital learning scales-up, with increasing dependency on data and IT infrastructure and increasing demand for real-time data to support learner analytics, universities will need to make IT departments more prominent in digital learning. This, however, presents many problems for established universities as their IT systems have largely grown in a piecemeal fashion e.g. student records systems, virtual learning environments, e-portfolios, making a unifying data environment difficult to achieve. Furthermore, IT people are not known for their communication, influencing and change management skills, particularly when dealing with what they perceive as alien cultures (e.g. academic!). This also needs to change.

7.2   *Big Data and Analytics*

The sector has been exploring data and learner analytics for a few years but is still in its infancy despite what some would like to promote. It does, however, have the potential to help academics to better understand how students are engaging with their courses and where there are problems. If used correctly and ethically this can help academics to better personalise their courses to individual students, particularly where student numbers are growing, as well as helping them to continually enhance their courses. However, there are preconceptions that it is all about feeding bucket-loads of data into a computer, turning the handle, and then receiving instant recommendations back. In my experience what data/learner analytics delivers requires to be carefully considered, contextualised and interpreted (including the quality of the data) before jumping to conclusions.

7.3 *Virtual Worlds*

Many would view virtual world technology as an example of a technology-led and over-hyped solution looking for a learning application. As an example of this, I remember working at one university which had made significant progress with scaling up blended learning but someone in the computer science department convinced the VC to spend a very large sum on a Second Life virtual world of the university. After a few months it was quietly forgotten due largely to it serving no real purpose and was an example of *style over substance*. Worse still, it diverted funds, effort and resources away from the real task of encouraging academics to adopt digital learning. Having said that, there are a number of specialist learning uses for virtual world technology for example working as simulators in sectors which have hazardous and unsafe environments, helping learners to experience these worlds without doing harm e.g. nuclear plant, aircraft simulators. It can be expensive to develop virtual world learning and it certainly does not fall into the academic DIY approach, so its future is largely dependent upon commercial models being established to provide the necessary development funding.

7.4 *Artificial Intelligence and Robotics*

I often get asked about exciting futuristic technologies such as artificial intelligence and robotics and my responses are usually rather pragmatic. I sometimes refer to these discussions as *displacement* behaviour where people do not want to face up to using technology in the present and find it easier to debate hypothetical futures which do not require them to do anything in the present. My pragmatic approach tends to be: fix your digital learning now and get your pedagogic approaches right before thinking you can influence the development of AI and robotics. Having said that, there are considerable opportunities in this area but the message from this chapter is that you cannot rely on the geeks alone to develop these technologies.

7.5 *When Bad Things Happen with IT*

As digital learning scales-up, there will be increasing dependency on the reliability and resilience of IT systems and unfortunately, cybersecurity threats will also increase e.g. hacking from students and outsiders and potential threats from states where censorship counts for far more than open and free speech. Users will expect systems to operate fully 100% of the time and IT departments will need to meet this need (an 'it just works' approach) which will most likely require increased resourcing to address digital threats, reliability and resilience and less emphasis on 'exciting' new innovative features.

7.6   *Student Cheating and Plagiarism in the Digital World*

I hear many anecdotes about student cheating and plagiarism such as students using essay mills, and I suspect it is generally rather downplayed in the sector. The more remote students are, the more difficult it is to know whether those taking online tests and/or submitting assignments are the ones who you think they are. Most universities use plagiarism-detection systems and I would argue that the approaches recommended earlier (e.g. high levels of student communications, engagement and community-building) support tutors in better *knowing* their students and hence able to detect unusually high-quality work. Important technologies that help in this area are biometric tools e.g. facial, voice and keystroke recognition, digital certificates, timestamp receipts and forensic analysis. To some extent student cheating could be overcome by requiring students to do a one-off visit to a centre to prove who they are and *register* their facial, voice and keystroke attributes and thereafter, whenever they submit assignments/take online tests, their attributes can be analysed and compared with those registered.

7.7   *New Entrant Universities and Big-Tech*

As I write this section, I am reading a Guardian newspaper article about the Dyson Institute of Engineering and Technology (opened in 2017) having been granted degree awarding powers, which is a sign that similar private sector initiatives will not be far away. There are also signs that big-tech companies such as Microsoft-owned LinkedIn will likely form partnerships with higher education institutes, most likely the big-brand ones. Such partnerships will have the opportunity to reinvent higher education for the digital world and will be largely unencumbered by the *baggage* of existing institutions i.e. bureaucracy, processes, ageing and fragmented IT systems, cultures etc. and will therefore be able to operate far more cost-effectively on a world-wide basis and probably change underlying business models.

8   Lessons Emerging from Lockdown Teaching

Over a 12-month period during lockdown, I supported large numbers of academics in rapidly converting their courses for online delivery. The majority were not digital innovators and most had minimal experience with online teaching. Programmes of support were provided to staff, customised for each university school and an evaluation of staff and student satisfaction was conducted. One of the key conclusions that emerged was that once tutors experience online delivery (that follows recommended good practice principles), then many make more informed and balanced judgements as to the pros and cons of digital learning. Significant numbers said that for certain types of learning it has distinct advantages over non-digital techniques with a general feeling that blended/hybrid approaches are the way forward. This is at variance with the general widespread impression that digital learning is only ever a *second best* option and not recognising the complexities of the landscape.

Another key conclusion that emerged is that an *all-in it together* approach is needed to drive and support change in academic practices, using a combination of strong and active leadership at a local level, external advice from experienced critical friends and pedagogic-driven digital learning advice from a mix of central and devolved professional support staff. Further details can be found in a paper (Specht et al., 2021) which describes a specific case study for the School of Media and Communications at a large post-92 university. The school achieved high satisfaction ratings from both students and staff relating to the period of online learning. I believe the *carrot and stick* analogy is at work here: earlier in the chapter I described how many years of Government funding for digital modernisation programmes in UK higher education largely failed to have a sustained impact (the *carrot* approach) whereas lessons learnt so far from COVID-19 have shown that the *stick* approach (i.e. tutors have had to engage with it) *can* have a much greater impact and most importantly, *can* develop belief in digital learning techniques in both staff and students. Having said that, it must be remembered that the transition to online learning over the lockdown period has been rapid and that it will take periods of reflection and curriculum review/development for pedagogic-driven best practices to be implemented across the board with more consistent approaches that students demand.

9   Review: To Conclude My Story

The media's simplistic view of digital learning, reflected in references to *online lectures*, underplays the complexities that universities face in implementing digital learning across the board. Not only do pedagogic models need to be redesigned to suit online and blended approaches and to cope with unpredictable futures, but institutions need to address deep-rooted cultural, structural, technical, management, commercial and behavioural factors that constrain institutionally embedding of digital learning. One can argue that COVID-19 has achieved more for digital learning than the UK Government's digital modernisation programme and certainly a lot more than the Government's TEF initiative. As with many ranking systems, the TEF focuses on simplistic metrics (which are not measures of teaching excellence), thereby encouraging gaming of the system and resulting in many unintended consequences, although I would argue these are thoroughly predictable.

COVID-19 has therefore had a positive influence on the scaling-up of digital learning and the development of belief in it amongst some (but not all) academics and students. However, it has happened too quickly for academics to fully redesign their courses with *future-proof* pedagogies suitable for fully online or blended learning approaches. There has been much goodwill from students who recognise the predicament universities have faced in the COVID-19 period, however this will not be sustained, and student expectations will escalate, particularly if course fees rise.

Many will still not be convinced about the full efficacy and value-for-money of digital learning although, if well-designed, it can go a long way to meet these criteria but not with the full rich social and cultural benefits of a campus experience. Universities will therefore need to find ways of engaging and communicating with students in more of a partnership approach to shape what the future student-tutor experiences will look like i.e. the *new-normal* of HE life.

Reference

Specht, D., Chatterton, P., Hartley, P., & Saunders, G. (2021). Developing belief in online teaching: Efficacy and digital transformation. *Journal of Perspectives in Applied Academic Practice*, 9(2), 68–76. https://doi.org/10.14297/jpaap.v9i2.486

CHAPTER 16

Technology and COVID-19

Remote Learning and Flipped Classes to Maintain Live Education

Riccarda Matteucci

Abstract

At the beginning of 2020, students and educators were catapulted into a worldwide experiment that no stakeholders had expected in terms of contents, lessons and assignments. Suddenly, these were located on-line overnight, but teachers worldwide were not properly trained to use new media effectively. There have been attempts to present innovative education, using technology to create and involve interest and render the teaching-learning process more appealing for students. An example is Flipped Classrooms (FC) that reverses traditional lecturing, because students learn content before class through readings and pre-recorded videos, freeing lectures for hands-on activities and discussion. There is a dearth of literature in education addressing flipped classrooms. This chapter discusses a student-centred framework for implementing this method. However, there has been scepticism and doubt about effectiveness of results. Remote Learning (RL), or a hybrid of this, is here and bound to stay. We are facing an extraordinary revolution humankind has ever encountered in term of education.

• • •

Don't let a good crisis go to waste.
WINSTON CHURCHILL

• •
  •

1 Introduction

As a result of the Coronavirus pandemic, people around the world are confined to homes with no clear idea of when life will shift to a new normal. While educators continue to adapt to conducting school during COVID-19, they are required to perform in different ways as to how they may best serve students, especially those who are most in needs.

Teachers have had to cope with the issue of RL and equity within an emergency context. Therefore, the main issue has not been concern for online learning, but more about what it means, from the point of view of equity, for children not having digital devices in their homes, while not physically attending school. Therefore, the COVID-19 crisis poses the question of how to engage educators to think about the best practices to satisfy the future needs of all learners.

Some argue that it is a cliché to talk about leveraging a crisis for change, while others claim human beings generally need a sense of urgency to create a momentum for altering practice. In his article that appeared on *Getting Smart Platform* June 12, 2020, Hiller A. Spires tends to belong to the second group. The COVID-19 needs to be seen as an opportunity, rather than a crisis, and this should be viewed as the case to change learning to meet needs of a 3rd millennium education.

The emergency has helped remove the doubt, if there was ever any, that we are globally interconnected and has highlighted that fact that key in educating our students is enabling them to understand this interconnection. They may navigate demographic and cultural lines of difference to leverage expertise and collaborate globally to improve the lifestyles of everyone. What we are experiencing at all this point of intersection shows clearly the kind of complexity we should be preparing the students to face.

This crisis is a clear lesson that the world will become progressively more problematic and complex rather than less. A contribution towards securing our future would be to involve students in more problem-solving skills and activities that address our real-world dilemmas. Schooling must focus on problem finding and solving, especially within ambiguous contexts.

2   Schooling in the Pandemic

When students and teachers returned to school in 2021 the general situation was not more promising than the year before. During the time of RL students should have acquired more independence and power: they were given more freedom in organising their schedules, deadlines and establishing their own learning pattern and final results. Whether in-person, hybrid or a 100% on line experiences, students need to find available something different than they have done in the past. Their learning experiences must be deeper, more personalised and more connected, to extend knowledge and skills. In this sense, the teacher role will shift from "sage on stage" to a "facilitator of learning experiences".

In his article "The 12 Shifts for Student-Centered Hybrid Environments" (July 22, 2020) in *Getting Smart Platform,* Kyle Wagner asserts that this transformation will be possible only if teachers make *12 key shifts*. He is author and founder/lead trainer of Transform Educational Consulting who thinks schools must create more social, emotional and globally aware citizens through project-based learning. The *12 Shifts* examined are the results of conversations and perceptions from worldwide practitioners (mentioned below) who have placed deep, student-centred project-based learning experiences at the core of their work. They have not just conformed to a certain education climate but increased and developed it. The following section summarises these ideas with the teachers' notes.

Shift 1 Learning Design: Teacher-Designed → Co-Designed and Curated
- Begin each learning journey by asking students what they want to know
- Organise content around topics rather than by standard criteria
- Provide choice in how students fulfil learning objectives (by Linda Amici)

Linda is a 5th grade teacher who enables 10-year-old students and above to produce a co-created and co-designed classrooms where they choose what they work on, who with and how they carry out tasks. In one of their projects, students were formally dressed, standing next to re-constructed models of ancient civilisations and had to explain, to an adult audience, why those cultures declined, fell and in some cases disappeared. The audience appreciated the pupils' performance full of documented details and exposed in a very clear way.

Shift 2 Learning Process: Led by Content → Led by Inquiry
- Have a plan, but do not be wedded to it
- Organise learning around topics and themes rather than subject-specific content
- Hold class meetings that give students a say in decision-making (by Rosie Westall)

As an early-years educator, at the Hong Kong Steiner Waldorf School, Rosie believes that 2020–21 scheduling will be a nightmare if learning is organised around content minutia. Her "democratic" classrooms start by discovering what topics her students are interested in, with objectives and curriculum organised around these. For example, in a "Future World" project, students imagined what creation will be like in 2025, building futuristic robots, renewable energy models, fake eye scanners etc. Rosie says her job is to build *trust* to spark joy that cannot be replicated. Only when this happens, teachers can sit back, listen and watch youngsters astound us.

> **Shift 3 Content/Skill Acquisition:** Isolated Content → Connected-Interdisciplinary
> – Sit down with colleagues outside your subject areas
> – Discover where content overlaps and which topics arouse common interest
> – Develop long-term projects and problem-based scenarios requiring integrated content to solve (by Loni Berqvis)

Loni believes that students are best served by planning interdisciplinary experiences running across subjects, disciplines and areas of expertise. This method has been widely applied in many European schools and in Italy; examples are Scuola I.I.S., C. Rosatelli in Rieti and Saverio Nitti in Rome (Sage & Matteucci, 2019, chapter 5).

> **Shift 4 Motivation:** Working for a Grade → Working to Solve Problems
> – Identify problems existing outside school
> – Identify academic content needed to solve them
> – Work with students to co-create rubrics for evaluation (by Mark Shulman)

Mark, an 8th grade Mathematics teacher, says we need different ways to motivate students in the years to follow. They need to partner with real business to help them solve problems. When seeing that work is not only to please teachers but for a larger cause and that people outside school are relying on them to achieve the planned results, this produces positive pressure to perform. Due to COVID-19, in the USA many schools/colleges abandoned grades in the spring quarter and shifted to work portfolios for admission to further levels of learning. In the education terminology, rubric means a scoring guide to evaluate quality of student's constructed responses. It is an assessment tool that indicates achievement criteria across components of any student work, written, oral and visual and there are 2 rubric types: holistic and analytical.

Shift 5 Student Work: Worksheets: Test-Based → Real Product/Services
- Be flexible with deadlines
- Establish community partners to support process
- Make time for continual reflection
- Introduce academic vocabulary (by Brett Carrier)

To make the shift to real world products/services, Brett, an English teacher, worked in an integrated team project at Park Maitland School, Florida, to build subject-specific content around a project needs. Brett designed the menu, food, logo and concept for a delivery food-truck to serve the community. The Math teacher advised on budgets and projected profits and losses; the design teacher provided 3D rendering and colour production and coordination. The team facilitated a business plan and product pitch. This shows how students developed skills impossible to obtain through worksheets and tests.

Shift 6 Inquiry: Teacher Questions → Student Questions
- Take a maker mind-set to learning and avoid perfectionism
- Transform a 'fixed classroom' into a flexible learning space
- Make inquiry part of a regular routine
- Display not only final products but work in progress (by Mark Bennet)

Mark suggests what the next uncertain school year will look like: "learning builds organically, with student questions driving the process" as in a constructivist approach. Being a makerspace teacher and consultant, he is an expert on this approach and uses it for projects with students. An example is a Renaissance project, on how to re-enact jousting battles or rebuild a printing press. In his "constructivist student-centred classroom" as he likes to define his working space, it is possible to touch things and neither students nor objects are hidden behind a glass.

Shift 7 Student Reflection: Value the Products → Value the Process
- Never throw away students' first drafts
- Provide quality feedback using simple protocols for students
- Celebrate the journey and failure as much as success
- Make the learning process highly visible (by Alfie Cheung)

Alfie is a Design Specialist and Project Manager at PolyU University, Hong Kong and writable classroom surfaces are covered by student works: post-its, notes, card clips, sketches, etc. Leaving tracks during a course helps students to keep in mind the whole process developed during the journey.

Shift 8 Task Completion: Independent Collaborative
- Balance student groups for readiness levels, affinity mapping, ability and skills
- Use structured processes and formative assessments (process journals) to monitor
- Use small group activities to establish structures and norms for collaboration in blended classes (by Kristin Damburger)

Kristin is a Learning Coach at the International School, Nido de Aguilas in Santiago, Chile. She says that if we want to create global socially and emotionally aware citizens, learning must be collaborative. The best way to obtain this is through projects. Students need to be accountable not only for their own work but also for that of their peers and group. "To experience success, students must identify their strength, divide work, resolve differences and pull their weight". Educational Robotics has this philosophy and practice (Sage & Matteucci, 2019, pp. 8–86).

Shift 9 Audience for Work: Teacher → Authentic, Public Audience
- Exhibit all work not just the best
- Involve students in deciding how work will be shared
- Partner with real business and professionals to serve as mentors, adjudicators or interviewers (by Matt Neylon)

Matt is a teacher of Visual and Performing Arts, at Mount Vernon School. He says low-quality work is the result of 3 missing elements: "a public audience, multiple feedback and student chances to ship work constantly". During RL, Mark worked directly with students, like many teachers worldwide. However, he added something more: he curated and exhibited student work in virtual museums for a public audience that showcased art pieces to integrated dance performances. Furthermore, students had opportunity to share work with peers, teachers and experts. He proved that when students ship their work regularly, they raise its quality.

Shift 10 Management/Evaluation: Progress Monitored by Teacher → Students, Peers, Experts
- Create stations and establish norms area for free working times
- Set up a small conference area for teachers and peer-led lessons
- Establish routines for continual work planning and reflection (by Keri Aspegren)

Keri applies a Montessori approach, using work-flow principles with students. They keep a log of work, reflecting on progress made, establishing goals and noting lessons from the teacher. Students monitor progress, organise meetings and conferences with other teachers and peers. The class 'runs itself', Keri says, with no teacher desk and events posted with materials for each lesson, normally shared with more than 25 teachers.

Shift 11 Discussion/Learning Experience: Teacher-Led → Facilitated/Socratic
- Build intrinsic motivation in kids to learn by tapping into what they care about
- Celebrate and discuss the process of great work as much you do the product
- Discuss projects as a way to transform lives, not just to deliver content (by Luna Ray)

A teacher of at-risk youth and former High Tech High Educator, Luna says to stop meeting standards the school has for you and meet those students have for you. Learning from mistakes, she begins project work with a Socratic discussion around questions and topics that excite her students' interests. The Socratic method is a form of cooperative argumentative dialogue between individuals, based on asking questions to stimulate critical thinking and to draw out ideas and underlying presuppositions.

Shift 12 Learning Delivery: School-Based → Community-Connected
- Develop relationship with nearby businesses
- Build maps of potential community partners and problems to solve
- Invite the community into classrooms to co-create with students (by Jill Clayton)

Jill works with students as young as 10 years. She connects and partners them with community members, considered co-teachers. She tries to solve complex problems, working with engineers, architects, urban planners, etc. Instead of limiting projects to school, she considers students as budding anthropologists, historians, citizen scientists and uses their ingenuity to solve problem.

Kyle Wagner is aware that *the 12 shifts* to student-centred learning cannot be made operative and profitable overnight. The same is the case for online learning as strategies require time, support and constant reflection to be effective.

Comment: It should not take a global pandemic for educators to re-think how we teach and learn. In 2020, we learned that the process can happen anytime and anywhere. Furthermore, learning is not seen confined to a physical place like school building, but rather as a mind-set that allows for constant repetition, refining and adaptation.

As educators we must provide the appropriate landscape. Let us hope the coronavirus is soon contained, if not, we know how to adapt and develop with other colleagues, students and stakeholders. Education will be seen less as a set of standards and objectives, but a gateway to better understand the world we live in. Teachers must help youngsters to feel comfortable with uncertainty and connect their learning. Kyle suggests that only by continually modelling for students how learning connects, they will develop the ability to see the whole picture.

Students must be free to develop their own learning pathways, address issues, make decisions and choose tasks more suitable for their abilities. We need to listen carefully to what students are interested in, provide provocative searching questions and activities to arouse curiosity and then let them take learning where it naturally leads. Therefore, the goal of each project chosen after an agreed topic is not to receive the highest mark, but to create meaningful impact. Learning, in this way, breaks routine and creates a risk-free environment that is both iterative and adaptive. Students are agile to transfer the mind-sets they gain through these experiences to new situations and scenarios.

All learning is social and sharable and educators must create an environment where anyone can be a teacher. We need to make classes more democratic, organising regular circle-time scheme meetings to discuss topic, make and share decisions. These are starting points to make changes to satisfy 21st century needs. In so doing, learners are given daily opportunity to share work with peers, teachers and a public audience. They become more agile and adaptable, improving their work and performances from each successive conversation. This is happening in Japan and many other nations where routines allow regular feedback and reflection.

3   Flipped Classrooms (FC)

In 1991–92, I attended a Human Communication course, at the Royal Central School of Speech and Drama, University of London. I consider this a turning point for my teaching career. The course enhanced my capability to communicate, because part of it included video presentations, observing speaker voice dynamics and body language during a performance. After the first two videos, I felt sorry for my students, who had to bear poor outputs and performances! Watching myself on screen helped correct mistakes. Rarely do educators reflect on what students think and take back after attending lessons or conferences. At the time, I was teaching at the University of Cambridge in a Faculty of Linguistics. How does this fit into flipped classroom approach, you may ask? It does, indeed, because I understood how important performance is and how beneficial is the use of technical aids in class. From experience, I advise a communication course should be compulsory for teachers, to enable them to engage and enthuse students and audiences.

From 2010–14, I regularly visited Africa, near Addis-Ababa, to teach in impoverished, scattered villages. I realised that technology could be the main tool to raise the education level there and in similar countries. To reach students in remote villages, teachers could use technology to record and deliver lessons for the benefit of youngsters unable to attend school. Most villages have a central building, occupied mainly by women taught literacy, cooking, sewing, weaving, hairdressing and other arts in order to make a living. These sites have electricity, Internet, telephones and screens and school buildings are normally nearby.

During this time, I involved Italian schools with case studies to prove how a FC approach could be used for them and African partners. In February 2020, in a Rieti school, where I worked for Robotic Education, I discussed this project with teachers and students. We agreed to film two lessons of 15/20-minutes. One held by an English teacher, who would have presented a Shakespearean sonnet, and the other by a Math's teacher on Geometry. Both lessons would have been posted on school web-platforms and students have the access to watch them. At the end of lessons, exercises were given and students had to hand them in, in class, the following day. Finally, I could make my dreams come true and demonstrate the importance of being filmed and rewind it in order to correct the mistakes or make any kind of necessary changes. With this approach, students can review content as many times as necessary for understanding and correcting inaccuracy. The agreed presentation date was March 9, 2020 just when the Flipped Classroom approach was adopted in Italian schools, due to the shutdown, and soon after worldwide all education system faced the same experience. Very quickly teachers had to learn it, almost overnight, in order to keep communication alive with their students.

Sharing this project with a highly professional psychologist, she said that never as during the pandemic she received calls and make Skype conferences with teachers who were suffering of panic attacks, because of fear of a bad performance while their lessons were recorded.

4   The Pros and Cons of Flipped Classrooms

The FC approach began is fairly new in teaching. Presented in the early years of the 21st century, it turns conventional methodology upside down. In traditional methods, teachers spoke and students listened. As we know, there are problems with this teaching mode: not all students learn at the same speed and in a similar way, with some left behind. Some learn by listening, others process better from visual input and all by actively implementing knowledge and sharing experiences. Teachers try their best to keep the class at the same level, but increasingly diverse students make this impossible. FC solves some issues and enables more personal learning. Teachers make videos on subject content to show on line to students before face-to-face lessons and in class deliver activities to apply content, check knowledge and progress. Pupils can review videos to understand content at any time, during *their time*, and return to class with questions needed to discuss and cover the subject with the teacher and peers. Keeping up with the class is no longer an issue, with initial independent learning. Instead of learning only by listening, students use class time to apply knowledge practically, with their teacher's support. This approach has more *pros* than *cons*:

– Recorded lectures can be viewed anytime and anywhere using digital devices to help students, missing school, to catch up with the rest of their class;
– FC aids transparency, as parents can access lessons, websites or blogs, that equip them with knowledge for helping their children;
– Teachers must trust that students have viewed lessons/lectures and prepared tasks. As FC places high accountability on students, a risk of poor preparation is always present;
– FC does not prepare students for the UK Standard Assessment Tests or similar used by other nations. Teachers must spend extra time preparing students for these;
– Lecturing without audiences is impersonal. Teachers may be unable to modify information to suit all audiences, traditionally done by observing students. Pauses, emphasis on key points and voice modulation may be less effective on pre-recordings. It is also more complex to receive and address questions. In cases when recorded time is more than 15/20 minutes, information is unlikely to engage audiences. This must be presented in short, highly-focused segments, with activities at the end.

The FC model has made a difference worldwide. Although it has disadvantages, it has proved effective under circumstances like the Coronavirus. Teachers have been free to decide with students and colleagues which classes to flip, thus delivering content in the most optimal method to assist learning. During the pandemic it has been the main method to keep the teaching-learning process alive.

5   COVID-19 and Future Education

When having babies, you are told that days are long but years are short. It is hard to believe that more than a year has passed since schools shutdown for COVID-19. We know little about how the future will look like and everyone is trying to make the educational system function for stakeholders. Distance learning is a difficult change that continues to improve, thanks to dedicated staff who most of the time go above and beyond their duty. In her article that appeared in the *Getting Smart Platform*, 'Sticky Buns and Distance Learning' Sara McKennon (June 7, 2020) questioned how can we support new learning experiences and ensure equity and safety to students gaining positive learning at home. In the same platform, Tom Vander Ark (June 1, 2020b) had brilliantly advised that schools and system leaders had a few months to make important decisions about the future of schools, that he summarised as:

– How to blend digital content into the core,
– Link it to an updated plan for remote learning,
– Plan for super hygiene and distancing onsite,
– Starting/partnering with an online school.

In what is likely to be most challenging ever, 2020–2021 academic year has clarified that education is a team-collaboration. Flexibility around common tools, resources and teaching strategies are critical to meet dynamic conditions and student needs. Vander Ark believes 3 innovation opportunities focus on success skills:

– *Thriving humans*
   Students return to school, with different needs from varying circumstances, eager to reconnect with teachers and friends. This is an opportunity to help them thrive by focusing on social and emotional wellbeing. They need to learn self awareness and self-management to build positive, productive relationships and make proper decisions. Team working and using educational robots will help them to achieve these important skills (Sage & Matteucci, 2019, pp.78–86). Students want to be seen, heard and valued, so consider social and emotional learning (SEL) as central to school culture and educational experiences. Vander Ark thinks that secondary schools should focus on SEL, adopting advisory periods and updating their approach to disciplines methods to redirect behaviour productively.

– *Meeting learners where they are*
   Learners come back from RL all over the place, some ahead but most behind. Meet students where they are and set goals for progress instead of pushing them to the next grade. Competency-based learning reconnects

learners, diagnosing learning levels and creating performance groups. It gives authentic evidence of learning and teachers will need to consider new forms of proof to help students progress or graduate. An appropriate way is encouraging learners to assemble portfolios of evidence to chart progress through all learning stages to Practitioner Doctorate level (Sage, 2010).

– *Work that matters*
   School closures and testing breaks have produced an opportunity to promote work that matters to learners and their community. Community-connected project–based learning has proved effective in Italian schools, where this was already adopted through the Education Robotics Curriculum, with great results for students, teachers and community (Sage & Matteucci, 2019). Sustaining work that matters needs teachers to raise learners' curiosity with interesting driving questions and give them chances to co-construct a project that results in a product valued by the learners and the community.

Social and emotional, competency and project-based learning offer opportunities to connect with the real world. This creates valuable learning experiences and schools that are more humane and more community-connected.

6   What Will Be the New Post-Pandemic?

We do not need futurologists to predict COVID-19 disruption. New baselines for work, learning, healthcare and governance are being established. Vander Ark and other analysts suggest 10 new aspects post-pandemic:

– *Big Class of 2040*: a spike in birth rates will result in big cohorts in schools.
– *More remote work*: companies will continue home smart-working, reducing leased space or becoming completely virtual. Prices of expensive urban real estate will decrease, with developers reducing constructions.
– *More personalised competency-based learning*: nations have released guidelines to schools saying, 'figure it out', find alternatives for students, make judgments about competency and eliminate what you can. Schools will rely on flexible timetables, contents, goals, etc. Educators will have less sit and listen professional development and more flexible, personalised learning/training.
– *More community-connected project-based learning*: school closures showed learning can happen anywhere, connected to local problems are valuable example of this point (Sage & Matteucci, 2019, pp. 88–100).
– *A new frame of meaningful measures*: Vander Ark considers the pandemic the end of an era of standards-based reform and preoccupation with

grade-level proficiency as the only measures of progress and school quality. In the pre-pandemic era there was growing consensus about the importance of success abilities, like communication, self and social awareness, collaboration, resilience and mind-set. These aspects increased during this period and schools must help learners build a comprehensive profile and assemble a transcript to reflect a personal learning journey.

– *More home-based and hybrid learning*: the US, following home-learning, forecast half a million students will not return to class. School districts will support home-schoolers with hybrid learning centres, as in Bethel, Connecticut and Da Vinci. Parents will turn home-school into a micro-school. Networks, like Acton Academy and Prenda Schools, will continue their explosive growth.

– *Fewer expensive schools and colleges*: private colleges and schools will not reopen, as parents seek less expensive, flexible alternatives.

– *Continuity of learning*: by the end of 2021, institutions will deliver a blended curriculum, learning platform, personal or take-home devices and support for ubiquitous Wi-Fi. In the post-pandemic era, people will acknowledge that education is a public service, no matter where it happens.

– *Better safety net*: people worldwide have been suddenly out of work forcing state legislatures to improve social safety nets fast. This will not only address short-term challenges but improve long-term ability to find a secure dislocation. People need to understand we have a long, bumpy ride of surprises, not all positive.

– *New mutuality*: is the basic change as we recognise our new mutuality. Education should focus on helping youngsters find and make their unique society contribution.

Comment: Students and families experience differing practical complications of school/college re-entry, so an inclusive approach must engage them. Jonathan Flynn, Head of Family and Community Engagement, at Brooklyn LAB, says that involving communities of colour and low-income in problem articulation and solution design is an equitable path forward. Many educators say this approach builds a process within schools and enhances the legitimacy of reopening the planning process. Given home Wi-Fi and digital learning, when not physically attending schools because of uncertainty about a COVID-19 resurge, educators must prepare for staggered schedules, medical fragilities and a permanent online learning options for the years to come. Practically, this involves creating tailored programmes for vulnerable students less able to learn remotely. Schools should research competency-based education, because it activates student capacity and ownership. Personalised learning plans are needed for larger student numbers, allowing shifts in approaches to happen quickly.

7   Equity during Pandemic COVID-19

Educators face remote learning equity for those without digital devices in emergency contexts. The pandemic is a "lesson" showing growing world complexity. Students need problem-solving abilities to deal with dilemmas. Hiller Spires (June 12, 2020), in his article "Education in the Time of Crisis", which appeared in the Getting Smart Platform, discusses students without home Internet access. Teachers phoned or travelled to reach students at home, delivering lessons or just talking with them to maintain contact. Parking lots re-opened to use school Wi-Fi, providing hotspots on school buses in local communities. Educators tried new ways to customise teaching and learning for those in poverty, for second language learners and for those with learning differences and special needs. While technology has provided stopgaps, many students live in communities with no technology devices or Internet. Moreover, his study reports that emerging technology, like Low-Earth-Orbit (LEO) and Starlink Satellite Services provide Internet in remote areas of the State of Carolina but could not solve the access gap. Unless the system addresses digital devices for everyone, some students will be further behind peers in attainment than before COVID-19.

8   Inequities Are Ongoing and Amplified with Remote Learning

David Ross in his article (April 24, 2020b) "As Distance Learning Turns on, Students Increasingly Tune Out" describes his visionary teacher experience, preparing students for the current crisis by maximising existing resources. In August 2019, he began tracking students submitting work via Google Classroom, as opposed to those taking a paper route. The first four months revealed that 80% of homework was submitted by paper because students live in disadvantaged homes with 50% receiving language, emotional or academic support. Articles have reported the dismal levels of online participation nationally among learners. NPR, a radio programme, reported that 4 in 10 American teens have not done online learning since schools closed and *The New York Times* head-lined: "As Schools Move Online, Many Students Stay Logged Out". This situation is due to a lack of technology or Wi-Fi, inexperience with software or devices, the need to share tech devices with siblings and parents, the lack of a safe working place, ill-prepared teachers needing upskilling and to general contrariness. The message that nobody would lose the school year meant students did not worry about final exams.

Ross compared online participation levels to pre-coronavirus grades. In the first week of April, the overall completion rate was 41%. In the last month of school, there was 91% of completion through a combination of phone calls, texts, emails, direct messages or Goggle Classrooms. Students were asked views about distant learning. In his article, he also highlights the extraordinary number of mental and emotional health issues that will be faced when schools fully resume, stating that these will matter more than student work progress. This is the same everywhere.

Another example of inequities reported in USA is in North Carolina. Already in 1997, the Supreme Court's decision in Leandro vs. the State of N.C. affirmed that the State has constitutional responsibility to provide students with an equal opportunity for a sound basic education and it was failing this responsibility. This means supporting children of every race and ethnicity economic level, family background and location from the most rural to the most urban. The Leandro Report shows inequities across this State Education System, before COVID-19 and now, amplified by remote learning.

The data in Tables 6.1 and 6.2 are part of an article by Laura Fay (2020): "Inequities are ongoing and amplified with remote learning", which appeared

TABLE 16.1   Percentage change in student participation – high, middle and low incomes

Decreased participation	Social group
+4.5%	High income
−30%	Middle income
−52.4%	Low income

TABLE 16.2   Percentage change in student mathematics progress – high, middle and low incomes

Decreased participation	Social group
+45.4%	High income
−0.7%	Middle income
−36%	Low income

in LA School Report that works in partnership with *The 74*.[1] As non-profit, non-partisan news site The 74 covers education in US, with a particular spotlight of how the coronavirus crisis is affecting students, teachers, and families.[2]

In these tables, schools are categorises as low, middle or high-income, according to the household median of the zip code where they live. It shows that the crisis is impacting low-income children and communities to provoke more troubles.

In the United States students from middle income ZIP codes decreased participation in on-line Mathematics coursework by 30%, and low-income went even worse reaching −52%, from January–May 2020,

In the United States students from middle income ZIP codes decreased progress in on-line Mathematics by 0.7% from January–May 2020. Nationally, high-income students increased their progress through Zearn Math lesson significantly, compared with their rates while school buildings were open. Instead, low-income students' progress slowed by 36% at the same time. Zearn is an online Maths Programme for students in kindergarten through to fifth grade.

Overall, the data suggest that school closures are not maintaining existing learning gaps but are widening them, affirmed David Williams who is the former senior adviser to City of Detroit Mayor. He is also the outreach director at Opportunity Insights, that is a non-partisan research and policy institute focused on improving economic opportunity. These data by Zearn Math offer a glimpse into the crisis and suggest that the pandemic may have exacerbated gaps, not only by leaving some students behind but also propelling privileged children further ahead academically.

From the information, not showing why students unfortunately dropped off or slowed progress, we can say that digital devices, teacher actions and/or district expectations played a role. From *Opportunity Insights*, economists note that Zearn data raise concern that COVID-19 may reduce social mobility and amplify inequality by having negative effects on human capital development for lower-income children. Research shows that distance learning is a poor substitute for in-person schooling, particularly for vulnerable students.

Totally different performance levels are achieved in Jefferson Parish, Louisiana, due to numerous interventions to keep students engaged after school shutdown. In fact, in Jefferson County the increase was an amazing 131%. A call centre, manned by central office staff and educators, was established and answered questions from 8 am–8 pm daily. Learning packs were handed to students with their grab-and-go lunches and stickers showed e-mail address families could use if needed. The district also trained teachers to use Google Classroom and they were partnered with an Internet company to provide low-cost service to families.

Furthermore, the district organised a policy that allowed students to receive grades for work completed in final weeks of the school year. This helped students "on the hook" says Jenna Chiasson, the Executive Director of Teaching and Learning, at Jefferson Parish schools, in Jefferson County. She suggests that it is necessary to "hold the bar and expectations for teaching and learning in years to come" and show grace and understanding for the current situation. Districts must execute strong, intentional plans for family communication and think as seriously about teaching and learning as they do about health and safety.

Comment: Schools must build flexible academic systems that accommodate transitions. Sociologists affirm that during a crisis, it is important to attend to all student needs, including health, academic, social-emotional and even financial needs. Transition, uncertainty and loss make vulnerable students discouraged and disengaged. We know how complex learners can be affected by their environment and we know how important it is to share information, so educators can incorporate approaches to meet diverse learner needs in schools. More than ever, schools must foster a holistic approach that integrates academics with healthcare and family support services. Students with a sick loved one that has lost a job, or is grieving, will need more than just academic support. Schools must help parents navigate financial, educational and wellness challenges. This relational support web helps students feel safe to re-engage learning in holistic, meaningful ways, hopefully filling the inequity gap. Schools have opportunity to cultivate wonder, curiosity and eagerness for learning. Plans need to restore and unlock creativity and power of every student and equip each one to shape a more just and equitable response to COVID-19.

9 Review

Most agree that remote learning cannot replace personal connections between teachers and students (WHO, Appendix). We witnessed educators conjuring magic to contact students during this crisis time. Also, families are facing economic hardship adding significant stress. Many parents/carers face challenges with navigating and supporting online schooling. It is necessary to reflect on the role of school in the current pandemic as basic assumptions are no longer valid from now on; specifically,

- Asynchronicity is key for RE and shows what is possible and how it could/ will enhance learning in future;
- Students, particularly older ones, could/will be engaged in online modules in an asynchronous fashion driven by their own interest and curiosity;

- Home or community learning could/will allow students to use time with teachers to workshop and to problem-solve, moving from a lecture model to one where students have more 1-on-1 time with educators;
- Funding for new construction and for the upkeep of the old premises could/will be redirected to increase human capital, meaning more teachers, counsellors, instructional coaches and support staff.

In the last two years, the world has experienced more educational change than at any time in our history and education will be divided into *before* and *after* 2020. It depends on us to shape and adjust necessary changes as we move along this innovative path, keeping in mind to serve all students well. We have mentioned that students need more voice, not only in the teaching-learning process. Italian School Union have organised strike and rallies to protest about quality of schools, involving students, teachers and temporary staff, when premises reopened.

In towns, slogans emphasised that "Government must take care of education" as a primary need and all stakeholders must work together for better provision. They denounced that classes are like chicken coops, with no benches and empty teacher desks, as not enough staff have been appointed to cover the necessities this crisis has brought. In Britain, the Sutton Trust (2020) reports that thousands of students in sixth-forms and further education colleges have had face-to-face learning halved, with classes only every other week. The future depends on how we build a suitable environment for youngsters. When the going is tough, the tough must get going!

Notes

1   www.the74million.org
2   It is possible to be updated at the 74million.org/coronavirus for latest news and analysis.

References

Belk, R., & Kozinets, R. (2005). Videography in marketing and consumer research. *Qualitative Market Research: An International Journal, 8*(2), 128–141.

Brunsell, E., & Horejsi, M. (2013). A flipped classroom in action. *Science Teacher, 80* (2), 8.

Bulu, S. (2012). Place presence, social presence, co-presence and satisfaction in virtual worlds. *Computers and Education, 58*, 154–161.

Chickering, A. W., & Gamson, Z. F. (1999). Development and adaptations of the seven principles for good practice in undergraduate education. *New Directions for Teaching and Learning, 80*, 75–81. https://doi.org/10.1002/tl.8006

Coates, H. (2005). The value of student engagement for higher education quality assurance. *Quality in Higher Education, 11*(1), 25–36. https://doi.org/10.1080/13538320500074915

Crews, T., & Butterfield, J. (2014, October 27–30). Data for flipped classroom design: Using student feedback to identify the best components from online and face-to-face classes. *Higher Education Studies, 4*(3), 38–47.

Demetry, C. (2010). *An innovation merging "classroom flip" and team-based learning* [Paper presentation]. Fortieth ASEE/IEEE Frontiers in Education Conference. doi:10.1109/FIE.2010.5673617

Evans, L. (2020, April 23). *How a Montessori classroom, online learning, and family engagement can work together*. Retrieved May 5, 2020, from https://www.gettingsmart.com/2020/04/23/how-a-montessori-classroom-online-learning-and-family-engagement-can-work-together/

Fay, L. A. (2020, September 10). *Zearn Math: Inequities are ongoing and amplified with remote learning*. Retrieved September 20, 2020, from https://www.the74million.org/article/new-data-suggests-pandemic-may-not-just-be-leaving-low-income-students-behind-it-may-be-propelling-wealthier-ones-even-further-ahead/

Feldman, K. (1984). Class size and college students' evaluations of teachers and courses: A closer look. *Research in Higher Education, 21*(1), 45–116.

Ford, J., Ford, L., & D'Amelio, A. (2008). Resistance to change: The rest of the story. *Academy of Management Review, 33*(2), 362–377.

Garrison, D. R., & Kanuka, H. (2004). Blended learning: Uncovering its transformative potential in higher education. *Internet and Higher Education, 7*(2), 95–106. https://doi.org/10.1016/j.iheduc.2004.02.001

Gerstein, J. (2012, May 15). *Flipped classroom: The full picture for higher education.* https://usergeneratededucation.wordpress.com/2012/05/15/flipped-classroom-the-full-picture-for-higher-education/

Glaser, B., & Strauss, A. (1967). *The discovery of grounded theory: Strategies for qualitative research.* Aldine.

Gusky, N. (2020, April 6). *Teaching online in the time of coronavirus.* Retrieved May 15, 2020, from https://www.gettingsmart.com/2020/04/06/teaching-online-in-the-time-of-coronavirus/

Herreid, C., & Schiller, N. (2013). Case studies and the flipped classroom. *Journal of College Science Teaching, 42*(5), 62–66.

Hodges, C., & Repman, J. (2011, September). *Moving outside the LMS: Matching Web 2.0 tools to instructional purpose.* EDUCAUSE Learning Initiative. http://net.educause.edu/ir/library/pdf/ELIB1103.pdf

Hughes, H. (2012). Introduction to flipping the college classroom. In T. Amiel & B. Wilson (Eds.), *Proceedings of EdMedia 2012: World conference on educational multimedia & technology* (pp. 2434–2438). Association for the Advancement of Computing in Education (AACE). https://www.learntechlib.org/primary/p/41097/

Keh, H. T., & Pang, J. (2010). Customer reactions to service separation. *Journal of Marketing, 74*(2), 55–70. https://doi.org/10.1509/jm.74.2.55

Keller, K. (1993). Conceptualising, measuring, and managing customer-based brand equity. *Journal of Marketing, 57*(1), 1–22. https://doi.org/10.1177/002224299305700101

Kim, J., Kwon, Y., & Cho, D. (2011), Investigating factors that influence social presence and learning outcomes in distance higher education. *Computers & Education, 57*(2), 1512–1520. https://doi.org/10.1016/j.compedu.2011.02.005

Kozinets, R. (2010). *Netnography: Doing ethnographic research online*. Sage.

Krueger, K. (2020, April 21). *Keep America's students learning at home*. Retrieved August 5, 2020, from https://www.gettingsmart.com/2020/04/21/keep-americas-students-learning-at-home/

Lage, M., Platt, G., & Treglia, M. (2000). Inverting the classroom: A gateway to creating an inclusive learning environment. *Journal of Economic Education, 31*(1), 30–43.

Lane, L. (2008). Toolbox or trap? Course management systems and pedagogy. *EDUCAUSE Quarterly, 31*(2), 4–6. http://net.educause.edu/ir/library/pdf/eqm0820.pdf

Lovelock, C., & Gummeson, E. (2004). Whither services marketing? In search of a new paradigm and fresh perspectives. *Journal of Service Research, 7*(1), 20–41.

McKeachie, W. J. (1980). Class size, large classes, and multiple sections. *Academe, 66*(1), 24–27. https://doi.org/10.2307/40249328

McKennon, S. (2020, June 7). *Sticky buns and distance learning*. Retrieved August 5, 2020, from https://www.gettingsmart.com/2020/06/07/sticky-buns-and-distance-learning/

Mizerski, R. (1995). The relationship between cartoon trade character recognition and attitude toward product category in young children. *Journal of Marketing, 59*(4), 58–70. https://doi.org/10.2307/1252328

Moreno, C., & Frishman, A. (2020, April 24). *Searching for the other side of the tunnel: Leading through COVID-19*. Retrieved May 5, 2020, from https://www.gettingsmart.com/2020/04/24/searching-for-the-other-side-of-the-tunnel-leading-through-covid-19/

Oreg, S. (2003). Resistance to change: Developing an individual differences measure. *Journal of Applied Psychology, 88*(4), 680–693. https://doi.org/10.1037/0021-9010.88.4.680

Parker, J., Maor, D., & Herrington, J. (2013). Authentic online learning: Aligning learner needs, pedagogy and technology. *Issues in Educational Research, 23*(2), 227–241. https://www.learntechlib.org/p/156411/

Poth, R. (2020, March 29). *Choosing the right tools for remote learning.* Retrieved May 5, 2020, from https://www.gettingsmart.com/2020/03/29/choosing-the-right-tools-for-remote-learning/

Reinartz, W. J., & Kumar, V. (2003). The impact of customer relationship characteristics on profitable lifetime duration. *Journal of Marketing, 67*(1), 77–99. https://doi.org/10.1509/jmkg.67.1.77.18589

Ross, D. (2020a, February 18). *Coronavirus offers teachable moments and wakeup call for all schools.* Retrieved May 5, 2020, from https://www.gettingsmart.com/2020/02/18/coronavirus-offers-teachable-moments-and-wakeup-call-for-all-schools/

Ross, D. (2020b, April 24). *As distance learning turns on, students increasingly tune out.* Retrieved May 5, 2020, from https://www.gettingsmart.com/2020/04/24/as-distance-learning-turns-on-students-increasingly-tune-out/

Russell-Bennett, R., Rundle-Thiele, S. R., & Kuhn, K.-A. (2010). Engaging marketing students: Student operated business in a simulated world. *Journal of Marketing Education, 32*(3), 253–263. https://doi.org/10.1177/0273475310377758

Rust, R. T., Lemon, K. N., & Zeithaml, V. A. (2004). Return on marketing: Using customer equity to focus marketing strategy. *Journal of Marketing, 68*, 109–127. https://doi.org/10.1509/jmkg.68.1.109.24030

Sage, R. (2010). *Using portfolios to develop effective professional continual development. Report to the GMC on training for medical practitioners.* London Medical Deanery.

Sage, R., & Matteucci, R. (Eds.). (2019). *The Robots are here, learning to live with them.* UBP.

Säljö, R. (1979). Learning about learning. *Higher Education, 8*, 443–451.

Sandberg, J. (2000). Understanding human competence at work: An interpretative approach. *Academy of Management Journal, 43*(1), 9–25. https://doi.org/10.2307/1556383

Snowball, J. D. (2014). Using interactive content and online activities to accommodate diversity in a large first year class. *Higher Education, 67*(6), 823–838.

So, H.-J., & Brush, T. A. (2008). Student perceptions of collaborative learning, social presence and satisfaction in a blended learning environment: Relationships and critical factors. *Computers & Education, 51*(1), 318–336. https://doi.org/10.1016/j.compedu.2007.05.009

Spires, H. A. (2020, June 12). *We can't put the genie back in the bottle: Designing next-generation education in the time of crisis.* Retrieved August 5, 2020, from https://www.gettingsmart.com/2020/06/12/we-cant-put-the-genie-back-in-the-bottle-designing-next-generation-education-in-the-time-of-crisis/

Steed, A. (2012). The flipped classroom. *Teaching Business and Economics, 16*(3), 9–11.

Strauss, A., & Corbin, J. (1990). *Basics of qualitative research: Grounded theory procedures and techniques.* Sage.

Sutton Trust. (2020). *Arrangement for addressing education for the disadvantaged in the 2020 pandemic.* https://www.suttontrust.com

Tinto, V. (1997). Colleges as communities: Exploring the educational character of student persistence. *Journal of Higher Education, 68*(6), 599–623. https://doi.org/10.2307/2959965

Tinto, V. (2006/2007). Research and practice of student retention: What next? *Journal of College Student Retention: Research, Theory and Practice, 8*(1), 1–19. https://doi.org/10.2190/4YNU-4TMB-22DJ-AN4W

Tucker, E. (2020a, May 7). *To reopen, America needs laboratory schools.* Retrieved July 5, 2020, from https://www.gettingsmart.com/2020/05/07/to-reopen-america-needs-laboratory-schools/

Tucker, E. (2020b, May 13). *Podcast: Eric Tucker on reopening schools with equity in mind.* Retrieved July 5, 2020, from https://www.gettingsmart.com/podcast/podcast-eric-tucker-on-reopening-schools-with-equity-in-mind/

Vander Ark, T. (2020a, March 24). *Hard reset: What will be new post pandemic.* Retrieved May 5, 2020, from https://www.forbes.com/sites/tomvanderark/2020/03/24/hard-reset-what-will-be-new-post-pandemic/?sh=185aa354153f

Vander Ark, T. (2020b, June 1). *Leaning into the innovation opportunity.* Retrieved July 10, 2020, from https://www.gettingsmart.com/2020/06/01/leaning-into-the-innovation-opportunity/

Vargo, S., & Lusch, R. (2004). Evolving to a new dominant logic for marketing. *Journal of Marketing, 68*(1), 1–17. https://doi.org/10.1509/jmkg.68.1.1.24036

Vygotsky, L. (1962). *Thought and language* (E. Vakar, Trans.). MIT Press.

Vygotsky, L. (1978). *Mind in society: The development of higher psychological processes* (V. John-Steiner, M. Cole, S. Scribner, & E. Souberman, Trans.). Harvard University Press.

Wachtel, H. K. (1998). Student evaluation of college teaching effectiveness: A brief review. *Assessment and Evaluation in Higher Education, 23*(2), 191–212. https://doi.org/10.1080/0260293980230207

Waddell, D., & Sohal, A. (1998). Resistance: A constructive tool for change management. *Management Decision, 36*(8), 543–548.

Wagner, K. (2020a, April 20). *Out with the test, in with PBL: How project-based learning is transforming remote learning.* Retrieved May 5, 2020, from https://www.gettingsmart.com/2020/04/20/out-with-the-test-in-with-pbl-how-project-based-learning-is-transforming-remote-learning/

Wagner, K. (2020b, July 22). *The 12 shifts for student-centered hybrid environments.* Retrieved August 5, 2020, from https://www.gettingsmart.com/2020/07/22/the-12-shifts-for-student-centered-hybrid-environments/

Weerawardena, J. (2003). Exploring the role of market learning capability in competitive strategy. *European Journal of Marketing, 37*(3/4), 407–429.

Wenger, E. (2000). Communities of practice and social learning systems. *Organization, 7*(2), 225–246. https://doi.org/10.1177/135050840072002

Wertsch, J. V. (1984). The zone of proximal development: Some conceptual issues. *New Directions for Child and Adolescent Development, 23*, 7–18. https://doi.org/10.1002/cd.23219842303

Zappe, S., Leicht, R., Messner, J., Litzinger, T., & Lee, H. (2009). *Flipping the classroom to explore active learning in a large undergraduate course* [Paper presentation]. American Society for Engineering Education Annual Conference, Portland, Oregon.

Appendix: Summary of Recomendations from the World Health Organisation (WHO) for Education Protocols (Appia 20, 1211 Geneva, Switzerland)

Education is a vital community infrastructure, playing a critical role in supporting the whole learner and not just their academic achievement. Guidance considers how to protect the health, safety and wellbeing of students, teachers, other staff, their families and communities. It is vital that administrators:

Coordinate, Plan and Prepare

– Engage and encourage education stakeholders to practice preventive measures and help institutions stay open
– Implement multiple SARS-CoV-2 mitigation strategies (e.g. social distancing, masks, hand hygiene and use of cohorting (bubbles))
– Communicate, educate and reinforce appropriate hygiene and social distancing practices in relevant, developmental ways for students, teachers and staff
– Integrate mitigation strategies into co- and extra-curricular activities (e.g., limiting or cancelling those where social distancing is not feasible)
– Maintain healthy environments (e.g., cleaning and disinfecting touched surfaces)
– Make decisions that consider the level of community transmission
– Repurpose unused/underutilised institution/community spaces to increase class space and facilitate social distancing, including outside, where feasible
– Develop a proactive plan for when anyone tests COVID-19 positive
– Develop a plan with a local health department for case-tracing in positive cases
– Educate parents/caregivers on the importance of monitoring and responding to COVID-19 symptoms at home
– Develop communication channels with local health departments to stay updated on COVID-19 transmission and local area responses

Role of Education

Education provides critical services to mitigate health disparities, like food programmes and social, physical, behavioural and mental health services. Closure disrupts delivery of critical services and places additional economic and psychological stress on families, to increase risk of conflict and violence. Their unique role makes educational institutions a priority for opening and remaining so, enabling students to receive both academic instruction and support as well as critical services. In order to prioritise this, communities should consider actions to mitigate community transmission.

Signs and Symptoms

COVID-19 symptoms include fever, headache, sore throat, cough, fatigue, nausea/vomiting and diarrhea. Many with the virus are asymptomatic (*no illness signs or symptoms*). Officials should make decisions about reopening education based on available data, including levels of community transmission and capacity to implement appropriate mitigation measures. Children seem at lower risk for contracting COVID-19 compared to adults. Adolescents, age 10–17, may be more likely to infect with SARS-CoV-2 than younger ones, but not at higher risk for developing severe illness.

There are currently a higher proportion of COVID-19 cases among Hispanic/Latino children compared to white non-Hispanics. Children and adults with certain medical problems (e.g. respiratory, endocrine, nutritional, metabolic and circulatory system diseases) may put them at increased risk for COVID-19 severe illness. Although rare, some children have developed multisystem inflammatory syndrome (MIS-C) after exposure to SARS-CoV-2. Most children hospitalised with MIS-C have recovered.

Data on SARS-CoV-2 transmission among children are limited. Evidence suggests that most children with COVID-19 were infected by a family member. For example, the first paediatric patients in South Korea and Vietnam were most likely from contact with adult family. Contact tracing of COVID-19 school students from France, Australia and Ireland suggests that they are less likely to transmit the virus to peers compared to household contacts. More research is needed on SARS-CoV-2 transmission.

What Is Known about Reopened Institutions and SARS-CoV-2 Transmission?

Education has responded to COVID-19 using many approaches. China, Denmark, Norway, Singapore, and Taiwan all required temperature checks at school entry. Most countries changed the way they operate to reduce class sizes, increase physical distance between students and keep them in defined groups to reduce contacts. Also, they have staggered attendance, start and stop times and created alternating shifts to enable social distancing. However, only certain students in some places have returned to education. Denmark was the first European country to reopen schools. It staggered student reentry in waves (e.g., one group started school first, followed by another at a later date), with limited class sizes using social distancing measures. Younger students (under 12) returned first, based on a lower health risk and need for more supervision. Class sizes were reduced to allow physical distancing. In Taiwan, students returned with mandatory temperature checks and face masks. Rather than national closures, Taiwan relied on local decisions to see if these were needed, based on infection rates.

There is mixed evidence about whether returning to education results in increased transmission or outbreaks. Denmark initially reported a slight increase in community cases after reopening schools and child care centres for students aged 2–12 years, followed by steady declines in cases among children between 1–19 years. In contrast, Israel experienced a surge of new cases and school outbreaks after reopening and relaxing social distancing. It is unclear what caused an increase in cases and what other school mitigation measures were implemented. In summer 2020, Texas reported more than 1,300 COVID-19 cases in childcare centres. Twice as many staff members were diagnosed as children, suggesting that the latter may be at lower risk of getting COVID-19 than adults. International school evidence suggests that re-openings are safe in communities with low SARS-CoV-2 transmission rates but not where it is high.

Why Is It Important to Open Education for In-Person Instruction?

Education plays a critical role in community wellbeing. It provides safe, supportive contexts, structure and routines for students, as well as other needed support services. Schools and colleges play a vital role in the economic health of communities by employing teachers and other staff and helping parents, guardians and caregivers. Institutions provide critical instruction and academic support, including tutoring, special education and learning.

Studies show that students have experienced learning loss during closure. In-person student instruction has advantages over virtual learning, particularly when not the planned format for instruction. Institutions may not have resources or capability to transition to virtual learning. Classroom instruction has teachers actively participating in student learning, providing feedback as they encounter challenges and promoting group engagement, particularly necessary for those with additional learning needs.

When institutions are closed to in-person instruction, disparities in educational outcomes could become wider, as some families may not have capacity to participate in distance learning (e.g., computer and internet access issues, lack of support because of jobs) and may rely on institution-based services supporting academic success. Persistent achievement gaps, prior to COVID 19 closures, like income disparities, racial and ethnic groups, could worsen, causing long-term effects on education outcomes, health and economic wellbeing of families and communities. Education plays a critical role in supporting the whole student, not just academic achievement.

Social, Emotional and Student Mental Health Is Enhanced through Education

Social interaction is vital not only for emotional wellbeing, but also for language, communication, social and interpersonal abilities. Some students have experienced social isolation and increased anxiety while not physically being in education due to COVID 19. Education can facilitate social, emotional and mental health through lessons that develop communication to recognise and manage emotions, set and achieve positive goals, appreciate other perspectives, establish and maintain positive relationships and make responsible decisions. Opportunities to be active through physical education help improve student feelings of anxiety and sadness. Continuity of other special services is important for student success.

Comment

The pandemic and the data collected has highlighted the issues of the *disadvantaged* students (background/disability. They are unable to adapt easily to the new blended learning format that is seen to be the pedagogical approach for the present and future. Some countries, like Turkey, have developed a strategy that gives them mire opportunities to concentrate on students with additional needs for what ever the reason. A national platform delivers basic subject content to all 18 million students allowing them to repeat digital delivery to acquire understanding. Teachers, therefore, can give time to those with additional needs and provide out of school support with an app and WhatsApp groups. Britain is viewed as coping less well with disadvantaged students compared with others in the OECD group of nations.

CHAPTER 17

The Maker Faire

Opportunities for Innovators

Riccarda Matteucci

Abstract

When we talk about technology in education we have to take account of the extensive MAKER FAIRE organisation, which holds events around the world. Wikipedia defines this as a "… Convention of do it yourself enthusiasts, started by the *MAKE* magazine in 2006. Participants come from a wide variety of interests, such as robotics, 3D printing, computers, arts and crafts and the hacker culture". This chapter presents the Maker Faire events to demonstrate their importance in life long education.

∴

Poor is the pupil who does not surpass his master.
　　　LEONARDO DA VINCI

∵

1 Introduction

In 2005, Dale Dougherty and Tim O'Reilly founded *MAKE*, a magazine that appears quarterly to showcase creative activities. The following year, the first Maker Faire was organised in San Mateo, California, in the United States of America (USA) to provide an opportunity for innovators to demonstrate their creations in a public forum. It was an immediate success and registered the presence of more than 20,000 visitors. This event rapidly became a cult activity and has expanded to more than 200 licensed Maker Faire groups in more than 40 countries around the world. The organisation is found in Europe, Asia, South America and Africa. The first Maker Faire in the United Kingdom took place on March 14–15, 2009, in the northern city of Newcastle-Upon-Tyne. It was a joint venture together with Newcastle Science Fest. Among the many events, one of the most unforgettable was held on June 18, 2014 at the White House, Washington, hosted by President Obama, who was then in office. This was the first ever Maker Faire event there and the only one run so far in this location,

The last Bay Area Faire was held in 2019 and the decision to end it was mostly financial, as attendance had dropped by more than 30%, but Dale Dougherty rebranded it as the *Make Community*. Due to the Coronavirus, which quickly spread worldwide in 2020, it was not able to function that year in either San Mateo or in New York City. This model was known as the *"World Maker Faire"* and the inability to function in 2020 was common in many other countries and parts around the world, due to the pandemic and a series of lockdowns in towns and cities.

On December 10–13, 2020, the *Rome Maker Faire* (8th version) and recognised as The European Edition, was organised in digital mode, on a platform where pavilions represented specific thematic routes. The stands were embodied on web pages, where the visitors and exhibitors could interact as in a traditional fair. This model has proved to be very successful so that the 9th version of the Rome Maker Faire will be held on 8–10 October 2021, in *phygital edition* both a physical and digital format. Phygital is the concept of using technology to bridge the digital world with the physical world in order to provide unique interactive experiences for the user. There will be a streaming marathon of innovation at this important event, virtual windows and many live activities. The programme is presently being organised to take account of the new presentation model.

2   What Is a Maker Faire?

Maker Faire is a gathering of fascinating, curious people, who enjoy learning and love sharing what they can do together in order to acquire knowledge and skills from each other and improve their designs. From engineers to artists, scientists to crafters, Maker Faire is a venue for these creators to present their hobbies, experiments and projects. It is also defined as the Greatest Show and Tell on Earth, a family-friendly showcase of invention, creativity and resourcefulness. To involve and attract people the Maker Faire community say: *Glimpse the future and get inspired.*

Internationally judged as the biggest show in the world devoted to inventions, creativity and ingenuity, Maker Faire is a celebration of the Maker

Movement. The exhibition allows people to present and demonstrate what they have produced and share what they have learned during the process amongst other interested people. The events unify science, technology and innovation, to create something completely novel and appealing. During the faire, dreamers, inventors and talented people merge and create a magical chemistry, so that you can learn much and enjoy new opportunities to network and perhaps cooperate and collaborate. We can speak of a kind of ecosystem, where the protagonists of the innovation scenarios meet, question and are questioned by others, to form new trains of thought and action as well as enjoying themselves and feeling fulfilment for all their hard work.

Typical of the majority of Maker Faire events is the blend of innovators with the general public. They become close, thanks to experimental ideas that make the visitors an integral part of the event. The one held in Rome is considered the most important in Europe, regarding innovation, robotics, AI, AR and VR, IoT, digital manufacturing and self-production.

3   Who Are the Makers?

The Makers are people of any kind, ranging from technology enthusiasts to creative scientists and also those who produce their inventions in the garage or the attic (Matteucci, 2019). Participants can be of all ages and come from any cultural background. When interviewing participants during the exhibition to ask: What does Maker Faire mean for you students? The following answers reflect their popular views:

Ideas are questioned and challenged through comparison with others
It is an opportunity to make personal progress by sharing experiences
Equality is demonstrated in the involvement of all innovative projects
A chance to present your ideas and tell your story to many others
It is education and training in a real context and allows one to grow in knowledge

The projects cover all fields, from disability to the environment, anything that could ameliorate daily living for the inhabitants of this world (Sage & Matteucci, 2019, pp. 87–101).

During Euro 2020, big data played an important role in proceedings. From the harnesses worn by players during sports' matches, it was possible to collect precious and useful information on activities and performances during both training and actual games. This is a typical example of an inventive idea presented at a Maker Faire.

4   The Make Magazine

These technological events, held annually around the world, are all recognised by the *MAKE MAGAZINE* and, as mentioned above, the most famous ones have been in San Mateo, Detroit, New York and Rome. Being the Maker Faire has been the first organisation completely dedicated to technological projects and DIY ventures, the Maker Faire inspires, unites, informs, connects and entertains a community of entrepreneurs and innovators. The magazine and its subsequent movement have transformed the world from the innovation, cultural and educational point of view.

The Maker people grow bigger and bigger ambitions and are kept closely informed of many different aspects of inventions and innovations through the magazine, that also helps them realise their incredible projects. These are mostly completed in their free time, or in schools tutored by teachers in great part giving their services on a volunteer basis (Sage & Matteucci, 2019, chapter 5).

MAKE offers the right to modify and mould any technology for working or pleasure requirements and provides a space on line to become informed about news and projects.[1] Furthermore, it offers a shop of kits, books and the Maker Shed to provide the necessary resources for schemes. A YouTube channel is available and in the section on projects there is a library of ones, describing how they were achieved step-by-step. In the book section, it is possible to find texts that cover fields such as an Introduction to Electronics, 3D printing, a Raspberry Pi, Arduino and much more.

Furthermore, the *MAKE MAGAZINE* has been assisting independent event organisers to produce small-scale Maker-Faire events in local communities.

5   Review

Students from 4 years old to undergraduates, graduates and post-graduates all benefit from participating in Maker Faire events. Positive outcomes are evident from the structure of the organisation that puts together different levels of people: beginners and also more advanced learners, who can share the knowledge and skills of different disciplines. Applying creative technologies to humanity issues can bridge the pervasive use of media. Makers can show dynamically their problem-solving ideas and test them by prototyping. They can make a connection between the algorithmic process and the subjects they are studying, when building, constructing and creating with technological tools and computing processes.

The future challenge is to have a community able to combine and mix emerging modes of media and humanities. As Dr. Fiorella Operto, co-founder of Scuola di Robotica in Genova, says about personal communication during the webinar *Breakfast Club 2021* (July 8, 2021):

> ... Unfortunately, we do not know Technology well enough ... and Technology needs more art and artistic figures, such as Dante, Raffaello, Michelangelo, Shakespeare, to broaden public knowledge and we have to keep in mind that we are only at the dawn of the digital revolution.

6 The European Edition Rome Maker Faire 2021, 8–10 October: The World Event for Technology Is Turning Pink

The most important European event dedicated to innovation and creativity, organised by the Chamber of Commerce, this year took place in Rome (see Figure 17.1 characterised by its *phygital edition mode.* It was an in-person event and also broadcasted in streaming and 2. soon was sold out with the attendance of 21 thousand people for the three-day exhibition. Held inside the Gasometro Ostiense Area, built in 1937 and renamed Industrial Coliseum, it served to store gas for the city. For a long time it was the biggest of its genre in Europe, now considered an example of industrial archaeology and for the Maker Faire Event 2021 opened to the public for the first time.

A highly skilled ecosystem was installed between in-person and online visitors involving makers, schools, universities, research centres, companies and

FIGURE 17.1   Rome Maker Faire 2021

enthusiasts in the name of innovation suitable for all. Arranged in 6 sections: Research, Life, Fabrication, Health, Arts, and Education with 225 exhibitors, it was a journey into past, present and future. The event seems to *turn pink* due to the big number of female participation as actresses in the numerous projects involved in the present and future time. Speaking with prof. Claudio Becchetti, consultant and organiser of technology courses at Istituto Massimo in Rome, he highlighted the presence of 'girls', who are most interested and passionate in technology. He affirmes that female students excel most if 'in' the projects before 11–12 years old. After that age it appears more difficult to involve them and technology will remain difficult to crack.

At Istituto Massimo, a comprehensive Jesuit Public School that has students from Kindergarten to Secondary High, technology is taught as an extra-curriculum subject through MakingOpen.net within the school. The team is made of professional volunteers (engineers, professors, doctors, entrepreneurs, etc.) who devote their time to organise advanced free-open-source courses related to hi-tech used for humanitarian projects. The courses and the achievements have been reported on national and international media. These vary from Making Drones (a project that won world record of maximum number of flying drones driven by kids), Making 3D printers (age 8–15), Making RoobotMagis (age 10–17), to Making Space Project, supported by Italian Air Force. The children (age 9–17) learned how to design, build and make fly-space vectors and experienced the chemical and physical phenomena of space environment involved. With the goal of helping students to enter in the space economy, boys and girls set the record for the simultaneous launch of 30 self-built rockets that reached a height of 330 metres, tested and performed at the Roma military airport of Furbara. In Making Electric Vehicles 2020 project, pupils (age 9–16) built 14 wooden-board karts run by electric propulsion, using recycled materials. Divided into teams, students competed for best driving performance, capability to manage the team in terms of marketing, brand, etc.

Figure 17.2 shows photos of 'girls' working on projects at Istituto Massimo site, with Professor Claudio Becchetti's permission.

Among the many projects, the startup *Windciti* presented by Edoardo Mier and Filippo Petrone, students at LUISS University in Rome, operates in the micro-wind sector (Figure 17.3). It has developed and patented a passive variable geometry turbine that enables energy production even with variable wind flow typical of cities and sea surface, by self-adjusting pitch, diameter and rotation. Turbines are poised to benefit both: customers, corporate energy managers, end-users, and environment, by significantly reducing CO_2 emissions.

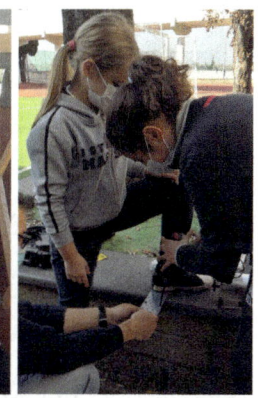

FIGURE 17.2   Maker Faire 2021: Professor Becchetti and students of Istituto Massimo

FIGURE 17.3
Edoardo Mier and Filippo Petrone present their
startup at Rome Maker Faire 2021

Note

1   blog.makezine.com

References

MakingOpen.net. (n.d.). Website.
Matteucci, R. (2019). Bullying: A widespread problem to solve using robotics as a solu-
     tion. In R. Sage & R. Matteucci (Eds.), *The robots are here: Learning to live with them*
     (pp. 74–82). Buckingham University Press.
Operto, F. (2021, July 5–8). *The breakfast club 2021* [Webinar]. Scuola di Robotica di
     Genova.

Websites
https://en.maker-faire.de
https://istitutomassimo.it
https://it.wikipedia.org
https://makerfaire.com
https://makerfairerome.eu
https://www.avvenire.it
https://www.eni.com
https://www.giuseppesimeone.it
https://www.innovacamera.it

https://www.raspberrypi.org
https://www.scuoladirobotica.it
https://www.schoolandcollegelistings.com
https://www.youtube.com

CHAPTER 18

E-Learning But Not Always E-Quality

Rosemary Sage

Abstract

E-learning has coped with the COVID-19 2020 pandemic, when face-to-face teaching activities have been impossible due to regular lockdowns. This has spot-lighted unfortunate inequality issues that have added to student mental stresses. Not only do some learners lack the necessary technology and home support to access on-line materials, but others are unable to process information without ongoing help. In the United Kingdom (UK) we have a National Curriculum that is highly prescriptive, with regular Standard Assessment Tests (SATs) and examinations. This system, therefore, focuses on *what* to learn rather than *how* to achieve knowledge and competencies effectively. Students who perform successfully in structured, supportive classrooms, have been floundering trying to cope without their usual, individual guidance. This has shown up their learning issues more acutely, based on linguistic deficiencies that have not been adequately assessed and identified. Stories have emerged during lockdown periods of their frustrations at not being heard. This chapter describes and discusses these problems with ideas of how to manage them to mitigate problems.

1 Introduction

As a speech and language therapist, psychologist and teacher, I have worked in Health and Social Services, mainstream Education and latterly in Universities. Studies in a typical Leicester primary school over three years showed all entries had language and cognition below age level (Sage, 2000) At the feeder secondary school, 80% of students were found to operate at a 5–6 year level on psycho-linguistic tests when aged 11–12, with the school continually in special measures. The Medical Research Council asked me to look at 300 children in this Midland area testing normally on intelligence (IQ) tests but failing in schools. The cohort all had problems with understanding and producing *extended language,* which component style IQ tests had not revealed. Therefore, a transmission learning style with extended talk and texts proved problematic.

© KONINKLIJKE BRILL NV, LEIDEN, 2022 | DOI:10.1163/9789004506466_023

Individuals can appear chatty and deal with conversation successfully when having some control over interaction, but have difficulty with lengthy language sequences in classroom talk and texts and on-line presentations. Their dialogue ability means that teachers assume they are language proficient but the monologue style of large class discourse is a problem, so they depend on direct or indirect help to complete tasks. During the pandemic, students, at all levels, have talked about missing teachers and classmates and the spontaneous conversations and relationships with them. The formal education context makes them keen to learn, holds them accountable and motivates to stay engaged. Also, learners acquire much knowledge from observing others, sharing information and gaining support and help when required.

Students, just described, would be viewed as having some degree of higher-level language disorder with the pandemic highlighting such issues. This is not only a problem at primary but also at the tertiary end of education, as some students say they cannot cope with webinars and so wander off. One suggested: "We'll pass courses anyway as universities don't allow us to fail". Transmitting information in the way we might do so face-to-face does not work for on-line presentations. These need material delivered in small chunks with more time to process outputs. There is a tendency for presenters to forget that those listening process at different rates, when faces do not reveal their non-verbal responses to assist the adjustment of input.

I have experienced problems on an online course undertaken over the past year. The webinars have been nearly 2 hours long with complex written input and a speaker expanding the content. As someone who is cross-lateral (both brain sides processing) instead of having a *left* or *right* side dominance, it means I need more time to process when there is simultaneous visual and auditory input. I found that the visual input had disappeared from the screen before processing it. Also, the auditory input was not always transmitted in a dynamic way, so it was easy to lose interest. Without an audience in front to transmit their non-verbal responses, speakers often lose their vocal variety. The experience has been frustrating, but fortunately there were recordings of all presentations to be processed at leisure.

It was interesting that in the Professional Learning Groups (PLG) most of the participants had experienced the same problems, but these were excellent events with a small group and a charismatic leader. On-line performances require specific presenter training to be effective as they rely on auditory and visual material, excluding haptic (touch, feeling, position in space) and non-verbal dimensions necessary for those learning best from real experience. This is vital for people with subtle communication issues. Also, there are many being instructed in a language other than mother-tongue, who similarly find nuanced information confusing.

Thus, the pandemic highlights students finding it difficult to work under their own steam and it is important to assess their communicative competencies to provide relevant support. One must consider ability to introspectively analyse (terms in the literature – inner speech/talk, self-talk, sub-vocal speech, mental verbalisation, internal dialogue/monologue or self-statement). Alongside *inner-talk* are external language dialogues and monologues (telling/ re-telling, giving instructions, reporting, making an argument etc.). However, the importance of *inner-talk* is rarely recognised, but Vygotsky (1986) suggested it depends on sequential language, which is vital for predictive thinking and action. If students have problems with this, they are unlikely to carry out tasks alone and need prompting for each stage. Articulating each step while doing it, repeating, recalling and stating the whole sequence is necessary to build mental verbalisation for completing tasks independently.

Hurlbert et al. (2013) have made *inner-talk* a focus for study and found that there is only an average 20% frequency of use. *External talk* is necessary for developing these internal self-statements. Is low frequency of *inner-talk* a result of technology as the preferred way of communicating? In countries, like Italy, Japan and Cuba, *talk* is the technology of learning and you do not find silent classrooms as students constantly verbalise to develop higher levels of speaking and thinking. Group work is more common than individual, so that participants constantly exchange ideas, reflect, review and refine performances. With students 4 years above UK counterparts in the *Dialogue, Innovation, Achievement and Learning* studies (DIAL) (Sage et al., 2002–2010) one has to take their approach seriously, as communication and relationships take precedence over subject learning. In Italy, the Roman tradition of Oratory and Rhetoric Schools is still seen today, with spoken examinations important for judging performance, so reflecting their normal life use. This is seen in Table 18.1.

TABLE 18.1   A comparison of teaching time for spoken and written development based on research by Steil (Feyton, 1991)

	Listening	Speaking	Reading	Writing
% Use in life	60%	20%	12%	8%
Learnt	First	Second	Third	Fourth
Used	Most	Next to most	Next to least	Least
Taught	Least	Nest to least	Nest to most	Most

When looking at this table one can easily see that primary language competencies get less attention than secondary ones in educational practice which experts suggest happens today.

2 E-Learning

Many issues are involved with online education but we cannot ignore the importance of it in times of a pandemic crisis. There are always solutions to fix problems. Technical difficulties can be solved through pre-recording video materials, testing content and having a reserve plan so that teaching–learning is never hindered. Online courses must be dynamic, interesting and interactive with information presented in small amounts, as it is not possible to judge audience understanding as in face-to-face contacts. Time limits, reminders and content summaries for students keeps them alert and attentive (especially important for those with language difficulties).

Efforts should be made to humanise learning so personal attention and initial face-to-face contact is vital for learners to trust and easily adapt to this new environment. Social media and group forums help connect students and educators. Personal communication is key when texts, messaging apps, video calls etc. prove difficult, as research indicates there is much miscommunication when non-verbal input is reduced (Sage, 2020). Deliver content with an applied task to follow so students can practise and hone skills. Encourage their feedback on these experiences and share this with the learning group. Support sets of 6–8 students are more suitable for such exchanges, as some find a 30+ group intimidating in an on-line forum, although others may prefer it to face-to-face contact.

The quality of courses should be continually reviewed, refined and designed to be creative, interactive, relevant, student-centred and group-based. Educators must produce clear, simple online instructions which facilitate feedback from learners and encourage them to question and expand course content. Institutions should focus on teaching strategies and emphasise collaborative, project and case-based learning. Their challenge is not only finding new technology and using it, but also reimagining their approach and helping students and staff wanting guidance on digital literacy. This is particularly important for those showing problems with language, who find the on-line mode more perplexing.

3 E-Quality: High Level Language Disorder (HLLD)

People generally know terms like *articulation, dysfluency, voice disturbances, language vocabulary, grammar, syntax and structure.* Problems in these areas will find their way to communication specialists. However, language can be affected outside of ability to produce a sentence with correct structure, vocabulary, articulation and voice dynamics. Subtle communicative components, known as *higher order/level language or executive function* can be impaired and more difficult to detect than defective speech sounds, limited grammar or disturbed voice quality. Those with HLLD often score well on basic language (e.g. vocabulary) and visual reasoning intelligence tests (e.g. Raven's Progressive Matrices) but struggle with verbal thinking and expression of in-depth explanations, instructions, story-telling or re-telling. Problems are more common than realised and include:

– *Sequencing*: impairment affects ability to organise and complete tasks independently and impacts on speaking/writing narrative events coherently or giving ordered instructions correctly. This presents as difficulty in recounting events coherently and delivering project steps to another person. These subtle abilities are underpinned by ability to sequence accurately within extended, connected language events. Difficulty in understanding and telling the time is common and interpreted wrongly as being dull or stupid.

– *Cause and effect* is ability to give a reason for a specific outcome. Without this competence one struggles to understand why something has happened and account for how an action leads to a certain consequence. If you did not grasp a sudden impact causes a glass to break, it would not be possible to appreciate that falling off a table might mean buying another one.

– *Inference and prediction* is being able to use verbal or visual clues to infer further information and make predictions based on these. From an instruction: 'Turn the headlights on', we deduce the person is driving as these are vehicle beams. We *infer* poor vision as the reason for this command and *predict* if we do not switch on the lights an accident might occur. Although information is not explicit, connections must be made for meaning. Talk & text depends on ability to *infer* & *cohere* content, so problems will affect learning.

– *Figurative language* is non-literal and includes idioms, metaphors and similes which are common in oral and literate activities. These do not convey a direct, concrete meaning and are abstract, depending on knowledge of language use. Problems with figurative words make jokes and humour difficult to fathom and speaking and reading more of a problem to understand.

Such glitches arise in the brain area called the *amygdala*, which is a small almond shape. This part of the limbic system is below the cerebral lobes and contains the *hippocampus, hypothalamus and amygdala*. The *hippocampus and amygdala* together enable memory processing. The *amygdala* encodes emotion and the *hippocampus* the details of happenings: settings, events, people/things, actions, results and reactions. We are most likely to remember things if having strong feelings and emotions about them.

Narrative processing, production and responding appropriately to significant auditory, visual or haptic stimuli are disrupted with problems in this brain area. Haptic is the non-language communication subsystem of physical awareness and contact – touch, feeling, movement and proprioception – sense of position in space. This is the basic human pathway and first to develop and last to be lost. It is the most effective learning channel but less used than auditory and visual ones in formal education experiences.

The *amygdala* is primary for perception and expression of emotional and social nuances and mostly responsible for understanding and producing spoken and written language. *Auditory neocortex* parts – from the *anterior* and *medial temporal lobe* and beyond the *insula,* including the *superior temporal lobe* and *inferior parietal lobule,* are partly evolved from the *amygdala*. It is suggested that the primary, secondary and auditory association areas, including *Wernicke's visual zone* evolved from the *amygdala* and are extensively interconnected with this nuclei via the inferior portions of the *arcuate fasciculus* and *claustrum*. When neocortical auditory areas are impaired, the *amygdala* can be disconnected and unable to extract or impart nuances to incoming or outgoing sounds and sights. The right (*large*) and left (*small*) *amygdala* are functionally lateralised, but both are vital for language perception and expression and maintaining functional integrity of neocortical auditory areas in R and L *temporal lobes*. These bi-lateral connections hierarchically organise language at the temporal neocortex level. The amygdala is a small almond shape in the middle of the brain.

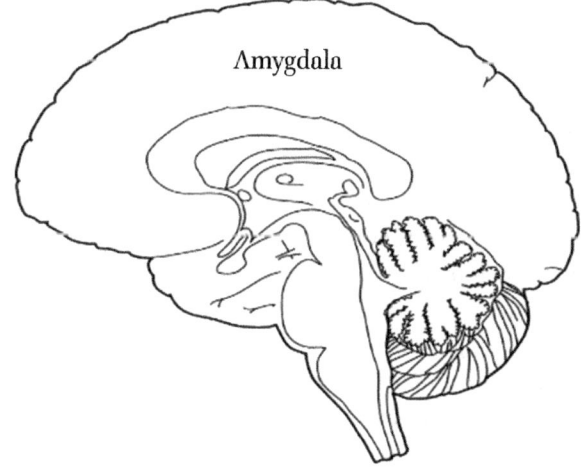

FIGURE 18.1
Brain section showing the
position of the amygdala

4   **General Indications: of Higher Level Language Disorder**

- Chatty & intelligent
- Speaking, reading, writing & spelling not to standard
- High IQ but academic achievements fail to match this
- Tests well on oral components (*vocabulary*)
- Tests badly on spoken/written narratives
- Not behind enough for assigned help but gains this from peers
- Lacks confidence & self-esteem
- Hides problems with ingenious strategies
- Often frustrated and emotional
- Considered lazy, careless, slow, dull, immature
- Behaviour problem or not bothered approach to work
- Often talented at art, drama, music, sport,
- Does well in marketing, sales, design, engineering & building jobs
- Visual & haptic abilities strong, seen in talents like model-making
- Learns best from hands-on experiences
- Likes demonstrations, experimentation, observation and visuals
- Problems maintaining attention, distracted, hyperactive or dreamer
- Easily loses track of time and gets lost

5   **Specific Indications**

5.1   *Vision, Spelling, Reading*
- Complains of dizziness when reading or head/stomach aches
- Confused by letters, numbers and words
- Sequences/explanations/instructions are difficult to understand
- Reading/writing shows repetitions, additions and omissions
- Substitutions and transpositions are commonly made mistakes
- Frequent reversals of letters, numbers and words
- Appears to have visual problems but not confirmed by tests
- Grumbles about seeing/feeling movements while reading/writing
- Reads and re-reads without full understanding
- Spells phonetically and inconsistently

5.2   *Hearing, Listening, Speaking*
- Easily side-tracked by noise & movements – fails to hear & listen
- Problems with putting thoughts into words
- Speaks haltingly in incomplete sentences

– Dysfluent when stressed
– Mispronounces words, transposes syllables, words and phrases

5.3   *Writing, Motor Ability*
– Trouble copying or writing, unusual grip, writing varies in legibility
– Uncoordinated, clumsy for sport, prone to motion sickness
– Difficulties with fine and/or gross motor skills and activities
– May be ambidextrous – often confuses left/right and over/under

5.4   *Time Management, Mathematics*
– Difficulty telling & managing time
– Problems dealing with sequenced information or tasks
– Computing depends on finger-counting and other tricks
– Knows answers but difficulty transcribing
– Can count but slow in calculating objects and dealing with money
– Can do arithmetic but not word problems
– Difficulty grasping algebra/higher mathematics

5.5   *Thinking, Memory Signs*
– Thinks primarily with images/feeling – not sounds/words
– Little inner-talk
– Limited memory for sequences, facts, information not experienced
– Excellent long-term memory for real experiences, locations and faces

5.6   *Personality, Behaviour, Health, Development Signs*
– Strong sense of justice, sensitive, strives for perfection
– Can be class clown, trouble-maker or too quiet in social situations
– Disorderly or compulsively disorderly
– Prone to ear infections
– Sensitive to foods, additives and chemical products
– Can be light/deep sleeper – bed wets beyond appropriate age
– Usually high/low pain threshold
– Symptoms & mistakes increase – stress/pressure/confusion/health
– Usually early/late development – crawling, standing, walking, talking

Not all signs are seen in a HLLD diagnosis, but 10+ would suggest this and will be observed in learning problems. Most of us will find that we have some of the symptoms above but manage them in daily life. It is not uncommon for people to have difficulties with letters (reading, writing and spelling) but have exceptional ability with numbers and mathematical operations. Many engineers and scientists have high numerical abilities but problems with oracy and literacy.

Generally, there is little concern about these signs until starting school when reading and writing are prioritised. Severe problems with these secondary language activities are often labelled as *dyslexia*, which is a descriptive not a diagnostic term, meaning "difficulty with words". Therefore, these literacy issues take precedence over subtle language ones and are frequently misunderstood and mismanaged in education.

Communication experts take a more holistic view and locate symptoms in the psycho-linguistic domain, with problems in integrating left (L-verbal) and right (R-visual) brain activities. Management is based on L-R brain integration (swimming, piano playing, etc.) and PACE brain patterning (Sage, 2000), as well as narrative language and thinking levels. When given learning strategies fitting a creative, visual, haptic, active hands-on style, progress is normally excellent. Those with HLLD signs often have high intellectual ability and develop exceptional creative talents with many geniuses exhibiting these issues. Adjustments are necessary for maximum performance. Sadly, these concerns are not often identified accurately or acknowledged, with people continuing to have life-long problems from incorrect management and frequent bullying behaviour from others in education and workplaces. On the positive side, many people with such difficulties learn to be resilient and determined.

6   Review: Consider Ideas for Effective E-Learning

- *E-learning* 3D situations and videos capture interest and stand out from Power-Points to be processed more easily
- *Video* images paint 1000 words but moving ones many more, by providing haptic input. A video, with a *context* & word *captions* for meaning, conveys more than still pictures
- *Relevant multi-media* for learning goals. If a course is about *language development*, a video shows growth stages more clearly than charts
- *Humour* gets over a point & keeps attention. Surprise learners to learn
- *Interaction* breaks up information and shares views for understanding. Some people are frustrated when interactions spoil information flow and these are hard to implement on mobile devices.
- *Narrative* e-learning should tell a story like a documentary film. It uses sets with video actors in a 3-D world. Be simple, amusing as appropriate to make output meaningful. Study television documentaries to see how messages transmit effectively.

– *Audience knowledge* decides relevant material. Today, these are diverse, with many students learning in a language other than mother-tongue, requiring more concentration and processing time. Research shows communication and language are always a problem in plural societies (Sage, 2020). Check for information overload, use short sentences in verbal transmissions, with pausing in between. Give important words and ideas suitable voice dynamics. Some find it difficult to integrate sound and sight together, so present a visual image/graphic first with suitable pausing to separate each medium. Follow with an explanation.

E-learning has accelerated in education as a result of the COVID-19 pandemic and we are all reflecting on how to use it more effectively with special attention for those not well suited to the predominately auditory and visual input. With preferred processing through the haptic sensory channel some will find e-learning, as an instruction mode, difficult and frustrating.

The Organisation for Economic Cooperation and Development (OECD) says that UK education is well supplied with technology, but staff are not trained sufficiently to deliver it effectively. The Director suggests Britain has made the slowest educational progress of the 37 OECD nations, because memorisation is the dominant learning strategy in a narrow, exam driven culture (Schleicher, 2020). He reports that education today is not about teaching facts, but developing a compass that integrates personal, practical and academic competencies.

Education must rebalance to develop a more holistic, world approach for coping with life – fixing on real not abstract issues. An OECD educational working paper (Bertling et al., 2020) reports education will never return to former teaching ways following the 2020 pandemic, with 50% preparing for a future of blended learning. There is an urgent need for ongoing professional development that monitors new teaching modes, using practitioner recording models to review evidence with colleagues. Since 60% of students worldwide do not reach required educational standards (Luckin, 2020), it is vital to review policies and practices at a time when education has been disrupted by pandemic lockdowns. The speedy introduction of e-learning has thrown up communication and language-based issues. These have previously received minimal attention in traditional teaching models. Communication matters. Let us make it matter more so that people struggle less with e-learning!

References

Bertling, J., Rojas, N., Alegre, J., & Faherty, K. (2020, October 14). *A tool to capture learning experiences during COVID-19: The PISA global crises questionnaire module.* OECD Education Working Paper 232. https://dx.doi.org/10.1787/9988df4e-en

Feyten, C. (1991). The power of listening ability: An overlooked dimension in language acquisition. *Modern Language Journal, 75,* 173–180. http://dx.doi.org/10.1111/j.1540-4781.1991.tb05348.x

Hurlburt, R., Heavey, C., & Kelsey, J. (2013). Towards a phenomenology of inner speech. *Consciousness and Cognition, 22,* 1477–1494.

Luckin, R. (2020, February 7). I, teacher: AI and school transformation. *New Statesman.* https://www.newstatesman.com/spotlight/2020/02/i-teacher-ai-and-school-transformation

Sage, R. (2000–2006). *Communication and learning* [Post-graduate course]. University of Leicester.

Sage, R. (2020). *Speechless: Understanding education.* University of Buckingham Press.

Sage, R., Rogers, J., & Cwenar, S. (2002–2010). *DIAL: Dialogue, innovation, achievement & learning studies, 1, 2, 3: Preparing the 21st-century citizen.* University of Leicester and the National Corporation of Universities, Japan.

Schleicher, A. (2020, February 4). Preparing the next generation for their future, not our past. *New Statesman.* https://www.newstatesman.com/politics/2020/02/preparing-the-next-generation-for-their-future-not-our-past

Vygotsky, L. (1986). *Thought and language.* MIT Press.

CHAPTER 19

A Blueprint for Learning

How World Events Are Changing Education

*Daryle Abrahams, Nigel Adams, Peter Chatterton, Stefano Cobello,
Joanna Ebner, Pierre Frath, Irene Glendinning, Susan James,
Riccarda Matteucci, Elena Milli, Gloria McGregor, Elizabeth Negus,
Juan Romero, Rosemary Sage and Emma Webster*

Abstract

This book represents the knowledge and experience of experts from many different areas of education and professional training. They all confirm that the present model reflects a time when societies were preparing employees to carry out routines for industrial and commercial work. Today, these procedures are increasingly implemented by intelligent machines (robots), so the roles of people are changing rapidly and are required to be more creative and collaborative, with better levels of communication and thinking. In Britain, a National Curriculum focuses on critical (linear, analytic), rather that creative (lateral free) thinking styles. The creative, right brain develops first (4–7 years) from freedom to explore, whereas the left one's period of growth is from 7 years onwards. If you examine the British educational curriculum we expect learners to approach left brain tasks, like analytic phonics for reading, as soon as they start formal schooling from 5 years onwards. Therefore, we are preventing the right brain developing and making it difficult for many people to reach their full potential. The top 10 countries educationally, work with brain development and do not start analytic work until after 7 years. This is a fundamental issue that educationalists must understand as well as the learning styles, evenly spread between top down and bottom up learners. Top downers require a very structured over view to what they are required to learn, whereas the bottom-uppers need personal stories and a narrative approach to information given them. It is possible to integrate both styles into teaching if having sufficient knowledge of brain information processing. Research cited in Sage (2000, 2003) shows how teachers give information in their preferred style, so that half the class is at a disadvantage. These are vital issues if we wish to improve levels of thinking and communication.

A blueprint provides a model for guidance with a suggested plan of action to help educational institutions to survive the rapid changes that are presently occurring in the world. It aims to guide collaborators through the process of designing and

© KONINKLIJKE BRILL NV, LEIDEN, 2022 | DOI:10.1163/9789004506466_024

contributing to the development of knowledge and competencies that are needed for life and work. Its purpose is to visualise the overall *architecture* to guide the design, development, and cooperation process. The following recommendations evolve from the content of the authors of this book.

1   Institutional Leadership

Effective institutions are based on deep and wide knowledge of appropriate policy and practice. They provide *conversational leadership*, with positive communication, inspiration, support and empowerment for stakeholders. Strong family, local, national and international community common attitudes and values back the educational goal of becoming effective, contributing, world citizens with the knowledge and competencies to progress our global society. Productive human relationships are key to successful organisations, with *trust* the critical factor. Finland easily attracts educators, although salaries are lower than some other European nations, by prioritising *confident communication*, with training at all levels, as effective co-operation and collaboration follow from this fundamental ability. Britain loses 40% of teachers within 1–5 years, due to problems of connecting and communicating with diverse learners, poor quality professional development and student bad behaviour. Appropriately trained teachers are vital (OECD, 2020a). *Community Early Learning Hubs* help parents with child development to understand the attitudes, values and abilities needed for life, with continuing specialist support available for those that need it. This is a vital input to reduce the large numbers of students requiring individual assistance in formal learning contexts. Now that students come from many different ethnic and cultural backgrounds, courses in getting to grips with intercultural communication are essential to promote equality and reduce the natural tensions that arise for individual differences (Sage, 2011).

2   Teaching and Learning Is a Communication Process: Make It a   Training Focus for All

Teaching relied on technology for instruction in the 2020–21 world pandemic. Blended learning (*technology and face-to-face*) is predicted as the future education mode, with *flipped classrooms* enabling more personalised support. Students review a topic at home, using virtual input to repeat as needed for understanding. Class time is dedicated to applying new concepts in peer group and community projects – proven to produce useful learning. The method connects up with local schemes, based on real people needs, to make learning creative and relevant, providing both *formal* and *informal* practical experiences, both inside and outside educational institutions. This provides for both top down and bottom learning styles more easily.

Equitable distribution of digital resources for students is problematic, with Britain prioritizing these, but the UK Department of Education reporting in parliament that 75% of educators view them as of less importance for learning. Virtual instruction requires a different approach to be effective, with brief information inserts, interspersed with relevant activities to review and apply concepts. Presenters of information must take account of the fact that without an audience, their voice dynamics reduce and it is difficult to adjust visual/auditory input for the varying processing needs of learners without their direct, continuous feedback.

The UK Oak National Academy provides technology design expertise, as does the Polo Europeo della Conoscenza *Robotics for Education* (courses and consultancy), but these opportunities must be validated by staff and students to be applied. Instruction in technology is usually necessary because teachers and learners are not by nature proficient ICT users (Chatterton, this volume, Chapter 15; Guggemos & Seufert, 2021). *Access* to technology resources is better than their *use* in most OECD (2018) nations. Teachers and students must rapidly know *how* to learn, using digital devices, for surviving the 21st century (EDEN, 2020). Commitment will ensure technology positively assists learning. Moves to technology learning require teacher training to be re-defined to focus on preparing students to recognise talents and interests for becoming contributing citizens. Present course cheating must be legally stopped as this has escalated even further during the pandemic. This is leading to a situation where more-and-more employers are disregarding qualifications and basing job offers on evidence of applying knowledge practically, with personal abilities to communicate, cooperate and collaborate effectively in work teams.

3   Formative Assessment Is Favoured by Employers so Establish It in Education

Technology requires different delivery to direct instruction so seek expert help. Assessment justification is that it improves learning, but *summative* methods (tests/exams) may skew teaching to marginalise student personal and practical development. Technology can reunite assessment and learning, advancing *formative personal portfolios* online that build through the educational system to doctoral level for permanent attainment evidence. These collections motivate authors, by logging meaningful materials, following internationally agreed criteria for stakeholders to reflect on and review progress. *Summative* information is not sufficiently accurate for evaluating existing individual knowledge or potential. Data from within rather than *on* practice has greater impact on progress. A *continuous record of achievement* develops *self-awareness* and *confidence* (OECD, 2020a) and countries like the USA are developing this mode of recording which universities, training organisations and work employers view as a more complete and accurate picture of applicants.

4   Review

Leadership style, quality instruction, facilitation and practical application, productive blended learning, portfolio assessment evidence, continual student and teacher consultation and appropriate support are all aspects needing regular review and updating. With the pandemic altering the pattern of life, it is an opportune time to consider the changes urgently needed to develop the broader personal and practical aspects of learning. These are the ones that must take priority if we are to achieve a smarter workforce that can cope with the higher-level tasks required now that intelligent machines can deal with the time-consuming routines of life.

References

EDEN. (2020). *Managing the next phase online*. European Distance E-Learning Network.

Guggemos, J., & Seufert, S. (2021). Teaching with and teaching about technology – Evidence for professional development of in-service teachers. *Computers in Human Behavior, 115*, 106613. https://doi.org/10.1016/j.chb.2020.106613

OECD. (2020a). *PISA 2018 results (volume V): Effective policies, successful schools*. OECD Publishing. https://doi.org/10.1787/ca768d40-en

OECD. (2020b). *Teachers' training and use of information and communications technology in the face of the COVID-19 crisis*. https//www.oecd.org>publications>teacher-training

Sage, R. (2000). *Class talk*. Bloomsbury.

Sage, R. (2003). *Learning to listen*. Bloomsbury.

Sage, R. (2011). *Getting to grips with intercultural communication*. INTERMAR: Project no. 519001 – LLP – 2011 – PT – KA2 – KA2MP.

CHAPTER 20

Epilogue

A Review and Reflection

Rosemary Sage and Riccarda Matteucci

Abstract

In 2019, a visit was made to Italian schools, colleges, universities and robotic education courses for teachers. The experience was inspiring and remains a precious, life memory. Italy retains value for oral expertise, seen in learner assessments and classroom activities. Student groups plan, develop and control tasks before presenting findings to others, seen in their *Education for Robotics* programme, where they devise projects to assist their learning and solve community problems, using available technology. In oral examinations, which often take priority over written ones, examinees must answer questions on subjects studied and present their reflections and refinements regarding their learning experiences. This educational pattern reinforces the importance of narrative thinking and language in student collaborations – enabling talk, ideas and creativity to flourish. Learning is a communicative experience, which must prioritise interactive involvement. The secret of education is that students instruct each other with teachers providing stimuli for them to talk, think and produce together (Webster, this volume, Chapter 6; Mattuecci, this volume, Chapter 17).

• • •

> What is the use of living, if not to strive for noble causes and to make this muddled world a better place for those who will live in it after we have gone.
>
> WINSTON CHURCHILL (1908)

1   Introduction

Delgado et al.'s (2018) meta-analysis on the effect of reading media, reinforces the importance of talk for developing and clarifying ideas, because a reliance on screens shows a worrying decline in understanding situations and events. We are less adept at reading all the non-verbal messages that provide 93% of the affective meaning of utterances (Mehrabian, 1971). The coordination of facial expressions, hand gestures, body language (posture and motion), voice pitch and tone, word emphasis, syntax sequential arrangements and pauses, along with context, act together to convey intent. Aleix Martinez, a professor of electrical and computer engineering at The Ohio State University, shows how important holistic communication competencies are for correct message interpretation and with 19 types of 'smile' identified to teach machine-learning algorithms, the communication system is complex (Arenschield, 2020).

Houghton et al. (2018) demonstrate how a population weaned on text messages is changing rules. Those communicating electronically break up thoughts by sending each as a separate message rather than using a *full stop* (introduced by Aristophanes of Byzantium in the 3rd century BC), which is now used to signal annoyance or irritation. Digital conversations depend on a nuanced meaning traditionally expressed non-verbally. Without the ability to convey meaning, new ways are created for clarifying messages. This explains why a recent PhD thesis had 17 lines of text and no full stops! Verbal and non-verbal communication is changing rapidly which reinforces a need to give these processes more attention in learning.

When learners enter structured education they shift from *informal dialogue* (where they have some control) to *formal monologue* (with less chance to regulate interactions), with many finding this difficult (Sage, 2020). Formal monologue requires processing *quantities of talk* in extended linguistic structures for tellings, re-tellings, instructions, reports etc. Thus, it is not surprising that the Organisation for Economic Cooperation and Development (OECD) endorses Italy for teaching that focuses on student talk. This is in contrast to Britain, showing the slowest educational progress of all OECD nations, because of narrow academic, trans-missive instruction and relegation of interactive communicative processes (OECD, Schleicher, 2020).

All nations must acknowledge changing needs in this new world, with intelligent machines taking over around 75% of routine jobs (Sage, 2020; Chatterton, this volume, Chapter 15). These now include autonomous robot burglars who can enter your house through a cat flap or letter box and scan it for valuables. A fierce robot dog will be a must for all of us! Such developments require us to become even smarter to keep abreast of intelligent machines. We need a broader knowledge and ability to communicate across languages and cultures for fresh job roles entailing more cooperative work for solving complex world problems of mobility, stability and population resourcing (Adams, this volume, Chapter 4; Abrahams, this volume, Chapter 5).

Thus, education must transform to cope with new demands and problems – not least a decline in language and thinking. This is exacerbated by British universities decolonising the English language and allowing misspellings and incorrect grammar in assignments, much to the chagrin of employers, who value clear speech and written communication. This has nothing to do with academic concerns. Linking the evils of colonisation with English literature is more about turning it into a political creed than studying different writing and author qualities. With technology rather than talk being the favoured way to connect, this presents a barrier to effective learning, now reinforced in education (Sage, 2020). Since 60% of world students do not reach required educational standards it is time to review policies and practices (Luckin, 2020). The book assembles world views on how education must progress. Views are we need teachers who are expert across the education sciences and open to new ideas and experimentation. Suggestions for change are given in the following sections.

1.1   *Recognise Talent and Diverse Views*

The full talents and views of everyone must be valued and employed. Business models, differing philosophies and economic stringencies may prevent this. Students lacking specific competencies demanded of a narrow, prescriptive, academic curriculum are dismissed as problems and may fail to get the support needed (McGregor, this volume, Chapter 14). There are many examples of people undermined and briefed against in education if having different ideas from management.

The Policy Exchange poll of 820 UK academics (Adekoya et al., 2020) shows wide support for staff discrimination, on political grounds, in publications, hiring and promotion, with chilling effects on research and teaching. Academics, finding superiors disagreeing with their views, courses, teaching and research focus may find contracts not renewed for reasons of non-standard practice. An increasing politicisation of staff appointments is a self-defeating, corrosive practice bringing lack of trust, respect and disincentive for talented people to take on lead positions.

Professor Nigel Biggar, Oxford Regius Professor of Theology, is leading an interdisciplinary inquiry on *The Ethics of Empire* (2017–2022), but has been condemned by colleagues, without justification, for being *racist* and *imperialist* for the study choice. Dr Kevin Fogg, from the Oxford Centre for Islamic

Studies has been fired for being gay and so not complying with the preference of its major funders, according to evidence supplied to the employment tribunal in October, 2020. Suppression and loss of wide knowledge, expertise and experience seriously damages progress.

A new set of moral attitudes and political adherence is weakening open debate and toleration of differences in favour of ideological positions. Those not in line with these find themselves cancelled (cast out) with reputations shattered. In the 16th century you were called *mumpsimus,* if you considered yourself right and others wrong, or an *ultracrepidarian,* if speaking on subjects of which you were ignorant. John Stuart Mill (philosopher) said such situations are social tyranny and the greatest threat to democracy. Bari Weiss (former New York Times journalist), suggests that cancelled people are rendered radioactive in an act of social murder. The Policy Exchange Report has received widespread comment with headlines in the *Daily Telegraph* (4/08/20) "Woke-ists have won, it's over for universities, staffed by intellectually identical robots!" The challenge of argument has been taken away. Students have responded on social media, warning prospective ones not to take up places, as courses are poor value for money and good staff have gone on the run!

Past/present scholars admit to being too scared to voice an opinion or put forward a view in case it goes against them and affects assignment marks. This issue needs urgent attention! Students must be encouraged in *how* rather than *what* to think, so that they can critically examine data. In September 2020, British Government Ministers ordered a review of the dumbing down of Higher Education, causing *spoon-feeding* of students, lowered standards and grade inflation.

At an employers' meeting recently, everyone complained about the superficial knowledge and limited personal and practical abilities of many of today's graduates. To achieve a Post Graduate Certificate in Education, considered the top British teaching qualification, all you need is 3 essays (40% pass mark) and to meet the required Teacher Standards, monitored from visits on teaching practice. This is different to 40 years ago, when you studied full-time and produced assignments in the 4 core areas: the *History, Philosophy, Psychology* and *Sociology* of Education. In a chosen core subject, you had to produce both practical and academic assignments with a substantial research project on an aspect of pedagogy.

1.2   Define Relevant Expertise

Appropriate personal abilities, knowledge and practical application must involve effective initial and continuing professional development (CPD) (Ebner, this volume, Chapter 8). UK teacher training is now mainly school-based, with less input from academics in a range of essential disciplines – the psychology and psycholinguistics of learning, human physical, mental, emotional and social growth, philosophy, communication sciences, sociology, history and use of new technology. In a plural society, deep knowledge of these areas is vital and all educators require awareness of *intercultural communication and human differences* to understand dissimilarities in languages, abilities, customs, values and attitudes that exist amongst students. The 2020 pandemic has focused on instruction through virtual reality, showing a need for people to alter approaches and attend to their performances (Chatterton, this volume, Chapter 15). Also, training in public speaking assists presenting to plural audiences, with differing processing capacities and language interpretations. Although not deemed primary in Britain, some nations take this seriously within teacher and student preparation.

1.3   *Develop Specialist Support*

In Britain, gifted amateurs are employed as teaching assistants, with general abilities but disconnected pedagogical experiences. They have responsibility for supporting students with learning needs, but often lack the specialised knowledge required to assist those with deficits or differences. In some countries, teaching assistants must have Masters level qualifications in the area supported, such as *Dyslexia* or *Higher Level Language Disorder*. Educators should have adequate expertise in learning difficulties for maximum impact on performance. There are nations with multi-discipline curriculum leaders, trained as speech pathologists, psychologists and teachers. The belief is that if you do not understand learning depends on communicative development and how it breaks down or fails to advance you cannot easily facilitate knowledge processes and personal competencies.

1.4   *Encourage School/College-Based Training*

Institutions need to create a properly-resourced *local* campus for training – reflecting the needs of their *specific* contexts (Ebner, this volume, Chapter 8). This happens in countries, like Cuba, where teachers have 6 years of initial graduate education in line with other professionals, like lawyers and medical practitioners. Fifty percent study for a Masters qualification over 3 years and many progress to doctorates. Educational establishments are grouped with a training campus located within one of them. University staff provide professional development directed at research *within* local practice. Educators must have chance to pursue specialist areas, with input from researchers to update knowledge and act as advisors to colleagues (Cuba/UK Universalisation Project: University of Leicester 2003–2006).

1.5   *Record Professional Development*

A practitioner model for recording CPD was developed and sponsored by the European Commission at the United Kingdom (UK) College of Teachers, involving 7 European partnerships (PEEP, 2011–2016). The record begins with an academic CV and a career review, detailing a theme for selecting evidence under 4 internationally agreed professional criteria: *acquisition and application of knowledge, continual professional development, mobility and partnerships.* If pursuing Masters or Practitioner Doctorates, a literature review demonstrates an up-to-date research and practice knowledge of the chosen theme (e.g. professional ethics), evaluating how data develops this in practice. Evidence, reflecting 20 *International Standard Classification of Education* (ISCED) Level 8 criteria, has witness statements to verify events, with feedback on achievements. A final, reflective statement shows how this has contributed to policy, practice and professional development. The submission is around 50,000 words for a Masters and 100,000 ones for a Practitioner Doctorate, including visual and auditory material if appropriate. (Sage, this volume, Chapter 10).

A review of the portfolio process for qualifications on social media commented on this approach being less open to abuse, with evidence of Masters and Doctorates being bought from unscrupulous institutions and websites (Glendinning, this volume, Chapter 11). Research *within* rather than *on* practice, involving participants also as subjects in investigations, demonstrates more impact on policy and practice than traditional approaches. Elizabeth Negus (this volume, Chapter 7), a Practitioner Doctor, endorses this qualification as focusing on personal work requirements for the greatest impact on progress. CPD portfolios are popular worldwide, allowing staff and students to regularly share their evidence to enhance everyone's professional and personal development. The UK 2020 school examinations were unable to take place because of the pandemic. This meant students initially received grades by means of an algorithm, which downgraded 40% of them from teacher predictions. We have sleepwalked into a situation where it is viewed as acceptable for biased computer simulations to decide the fate of individuals in an unchallenged march towards a modern form of tyranny!

In the United States of America (USA), 150 schools use work portfolios instead of examinations, which are accepted by universities, training institutes and workplaces. This is a sensible development, as examination grading changes annually to suit political requirements. Thus, summative evaluations are not always reliable indicators of potential, as they are marked according to criteria which will inevitably disadvantage some students. The Italian system places more reliance on oral assessment, by a panel that includes experts within and outside schools. This is viewed as a more reliable, efficient way of judging knowledge and expertise.

1.6   *Workplace Intermissions*

A practice of giving staff remission to either study or visit other institutions abroad energises the individual and benefits colleagues from knowledge and experience shared. This assists *mobility* (global links) and *partnerships* – regarded as necessary for all professional roles with links worldwide. Schools/ colleges that encourage national and international contacts are assisting students in becoming effective global citizens, by giving opportunities to understand the varying lifestyles that have evolved from the different physical characteristics of world areas. It helps us see we are all part of a greater whole.

1.7   *Conversational Leadership* (CL)

This has been widely accepted but not adopted. Leaders must improve workplace dialogue but *'the culture'* is a barrier. Employee expectations and the external context have changed, but outdated practices and mind-sets persist. To achieve this: Have a conversation about conversations: How do we talk to each other in this workplace? Review what inhibits open talk. Is it process, opportunity, mindset, competencies, or these together? This promotes effective conversations by encouraging awareness, working with rather than against the culture.

1.8   *Leaders Must Move from Having Right Answers to Asking Right Questions*

Leadership with a conversational approach replaces the complexity of monologue with the simplicity of dialogue. This enables open and flowing rather than closed and directive dialogue. Leaders must cultivate listening to all people and speaking *with* rather than to them – directly, sincerely and regularly.

1.9   *Leaders and Managers Must Learn the Strategies of Better Conversations*

Techniques to improve talk, like inquiring, reporting, reflecting, challenging and dealing with conflict, can be taught. This is vital to increase confidence for *difficult* conversations.

– Command & control is not effective for leaders to run workplaces
– Conversation Leadership is open meaningful, genuine dialogue between employees & leaders that compromises & accepts views
– A more conversational culture arises from talking a subject through, sharing & refining ideas to equip with competencies for decisions
– Conversational, distributed leadership is vital & inevitable, in line with the future world, with equality & discrimination issues to solve

Comment: The award winning teacher, John Taylor Gatto details education deficiencies in his thoughtful book, *Dumbing Us Down* (2017). Strimpel (2020) quotes the experience of *Careers Collective*, which reports that graduates now struggle to find jobs as grade inflation means their degrees have lost value. Employers are adapting to a future in which university qualifications become the exception rather than the norm for highly-skilled work. Companies like Apple, Google, IBM, Ernst & Young, Random House and Penguin have opened up employment to non-graduates, resulting in applications offering better levels of personal and practical competencies.

Prescriptive curricula undermine and limit student abilities to think, communicate creatively and critically as well as behave appropriately. Given state involvement in many life aspects, it is unsurprising that there is an epidemic of bullying and disruptive behaviour across education sectors, which a world study is investigating (Cobello & Milli, this volume, Chapter 13). UK Government statistics reveal that 438,300 school exclusions happened in 2019, equivalent to 2,307 daily. Disruptive behaviour remains the common reason for suspensions, including bullying, assaults, drugs and alcohol-related incidents. Such behaviour shows an absence of *theory of mind* (Appendix), with inability to understand consequences of actions, depending on language narrative competence. Language and behaviour research shows a reduction of brain grey matter in the orbito-frontal cortex, implicated in impulse control and decision-making, to explain inappropriate conduct (Sage, 2020).

International comparison tables mean education has global similarities but negative costs. Staff and students must reach standards in ways not always encouraging effective teaching, or engaging with those unable to respond to abstract, academic methods. This causes pressure to achieve, so encouraging bullying and unfitting behaviour of staff and students like cheating! The *Wellcome Foundation Report* (Farrar, 2020), on university staff culture, found 78% had witnessed aggression; 43% experienced severe bullying and harrassment; 53% sought help for depression and 20% felt creativity had been stifled. Taylor Gatto (2017) focussed on the *group sociocultural system* to examine issues holistically.

1.10 Social Capital Theory

Social capital theory sheds light on behaviour, used to obtain and protect personal position, which fuels power with resources to act. In contrast, those lacking *social capital (specific learning needs/lower staff positions)* find it difficult to shed a lesser status and see themselves as inadequate, reinforced by peer/colleague responses.

1.11 Desire for Dominance

This is a motivating factor in all group situations, used to acquire both *individual and group social dominance*, seen more commonly in plural societies.

1.12   *Humiliation of People*
This is a consequence of *social domination*, resulting in negative outcomes like depression, anger & enduring memories for those who are unsuccessful.

1.13   *Organisational Culture*
This is affected by those failing to reach standards, so reinforcing their low position in the group/s (students/staff), with a negative presence impacting on the climate. It highlights need for a holistic approach to learning and organisation.

•••

Thus, social capital, dominance, humiliation and organizational culture theories explain group behaviour, shedding light on how professionals can collaboratively manage learning. Experts confirm the importance of these analytic methods in a world requiring a more holistic perspective to explain complexity. Unfortunately, traditional linear approaches, promote studies *on* rather than *within* practice, with narrow interpretations of situations, which focus on individuals but not their interactions.

2   How the Pandemic Is Rewriting Principles

With the population in full/partial pandemic lockdown for months in 2020–21, there has been a drive by some people insisting that human life must be understood through the prism of identity politics. They say that individuals must be defined by the apparently homogenous experience of the group to which they belong, *race, religion, sex, age*, etc. A focus on groups, whose virtue is their marginality, neglects our common culture. This is replaced by a fractured society playing to those characterised by a hostile separatism, leading to culture '*wars*'. An example is a statue of Sir Winston Churchill (*British Prime-minister*), who defeated fascism. It was defaced by anti-racists and then defended by fascists during lockdown. In France, anti-racists want to suppress everything of Colbert (Louis XIV Minister) as he published a *Code Noir* regulating slavery. However, this was progress of sorts and a step to abolition, recognising slaves and introducing them into the legal framework. Writers, like Mazarine Pingeot, argue that cheap indignation and moralism has replaced politics. If wanting to fight for minority rights, political action is the way, not shaming & threatening people into submission (Frath, this volume, Chapter 9).

Traditionally, national institutions have encouraged us to always compromise and make sacrifices for one another, respecting our community and common good. Pericles, the Greek, said that Athenians pride themselves in being free and tolerant in private, but in public are obedient to the established law, social attitudes and customs. Sage (2020) presents research to show how common views, values, attitudes and appearances are vital for peaceful co-existence of citizens. This is the secret of Western civilisation – secular laws within a jurisdiction allowing liberty. The bond between free and equal citizens must not be broken. It is not one of race or religion but loyalty to the nation and love for its land, laws, language, values and culture.

However, Western nations are not cohesive societies today. In Britain, the wealth of the richest 10% of families is 5 times higher than the rest combined (Office for National Statistics, 2020). Where is equality here? (Romero, this volume, Foreword). The Food Foundation reported that in Autumn 2020, 3 in 10 British children (2 million) are registered for free school meals, with 65% from families with higher income occupations. Also, there is the pernicious effect of cultural liberalism and militant identity politics. Elites debate the lack of black students at Oxford, but fail to acknowledge that white indigenous pupils are less likely to go to university than other ethnic groups, whilst the white working-class fare the worst at school.

Professor Peter Edward's evidence to the September 2020 UK Education Select Committee warned of the plight of the white working class, as raising their issues is deemed unfashionable, taboo and not worthy of consideration. As a teacher, in the 1980s, this was experienced in a Midland city school with a majority of immigrant pupils. The immigrant children had Home Office funding for daily extra individual support, whereas the indigenous ones, who had low levels of thinking and language, needed speech and language help, which meant long waiting lists and loss of learning. When bringing this to constant attention with bosses, the problems were continually brushed aside. Such dismissive views are attributed to hard-right politics. As a working class lad, who now is an Oxford academic, Professor Edwards knows what he is talking about. Those raising plights of white working classes are cancelled as cranks and if backing unifying identities as *patriotism* are ridiculed as reactionaries. Data from the Annual Population Survey (Office for National Statistics, 2020) shows that young white Britons, aged 16–29, earn less than their BAME peers. This is unsurprising as the indigenous students often have received less help.

Today's liberal thinkers follow views of those like Michel Foucault (1966), the French philosopher, who argued all discourse is oppressive, with social realities imposed through language, customs and institutions. These maintain exploitative hierarchies, so the pursuit of equal rights is a trap to be overturned, because power has historically been with white men. This influenced *intersectionality*, highlighting the different experiences of racial and sexual groups.

Intersectionality is a theory of how aspects of a person's social and political identity (gender, sex, race, class, sexuality, disability, appearance, height, etc.) combine to create unique modes of discrimination and privilege. Ethnicity and sex affect us but do not define us. Our abilities, character, beliefs and values count as much as skin colour and reproductive organs. *Intersectionality* neglects factors, like social class and economic geography (twice as many disadvantaged students from London go to university compared with elsewhere), but is now in government, workplace and legal policy.

Oppression Olympics state some identity groups are suffering with others as the cause. Together with a belief that we oppress through language and actions, this renders us guilty, regardless of intent or meaning, so making woke racism acceptable. It is a characterisation of marginalisation as a competition to determine the relative weight of the overall oppression of individuals/groups. It compares race, gender, socioeconomic status or disabilities – to determine who is the worst off and most oppressed. This arises within debates about ideological values of identity politics, intersectionality and social privilege.

Liberal thought is based on a misconceived model of human nature and political organisation that underestimates the cultural and institutional context as well as the history of communities. Viewing countries as a stage where anyone in the world can enter, live and work with only minimal obligations, liberalists regard borders as restraints on personal freedom. However, ethnically diverse nations are more likely to ditch attachments to the majority culture and identity. Research shows that the more diverse a society the less trust and reciprocity there is, with reluctance to pay taxes for public and welfare services (Matteucci, 2017). Therefore, liberalism can become illiberal and intolerant. Racial prejudice is fear of outsiders, who might overwhelm and disrupt normal expectations – customs, attitudes & way of life.

A debate on *code-switching,* when people normally change their way of speaking and behaving to suit conventions of situations, shows how some immigrants resist this as discrimination. A stable society, with strong community ties, can absorb new arrivals with calmness and kindness, realising enrichment comes from weaving in and out of each other's cultures. However, the large numbers of immigrants continually arriving in the West have brought anxiety, because the traditional ethos is changing to break boundaries that give existing citizens security and stability. The move to axe *Rule Britannia* and *Land of Hope and Glory* at the 2020 London Proms is an example, receiving resistance from patriots, because words have been wrenched from their true historical context to prove British tyranny. This signals a loss of British identity.

A strong view exists, particularly amongst those with little voice, that there is now an attempt to impose a single, hostile narrative, which wants to efface the national story and retell it as racial oppression. The illegal army, *Forever Family Force*, dressed in black, with the clenched fist of the 1970s *Black Power* movement, has been marching with the *Rhodes Must Fall* and *Extinction Rebellion* groups to demand slavery reparations from government. Edmund Burke, the philosopher, said that rage and frenzy will pull down more in half an hour than prudence, deliberation and foresight can build up in a hundred years.

This hounding is reminiscent of *Mao's Chinese Cultural Revolution* (1966–1976), which wrecked this ancient civilisation. The only way someone accused of thought-crime could escape punishment was through public confession and re-education, in which they were humiliated. The present *woke movement* – a concern for justice, but now used for intolerance of anyone not supporting your views and attitudes, has reinvented this ritual to stamp on views that do not fit. Teachers, professors and others try to hang on to jobs and not be *cancelled*, the new word for this action!

Professor Greg Patton, a communication expert at the University of Southern California, was teaching business students about Chinese culture, saying the expression *neige* (pronounced nee-gah) was often used as a *pause* in negotiations. The students complained, saying this racial slur badly affected their mental health. This was nothing to do with the N-word and the context did not suggest a racist interpretation. The University backed students and suspended Professor Patton (Hacker News, 7 September 2020). Increasingly, people behave in irrational, intolerant, unpleasant ways. Universities, traditionally upholding different views, have fallen to intimidation.

Today's email and social media makes situations like this worse than the Chinese revolutionary form, as the destructive ideology is global not local. The aim is to dictate how we deliberate and operate, with people told what they must think, say, read and follow. There is no longer free thought and if holding ideas different to those in power, or saying something that is clearly wrongly interpreted, you may suffer injustice. Symptoms are continually around us but we are generally not interested in understanding causes.

Traditional accounts about our existence have now collapsed. Religion was first – from the 19th century onwards. During the last century, secular aspirations of political philosophies followed. The post-modern era (late 20th century) dismissed out-moded narratives about life's meaning. In the wealthy, Western democracies, the modern reason for living is to get rich and have fun. Finding meaning now is by waging war against anyone not thinking like us. The justification for this is to bring harmony, but it promotes division, as experts have shown.

3   The Importance of Boundaries

Professor Furedi (2020) in *Why Borders Matter: Why Humanity Must Relearn
the Art of Drawing Boundaries,* presents the price we are paying for corrupting
age-old certainties. Boundaries are key in making moral distinctions between
right and wrong. In Europe, the Schengen Agreement (1985) abolished many
frontiers, indicating that national borders were artificial, exclusionary, unjust
and anti-human. By not drawing lines between nation states, distinctions
between different people cannot be made. Thus, history and human development's role in creating peace and security is ignored, with national sovereignty
belittled as irrelevant in a global world. Also, blurring of lines between generations and different ethnic cultures confuses roles and responsibilities, with
value systems not consistently upheld for children to learn how to interact and
behave in the place where they live.

Furedi says university students are "infants", unable to be independent in
thought or action, which augurs badly for their contributions to life and work.
Gender neutrality is another example, with directives by New York's Commission on Human Rights to fine landlords/employers up to $250,000 (£200,000)
if using the wrong pronouns with binary employees. *Who Are You? The Kid's
Guide to Gender Identity,* by Brook Pessin-Whedbee, takes readers through
identities, like gender-queer, non-binary, bigender, neutrois (neutral/null identity) and two-spirit – a person with male and female spirit).

The book teaches that the gender concept is fiction not fact, to contradict
obvious physical differences. Another advance of the boundary-less movement is the undermining of public and private, encouraging people to openly
express themselves and prevent mental health issues. Although talk is positive
to release negative emotions, some privacy is vital as it is unwise to always
express views and feelings publicly. In a narcissistic age, "I" and "me" are central
to vocabularies, demonstrating an individual is more important than society.
Furedi says that rejecting boundaries weakens communities and nations –
leading to destruction and decline. Such issues need review to achieve balanced views to allow positive progress as *all lives* matter.

4   How Can Education Manage This New World Order?

With people returning to education following lockdowns, the sector wonders
how to address the present political, economic and social scene, feeling pressure to do something. Whilst it is crucial to address current events, it is unwise

to introduce the topic of how the world is changing things into pastoral teaching. To restructure the curriculum, without reflection and consultation, may harm learners. Public demonstrations revolve around divisive identity politics, using phrases like *white privilege, white saviour* and *white fragility*. The demand that Britain must make amends for African slavery indicates that whites are forever responsible for black woes. However, an African colleague says that if his ancestors had not been slaves in the West, he would not have had the chance to become a doctor.

Historians have said that these issues should not be presented as unchallengeable facts. For example, cries to remove a statue of Cecil Rhodes at Oxford University, because of a fortune made from slavery, are disputed, as this was abolished in the British Empire long before his birth. Rhodes Oxford Scholarships have no colour-bar and are globally regarded as the most generous in the world. Also, the Archbishop of Canterbury's move to change the ethnicity for Christ's portrayal ignores the fact that in other countries he is depicted as one of themselves, so this action could be viewed as insulting to white British.

Goodhart (2020) says that provision of detailed, accurate evidence has not been a strong point of the *UK Black Lives Matter* movement, which highlights discrimination against people of colour. British Indians do much better than white in labour market outcomes. 35% of British Caribbean men are in the top two social classes, only slightly less than the white proportion. On the police stop and search argument, the disproportionality for black citizens falls away when you consider where this happens, in city areas of high violent crime (Office for National Statistics, 2020).

The classroom is not a place for *Critical Race Theory* (CRT) – the field of study giving rise to controversial ideas and terms of suppression. Does the logic of this theory suggest that a mixed-race child should perceive one parent as the oppressor and the other as the oppressed? CRT thinks truth, correct spelling, mathematics accuracy, time-keeping and discipline are white supremacist ideas, so confirming the rejection of behaviour boundaries. *Uncommon Schools* have issued a policy that they will no longer encourage pupils to listen in class; ties are not a present uniform requirement; trainers may replace shoes; detentions are only for major infractions; staff will undergo unconscious bias training and teachers must manage emotions in conflict situations. The USA Kipp Chartered schools have eliminated their "Work Hard. Be Nice" slogan, as it values compliancy and submission. Also, a London University academic published tweets claiming that a teacher correcting student grammar is being punitive, oppressive and discriminatory (August, 2020). Do these examples suggest that words like *dedication, kindness, resilience* and *accuracy* are unacceptable? Best-selling children's books along CRT lines are *Feminist Baby*

(Loryn Brantz), *Antiracist Baby* (Ibram X Kendi) and *The Little Girl Who Gave Zero F*cks* (Amy Kean).

The Chartered College of Teaching supports the CRT approach, providing resources for schools to teach about whiteness, white racism, white identity, privilege, power and intersectionality. Mandatory reading lists include one-sided perspectives on race relations, presenting a single view as unquestioned truth, with little or no empirical evidence. In education, opinions should be challenged and facts backed up with proof and balanced literature. Attempts are made to de-colonise the curriculum, with Birmingham City University and the Youth Music charity launching campaigns to erase Mozart from the curriculum and replace him with Stormzy to shake up teaching. There is much to be learnt from Stormzy's top hit, *Shut Up*, but it does not compare with Mozart's technical symphonies, which inspire and revive. Also, black history curriculum campaigners often argue from uninformed positions. There are influential black people on the syllabus, like *Rosa Parks* and *Mary Seacole*, taught from UK Key Stage 1.

Youngsters do not see race as their sole identity. They must understand that people are individuals and part of a greater whole. History belongs to all of us and unites us regardless of race, belief or religion. However, London Royal Academy of Dramatic Art (RADA) students have produced an *Anti-Racism Action Plan*, because College experience is "filtered through the History of the West – imperialism, colonialism and white supremacy". They propose to rename the *George Bernard Shaw Theatre*, as this playwright was sympathetic to eugenics and fascism. Will they return the annual £80,000 tainted money, paid to RADA from the Shaw estate over 70 years (around 6 million)? Also, they have *cancelled* the Restoration comedies, because characters are figureheads of the Empire, which experts say is incorrect. Decolonising the curriculum is now common practice. Education should be about passing on knowledge and teaching the best available, rather than focusing on popular trends and erasing history, so preventing opportunities to review past practices for improvement and progress.

Not only is the curriculum under threat but teacher training is at risk. Knowledge is being tainted by divisive identity politics employing *unconscious bias training*. Attending such a session, teachers were told that children should never read the *Black Sambo* books. This series give a positive image of a different culture with gorgeous *black mamas*. Trainers are using Harvard University's *Implicit Association Test* to highlight *unconscious bias*, despite the authors and the diagnostic community exposing it as unsuitable for general use. Using assessments reliably require training to professional standards, as data may be interpreted inaccurately. However, these tests are being used without expert training, which is dangerous and unethical. The idea that one may be racially biased without knowing is malicious. Teachers are advised to read *White Fragility*, by Robin DiAngelo – claiming all white people are racist with denials providing proof. Challenge this and one is dismissed as expressing white privilege – an intellectual trap planned for the naïve.

Although measures from curriculum alterations to teacher training are implemented by the well-intentioned wanting to do the right thing, they risk stoking up racial tension, where there was little or none in the first place. This causes potentially long-standing issues among vulnerable youngsters, who should be taught *how* rather than *what* to think. Also, it would be considered a breach of the UK 1996 Education Act, with a duty to maintain political neutrality. However, there is growing opposition to CRT for following moralised, politicised one-sided perspectives. Increasing liberalism and lack of boundaries to actions and places are creating a society where *anything goes*. This was brought to attention in the summer of 2020, when fewer UK people took holidays abroad, because of the pandemic, so making for British beauty spots. These have been left as rubbish tips with residents of Cumbria saying that regular, respectful visitors have come expecting William Wordsworth and have encountered scenes befitting London Wandsworth.

In 2017, La Boeuf (American Actor), Ronkko (Finnish Artist) and Turner (British Artist) came together in *a* New York Performance Art Project, focusing on *Don't Divide Us,* which has become the international melting pot of ages, races, genders, sexualities and beliefs. In 2020, an online petition opposed the Australian Government's move to establish discriminatory laws, making it easier for people to impose their beliefs on others. Also, a coalition of teachers, academics, artists and others from different backgrounds was launched in 2020 by *Anglican Mainstream*. This campaign is concerned about a toxic, radicalised agenda increasing division and cultural conflict worldwide. It is supporting education through this mine-field, with fact-based investigations into the roots of social problems. It does not aim for quick-fixes or simplistic, inaccurate explanations, which have been tumbling out from media sources. It offers a way to help learners understand the world rather than the faux-science of CRT and the anti-capitalist, -imperialist, -Western and -Semitic rhetoric of many identity political movements. *Don't Divide us* is an important mantra for learners to comprehend, with a message of communication, cooperation and collaboration, hailed by business and commerce as vital for solving world problems (Abrahams, this volume, Chapter 5). Forging a shared identity brings solidarity – making compromise, tolerance and sacrifice possible to build a politics of common good. We must absorb the wisdom of the famous American Civil Rights Leader, Martin Luther

King, who dreamt of a future in which people were judged not by skin colour but character content.

5   Review

Empirical research has been presented and interpreted in this book, which recognises and explains education complexity (Matteucci, this volume, Chapters 16 and 17). Learning is contextual, mediated by situated relationships between individuals in social contexts having their own norms and practices. Multiple settings and groups, in which individuals interact mutually, create their behaviour, attitudes, social relationships, identities and values (James, this volume, Chapter 12). Learning and teaching are interpreted differently as society changes – experienced and responded to in various ways.

Sociocultural perspectives force us to move attention away from the individual teacher-student dyad and focus on contextual, historical and institutional influences that surround teaching, learning and behaviour (Cobello & Milli, this volume, Chapter 13). This assigns greater responsibility to others with whom a student interacts, whilst challenging certain community–based norms, which may regularise certain interactive styles or negative behaviours. Adopting a sociocultural interpretation recognises various influences on individuals and reinforces the importance of tackling all levels of the system (Bronfenbrenner, 1979). We need to move from relying heavily on individualised, blame-based or punitive approaches for researching, assessing and addressing learning.

Contextual factors operating around students must be considered, which result in particular behaviour patterns. This means shifting attention away from isolating particular variables that influence education, as in many assessments and traditional, linear research methods, which narrow evaluations (Frath, this volume, Chapter 9). It is important to recognise wider influences that interact together to create a situation. We must understand what triggers might be important for initiating particular patterns of learning behaviour, interactions or responses in specific circumstances and what conditions might inhibit practices. It is vital to study reciprocal interactions between people, as part of their membership of many, intersecting communities and recognize the role of identity through participation and ongoing meaning-making (Ttofi & Farrington, 2012). This assists understanding of what helps and hinders learning management. We are often directed towards certain issues and so neglect the big picture.

Sociocultural educational research addresses context to explore meaning-making, interactions and relationships *across time*. There are challenges here, suggesting that adopting multiple methods to study a topic or question enables the flexibility and sensitivity required to capture relevant nuances. A high proportion of empirical work presents as a-theoretical, because of a lack of specific reference to models. This is not a criticism, because no theory provides all answers to questions. Therefore, it is vital to consider what works and is appropriate in a *particular* context (Menesini & Salmivalli, 2017)

Evidence from real situations supports practitioner models of qualification, such as doctorates. The potential of sociocultural perspectives for understanding education issues has not been fully realised in most studies. Additional insight is gained from applying these to what is known (and still unknown) about effective instruction and human information processing (Sage, this volume, Chapters 1, 2, 3, and 18).

For researchers undertaking empirical work, approaches should be reviewed and questions posed as work progresses (as advocated in the practitioner doctorate model) rather than just at the beginning of a study. This allows additional interpretations and potential alternative explanations for data trends to be considered. Sociocultural tools enable issues to be considered from many perspectives to help work through issues. Over-reliance on self-reports (e.g. questionnaires) run a risk of confusing what people say they do with what actually happens and experience shows these can be unreliable. Being mindful not to assume too much from data, brings possibility that people will act differently in situations depending on circumstances. Sociocultural theory overcomes potential pitfalls around what is a representation and an action, as it centres on real activity and meaning. It challenges stability in behaviours, characteristics and interactions – recognising that roles and actions are complex, involving subtle judgements and complex relations. This is why practitioner modes, investigating workplace activities over time, are gaining ground. They move through the rhetoric of objective views from traditional, linear, research, which rarely mirrors reality accurately. Answering a narrow question and collecting data on just one brief occasion provides a narrow, restricted view.

With regard to teaching intervention, there is interest in studying contexts influencing learning. Cowie's (2008) whole school/college approach considers these – referred to as *risk factors* – operating at different levels to impact on student engagement. This resonates with the *Ecological System theory* (Bronfenbrenner, 1979). At the *individual* level, consideration is about personal characteristics and elements of biological, personal history that might make people vulnerable to learning difficulties. At an *interpersonal* level, discussion is about an individual's family and peer relationships, with types of behaviours normalised and valued. At a *community* level, factors operating in school/college or neighbourhood, like gangs, school/college ethos and unemployment problems are examined. At the *societal* level, social and cultural norms, which might normalise acceptable means of interaction are presented. If we want to successfully address learning, we must adopt approaches operating at a societal and school/college level as well as interpersonal. This means educational institutions working in partnership with families and communities, alongside support efforts within formal learning.

Literature on management, intervention and support favours holistic approaches with outside involvement (DfE, 2014). The most effective interventions are those adopting whole-institution, classroom and individual levels, whilst involving families plus the wider community (Cowie, 2011). A reason why programmes like Educational Robotics (Poloeuropa world initiatives to develop learning for 21st century citizens) are successful is the way they address the multi-layered influences operating in student experience and recognise the various contexts in which they participate. 'We need to focus on changing the system rather than the individuals within it' (Monks et al., 2009, p. 154). Therefore, a sociocultural perspective is advocated, in order to understand, explain and address *inequality* highlighted in the 2020 pandemic.

In the 21st century, we have created much knowledge from which people have accomplished great things. However, information is often unmanageable and what we know exceeds our ability to deliver the benefits reliably. Knowledge burdens as well as assists us in making progress. We need a strategy for overcoming failure based on understanding and supporting communication. This is common in therapeutics (e.g. Speech & Language Therapy), but less so in education. Where there is a will there is a way. Let us make this a year for action! Recently, the media reported that parents consulted faith healers to adjust their youngsters' school leaving grades upwards, so confirming we are in a time of anxiety and uncertainty! However, we must not base all decisions on fear, but let hope have a look in as well. Maybe we can build nations that belong to all who live in them and provide equal opportunities to make the most of their talents and interests. With 1 in 5 UK students leaving education functionally illiterate it is time to realise that high quality teaching is the best chance to fulfil potential.

To achieve this we must resolve the issue of *love* and *hate* that exists in all of us and society at large. If *hate* wins, learning is disrupted for individuals and groups. Britain has just done an analysis of 120,000 police recorded hate incidents and reports that none can be considered crimes. They include a man whistling the *Bob the Builder* theme tune as he passed a neighbour, a teacher who allowed a child to bang his head against the pool-side, which the mother said was due to his ethnicity and a person who dropped a burger outside the house of the Portuguese owner, who alleged it was due to his colour. Such police records damage a person's career. The legend of the *Two Wolves* is applicable here. This popular legend of unknown origin, is sometimes attributed to the Cherokee or Lenape people. It is a story of a grandfather using a metaphor of two wolves fighting within him to explain his inner love-hate conflicts to his grandson. When the grandson asks which wolf wins, the grandfather answers: "Whichever he chooses to feed is the one that wins".

6   Postscript

Since this book was sent to the publishers in October 2020, much has happened in the following months. The pandemic shows no sign of abating and talk about technology is to the fore. What about us humans? Are we going to be replaced by robots? Will we become less relevant as intelligent machines take over more of our roles? Are we still evolving? This is the decade when the *Internet of Things* (IoT) will force the evolution and gradual dissolution of the traditional understanding of homo sapiens. The web has become the way for most of us to access the internet with Google as the search engine. The question is: Are we being pushed and manipulated as we search? Do we want advertising jumping up at us whenever we switch on? Do we want our data tracked, traced and revamped to influence us in restricted ways? Do we want to be profiled by algorithms?

When buying online, one must click *accept* on the privacy policy which means that what has been purchased is not private at all. Personalising the web is about persuading you to part with your money, with everything tailored to help. This new customer model means you pay twice, with cash for goods and personal information transmitted. In fact, online giants raise prices of everything bought if you have an expensive laptop, so regularly ripping many of us off (Fairer Finance consumer group statement). Our clicks and likes determine *Editors Picks*, ensuring that the little we know and our personal biases will be looped back to us repeatedly. This means different ideas and a wider view disappear to make us narrower in thinking and deeds.

Consider a world with no private thoughts or actions. The internet of things allows any object to act as a computer. Your fridge totals the food bought and consumed. If having a diet app, the fridge helps by ordering the correct food to eat and self-locks if you break the rules. Smart beds warm or cool, manage light flow and report your state of sleeplessness to the automated doctor for medication if needed. In the kitchen, the toaster reminds you it is a no-carbs day and the toilet assesses the contents of anything you drop into it! Of course, there are advantages in this unified connectivity – boring tasks are removed from life. This new reality is sold to us as empowerment not surveillance. Elon Musk's Neuralink Company works on brain-computer interfaces, allowing human ability to control computer operations through their thoughts, with people trials over 2020–21. Modern medicine has retuned biology, as we live twice as long as our ancestors. Silicon Valley is researching how physical and mental decline can be reversed to survive for longer. However, these medical advances now mean over population on our planet and grave shortages of natural resources. AI systems suffer no such losses and declines and can augment, version-up and get smarter. However, we must not imagine that the AI world is perfect. Robots collided in a major distribution depot in SE London with 3,500 of them programmed to pack deliveries. A terrific blaze was the result of this July 2021 collision with 100 firefighters involved in extinguishing it. This is the third blaze in an Ocado warehouse in under 2 years where buildings have been destroyed. Although merging with AI is a logical outcome for the new form of homo sapiens, outcomes often resist predictions and expectations. What is predicted confidently is *personalisation* – your smart house, car, life-style, personal shopper, teacher or therapist etc. to replace out-of-date privacy. The new analogue human will find it difficult to be off-grid at times! At the moment, we can leave phones at home but soon smart devices and implants will become normal and there will be no logging on. As Winterton (2021) says you are in and on for life – from sci-fi to Wi-Fi to my-wi.

The 5Rights organisation is fighting to protect children, who are tech savvy but tech vulnerable. Online grooming is escalating and in the UK 5Rights report that in one month of 2020 over 9 million attempts to view child-abuse images were blocked. In primary schools visited, we are regularly told that about 3/4s of 10 year olds constantly access pornography. There does not seem enough concern about exploitation of children by phones, which includes addictive gaming, the despair of dislikes/likes as well as porn habits.

What happens about this lack of division between the real and on-line worlds? The goal of the Silicon Valley digital masters is there will be no off-line. It may be that issues of privacy and data usage are temporary problems. We assume that human interests and actors will remain dominant in all aspects of life. However, if AI becomes super-intelligent and an actor and not just a tool, then the future for humans may not be so important.

The problem with humans is their disregard of problems. For example, the issue about climate change is it could mean we have to eventually fight for food or starve. As we are life-limited, there is a general lack of concern for what may lay ahead when we are pushing up the daisies! Although the world may become poorer as a result of the huge expenses of the COVID-19 pandemic, the virus gives opportunities for tech giants to become richer with even more world control. Eric Schmidt (American technology businessman and software engineer; CEO of Google 2001–11 and Executive Chairperson 2011–15) talks about home-schooling for all using platforms replacing contact in the pandemic (teachers take note!). This means new connection types. Virtual-reality avatar sessions are being trialled by Face-book and will soon become common place like Zoom. However, all these innovations are presently costly at a time of likely world recession due to the pandemic.

Moreover, AI is an energy guzzler and our fossil-fuel will never be sufficient for this new future. Chris Mason, Professor of Physiology and Biophysics (2021) at Weill Cornell Medical School, New York, argues that humans will be able to engineer their bodies to survive extra-terrestrial conditions and live on new planets when earth can no longer sustain life. Another constraint is *Moore's Law,* observing that every 2 years the number of transistors fitting on a square-inch of microchip will double. It is 50 years since Federico Faggin, the Italian genius, produced the first Intel microchip – the computing power that once filled a large building with hardware that now fits into a smart watch on your wrist.

There is an obvious limit to this progress and the next projected jump is into quantum computing, to increase speed and commands, with reports that China has made this breakthrough. Google and IBM claim they are close to this possibility. Quantum computers perform calculations based on the probability of an object's state before it is measured – instead of just 1s or 0s. Thus, they have potential to process exponentially more data compared to classical computers. A single state, such as *on* or *off*, *up* or *down*, *1* or *0*, is called a *bit*. Quantum computers will be remote from reality so we are building something that only a few people will know how the systems that control us actually work. Questions of what is "you" and how far there can be control over life arise, George Orwell (2000) was not wrong when in his book *Nineteen Eighty-Four,* he said "You had to live – did live, from habit that became instinct – in the assumption that every sound you made was overheard and except in darkness, every movement scrutinized" (p. 25).

Humans are adaptable. Those of us who are old, mourn the past, simpler life, but none of us would wish to return to the world of two centuries ago. We dislike modern web intrusion, but who would be without their smart phones today? We can see a world becoming less democratic but it may be less stressful with many irritating tasks taken off our hands by our robot colleagues. More decisions will be taken by intelligent machines, which are more predictable, reliable and accurate than fallible humans.

Recently, we have been working with teenagers from selective grammar and public schools on practical tasks like cleaning cars, mowing lawns, weeding flower beds and chopping wood. These are students who do well in school exams. However, they find it difficult to carry out 3 instructions and continually fail to use initiative and ask for help when they should be able to solve a practical problem. They never go through their jobs, to check and review outcomes, so that things are missed like the unwashed car windscreen. These young people are constantly on their phones, which come out at every opportunity, even when asked to put them away while executing their tasks. Although excellent at learning facts, which are checked in exams and tests, their application of these needs attention. We cannot blame them, as our UK system is skewed towards competitive testing and worldwide comparisons through league tables, with factual knowledge easier to mark rather than their use in real life situations. The students demonstrate lack of inner language narrative thinking to complete tasks alone, which is the competence mentioned as lacking in workplace reports of employee performance. This ability is learnt through opportunities to use spoken language continually with others, in order to develop inner thinking. Education must make more effort to improve student internal and external communication processes and give teachers the knowledge they need to develop this complex activity. It is a vital ability to keep robots in their proper place – helping but not suppressing us humans! Do not let the advancing robot army destroy us.

References

Adekoya, R., Kaufmann, E., & Simpson, T. (2020). *Academic freedom in the UK: Protecting viewpoint diversity.* Policy Exchange. https://policyexchange.org.uk/wp-content/uploads/Academic-freedom-in-the-UK.pdf

Arenschield, L. (2020, February 15). Facial expressions don't tell the whole story of emotion. *Ohio State News.* https://news.osu.edu/facial-expressions-dont-tell-the-whole-story-of-emotion/

Baron-Cohen, S. (2011). What is theory of mind and is it impaired in ASC? In S. Bölte & J. Hallmayer (Eds.), *Autism spectrum conditions: FAQs on autism, Asperger syndrome and atypical autism answered by international experts* (pp. 136–138). Hogrefe.

Biggar, N. (2017–2022). *Ethics and empire* [Interdisciplinary project]. The McDonald Centre, University of Oxford.

Bronfenbrenner, U. (1979). *The ecology of human development.* Harvard University Press.

Burke, E. (n.d.). Edmund Burke quotes. https://www.goodread.com/author/quotes/17142.Edmund_Burke

Cowie, D. (2008). *New perspectives on bullying.* Open University Press.

Delgado, P., Vargas, C., Ackerman, R., & Salmerón, L. (2018). Don't throw away your printed books: A meta-analysis on the effect of reading media on reading comprehension. *Educational Research Review, 25,* 23–38. https://doi.org/10.1016/j.edurev.2018.09.003

DfE. (2014). *Preventing and tackling bullying: Advice for head teachers, staff & governing bodies*. Department for Education.

Farrar, J. (2020). *What researchers think about the cuture they work in*. Wellcome Institute. https://wellcome.org/reports/what-researchers-think-about-research-culture

Frey, C. B., & Osborne, M. A. (2013, September 17). *The future of employment: How susceptible are jobs to computerisation?* [Paper]. Oxford Martin School, University of Oxford. https://www.oxfordmartin.ox.ac.uk/downloads/academic/The_Future_of_Employment.pdf

Foucault, M. (1966). *Les mots et les choses: une archéologie des sciences humaines*. Gallimard.

Furedi, F. (2020). *Why boundaries matter: Why humanity must relearn the art of drawing boundaries*. Taylor & Francis.

Goodhart, D. (2020). *Head, hand, heart*. Penguin.

Houghton, K. J., Upadhyay, S. S. N., & Klin, C. M. (2018). Punctuation in text messages may convey abruptness. *Computers in Human Behavior, 80*, 112–121. https://doi.org/10.1016/j.chb.2017.10.044

Luckin, R. (2020, February 7). I, teacher: AI and school transformation. *New Statesman*. https://www.newstatesman.com/spotlight/2020/02/i-teacher-ai-and-school-transformation

Mason, C. (2021). *DNA editing*. https://research.cornell.edu/researchers/christopher-e-mason

Matteucci, R. (2017). Communication in the multicultural classroom: A challenge in 21st century education: Teachers, students, families and administrators. In R. Sage (Ed.), *Paradoxes in education*. Sense.

Mehrabian, A. (1971). *Silent messages*. Wadsworth.

Office for National Statistics. (2020). *Annual population survey*. www.ons.gov.uk

Orwell, G. (2000). *Nineteen eighty-four*. Penguin Modern Classics.

PEEP. (2011–2016). Policy for educator evidence in portfolios. Project no. 521454-LLP-1-2011-1-UK-KA1-KA1ECETB. Grant agreement 2011–4133/008–001. Key activity one: Policy co-operation and innovation.

Sackstein, S. (2015). *Hacking assessment: 10 ways to go gradeless in a traditional grades school*. Times 10 Publications.

Sage, R. (2020). *Speechless: Understanding education*. University of Buckingham Press.

Sage, R., & Matteucci, R. (Eds.). (forthcoming). *Teaching with technology*.

Schleicher, A. (2020, February 4). Preparing the next generation for their future, not our past. *New Statesman*. https://www.newstatesman.com/politics/2020/02/preparing-the-next-generation-for-their-future-not-our-past

Strimpel, Z. (2020, October 11). Covid could spell the end for university life. *Sunday Telegraph*.

Taylor Gatto, J. (2017). *Dumbing us down: The hidden curriculum of compulsory schooling* (2nd ed.). New Society Publishers

Ttofi, M. M., & Farrington, D. P. (2012). Risk and protective factors, longitudinal research, and bullying prevention. *New Directions for Youth Development, 133,* 85–98. doi:10.1002/yd.20009. PMID: 22504793

Winterson, J. (2021). *How we got here: Where we might go next.* Jonathan Cape.

Appendix: Theory of Mind

– Ability to understand the mental states of others and recognize they may differ from our own.

– Plays a vital role in solving conflicts, developing social abilities and making judgements

– Understanding starts around age 4, but research suggests it may develop earlier

– Studies show that persons with Autism may have more difficulty answering theory of mind questions correctly, which may explain why certain social situations confuse them (Baron-Cohen, 2011).